THE CHILDREN'S ASTROLOGER

THE CHILDREN'S ASTROLOGER

Dodie & Allan Edmands

HAWTHORN BOOKS, INC.
Publishers/NEW YORK
A Howard & Wyndham Company

To Oona, the firstborn

Permission to quote from the following sources is gratefully acknowledged:

Winnie-the-Pooh by A. A. Milne. Copyright © 1926 by E. P. Dutton & Company, Inc.; renewal 1954 by A. A. Milne. Reprinted by permission of the publisher, E. P. Dutton & Company, Inc.

Tootle by Gertrude Crampton. Copyright © 1945 by Western Publishing Company, Inc. Used by permission of the publisher.

The Youngest One by Taro Yashima. Copyright © 1962 by Taro Yashima. Reprinted by permission of The Viking Press.

Tawny Scrawny Lion by Kathryn Jackson. Copyright © 1952 by Western Publishing Company, Inc. Used by permission of the publisher.

Adaptation of *The Saggy Baggy Elephant* by K. and B. Jackson. Copyright © 1947 by Western Publishing Company, Inc. Used by permission of the publisher.

"Rapunzel" from *Fairy Tales* by Jacob and Wilhelm Grimm. Copyright © 1947 by the World Publishing Company. Reprinted by permission of the publishers, William Collins & World Publishing Co., Inc.

Susie's New Stove by Annie North Bedford. Copyright © 1950 by Western Publishing Company, Inc. Used by permission of the publisher.

Animal Friends by Jane Werner. Copyright © 1953 by Western Publishing Company, Inc. Used by permission of the publisher.

The Color Kittens by Margaret Wise Brown. Copyright © 1949 by Western Publishing Company, Inc. Used by permission of the publisher.

THE CHILDREN'S ASTROLOGER

Library of Congress Catalog Card Number: 78-53406

ISBN: 0-8015-1227-1

1 2 3 4 5 6 7 8 9 10

Contents

PART THREE:
Appendixes

Acknowledgments

We are sincerely grateful to the following people, without whose personal contributions or published research this book would not have been possible:

Sandra Choron, our editor, whose bright idea sparked it all and whose continuing encouragement nourished it into existence;

The late Arnold Gesell, M.D., whose delineation of the stages of child development focused our perceptions both as parents and in the writing of this book; and Louise Bates Ames, Ph.D., and Frances L. Ilg, M.D., colleagues of Dr. Gesell, whose warm and lively presentations of their continuing research with young children gave us wisdom as first-time parents and kept us on the right track here;

Judi Bachrach, our daughter's nursery school teacher, whose thoughtful comments and suggestions inspired many changes;

And most of all, our friends and fellow parents—in particular, Merrily Blum, Glory and Rick Brightfield, Merle Cosgrove, Ursula Degenhardt, Louise Flesher, Virginia Gerson, Louise Hartman, Betty and John Phillips, and Nancy Rullo—who generously gave of their time to talk with us about their children and whose anecdotes allowed us to bring the astrological abstractions down to earth.

PART ONE:
Children and Astrology

Introduction

This is a book for parents, grandparents, teachers, baby-sitters, and all those who love and care for young children. It endeavors to describe the individual personalities of these as yet unfurled beings through the wisdom of astrology.

A book such as this will naturally be turned to by all those who are eagerly curious to find answers to the intriguing question of what kinds of people their newborn infants will be. On the surface they all seem to be not much more than perfectly organized masses of protoplasm, smiling, squawking, gurgling, cooing, spitting up, and sleeping; yet even from the start some differences begin to emerge. We ourselves vividly remember wondering what kind of person our first child would become: Would she be beautiful, brilliant, talented, wise? We had no doubts that she'd accomplish amazing and wonderful feats, but which ones they were we weren't sure. It was very hard at first to adjust to the idea that this helpless creature who had so lately been a part of her mother's body was actually a person in her own right, so hard that we'd make ludicrous slips in the early months such as, "She's doing that just the way humans do!" We cared for her needs. We loved her as much as anyone could love a projection of themselves. But who was she?

And even though we were both astrologers (and thought we held the key to the mysteries of our own and everyone else's personality as a result of the birth charts we collected and studied), we still seemed to be only a small step ahead of the game. For one thing, no books like this one had yet been written, books in which the basic adult personality archetypes (what we call the signs) are expressed in terms applicable to the infant and young child. Astrology gave us a practical understanding of the kinds of life experiences and psychological dilemmas that adults (and even older children) have to deal with, but it left us relatively unaided when it came to focusing in on these bright, seemingly carefree young ones.

This book is designed to answer that need. We hope that it will introduce you to the person who is your child if you haven't made his or her acquaintance already. However, it has another purpose besides the satisfaction of curiosity. Since your children will more or less develop according to their own inner natures, regardless of the accuracy of your guesses, what we really seek to do is to open up to you the wisdom astrology can give at this extremely formative time in a human being's progress toward maturity—that is, the first six years of life.

Where Do Personality Differences Come From?

Children are fundamentally themselves from the beginning. This is one of the insights astrology gives us, and we shall expand on this momentarily. The conception that children are clean slates upon which we write their character with every nuance in our handling of them is of fairly modern origin. To older, more traditionally oriented parents, the children who were hard to handle or who followed interests of their own were sometimes considered "difficult"; whereas those who were more compliant, who accepted the family's creed and fulfilled their parents' expectations, tended to be thought of as "good." But new theories of the unconscious have given rise to a more psychologically oriented approach to child rearing in which the role of parents in effecting this "difficult" behavior is highlighted. Although, in our opinion, this new understanding represents an important growth in awareness, it still tends to place an extremely heavy and unwarranted burden of responsibility on parents. Either way, old-fashioned or new, in general the individuality of the child is discounted or ignored.

The study of astrology reveals that what we call personality is actually a unique pattern of tendencies with which each one of us is born. The astrological symbols in no way *prescribe* behavior; rather, they *describe* it. The newborn person can be likened to a seed, which carries its future traits and the program for much of its development encoded within it. The seedling organism may be exposed to nurturing conditions or adverse ones, and these, too, will affect its growth. But whatever makes it an individual is something that is born with it, waiting to unfold with time.

Astrology is not the only study that asserts the existence of inborn personality differences; there is also increasing confirmation from more widely respected, scientific and academic sources that this is so. For example, researchers at the Gesell Institute of Child Development, even as they posit certain standard developmental stages that all children go through, emphasize that there are definite individual differences that will qualify the particular child's expression of the typical behaviors they describe. Dr. William H. Sheldon's theory of basic contrasting body types is well known, in which personality characteristics are thought to derive to a great extent from the kind of physiological constitution a person is born with. Drs. Stella Chess and Alexander Thomas and their colleagues have made long-term studies of children, from which they've been able to outline certain distinct temperamental differences having to do with activity level, adaptability, intensity of reaction, quality of mood, and so on; and they've shown that these can be observed from earliest infancy on. Of course, these studies only restate in scientific terms what parents of large families have always known: Children differ.

So we parents shouldn't blame ourselves for the child who is hard to handle (he is "shaping" the interaction between us as much as we are influencing him) nor take all the credit if we are blessed with an easily manageable child. Most of these patterns of behavior are the result of innate ways of experiencing, whose origin no one has yet been able absolutely to pinpoint. Astrology, however, helps us to define these patterns more clearly.

How Astrology Helps Parents Help Children

The period of early childhood can be considered formative because it is a time when innate tendencies can either be made the most of, thus setting the child on a strong course for life, or be suppressed into more negative means of expression. To take up the analogy to the seed once more, it's the difference between a plant that is watered, fertilized, pruned, and given the sunlight it needs and the one that is cast off and left to struggle for itself.

Astrology can help us to recognize clearly our children for who they are and to accept their right to be that way. Only then can we really begin to respect their differences—both from each other and from ourselves. We will not try to make them into something they are not and will not suffer deep disappointment as a result of their unique style of approach. This is the way in which we do "form" our children—by our acceptance or rejection of them for who they are (as opposed to what they do).

Ironically, the more fully we accept our children, the more able we will be to guide them into desirable ways of expression, for our knowledge will help us set up the most conducive conditions for their growth as well as the most effective techniques for discouraging their excesses. And above all, our tolerance and acceptance of them—even more than our elemental bond of love—will provide the basis from which they will derive their own tolerant understanding of themselves and go on to become the conscious, willing gardeners of the next generation of seedlings.

The objectivity astrology offers can also help free parents of much of their anxiety about their children. As stated earlier, the less personally identified we are with the way our children behave, the more able we will be to cultivate a calm center within ourselves and in turn be patient with them. But when we do find ourselves pushed beyond our limits, our confidence in ourselves as able parents should remain intact, for we'll understand that we are only the caretakers of their flowering young spirits and not the gods and goddesses we are sometimes mistaken for. If we can be realistic in our expectations of our children, our pleasure in them should grow as we observe them doing the best they are able with their own unique talents and abilities. Worries about their rate of development or about how they compare with our friends' children should also leave us as we come to value these individuals for what they alone have to offer. And finally, and perhaps most practically, since our accurate recognition of the individual needs of our children should lead us to the most appropriate methods for handling them, we'll cease to fight those losing battles that are so discouraging, and life should become easier and far more gratifying for all.

What Is Astrology?

Astrology can be a profound teacher for achieving this objectivity. Progenitor of both astronomy and psychology, it is a countless-thousands-year-old symbolic system—a language, really—consisting of amazingly apt metaphors for inner realities we still perceive as functioning today. The mere fact of astrology's extraordinary endurance is enough to warrant it a place in our respect.

Precisely how it works is not a subject we can speculate about here; in fact, no one really knows, though as modern science develops increasingly sophisticated methods of data collection and analysis, some interesting evidence begins to flow in.

What we do know is that astrology is a way of focusing in on the underlying structure of personality. And it does this in terms so universal that they can be used and grasped at almost every possible level of a human being's understanding.

Astrology helps people to see themselves—and, more specifically, their children—better. When properly used, it gives us a *nonjudgmental* framework for sorting out our children's genuine strengths from our expectations of them.

Naturally, we must remember that nonastrological variables influence all human beings. In addition to cultural and socioeconomic circumstances, we must also consider, for example, a child's sex. Even without cultural pressure, boys as a rule are a little wilder than girls, they develop more slowly, and in contrast to girls, they tend to prefer blocks and toys with wheels to dolls and books. The child's position in the family also plays a major role: Is she an only child? The firstborn? Secondborn? Does she have older brothers? Younger brothers? Older sisters? Younger ones? The child's developmental age, too, is extremely significant (and we shall call explicit attention to this throughout the book). We expect a child of five to behave differently from one who is two and a half, not just because of his wider experience but because he is feeling different internal stresses. Finally, how do you behave as parents? As we've already discussed, although parental handling isn't everything, it does have a marked impact on the child's personality.

Without astrology we might be perplexed by the tremendous dissimilarity between two children whose backgrounds seem so alike in every other respect. Astrology sheds light on these *hidden* distinctions; it reveals the different possible responses children might have to the same biological or environmental influences.

Why We Chose This Age Group—Birth through Five

We have chosen to limit ourselves to preschoolers—boys and girls under six—for a number of reasons. First, as stated earlier, we hope that our book will give parents one more way of looking at their children at a time when they can use all the help they can get. It is a time when our children are closer to and more dependent on us than they will ever be again. Never again will they be so fully open to us, so easily and deeply affected by how we feel about them and by how successfully they can handle the kinds of situations we expose them to.

Second, it gives us the opportunity to deal in depth with an age group that, though it has certain major cyclic reversals within it, is relatively of a piece. We see this age as being circumscribed more or less by birth at one end and the entry into first grade at the other. The changes that occur in this brief period seem truly astounding from the slowed-down perspective of adult time. In our research for this book we have given major attention to the developmental stages first delineated by Dr. Arnold Gesell and his colleagues and later adopted by modern psychologists in general. But you should remember not to take these developmental gradients too rigidly. Each child is an individual in his or her rate of development too. Some children arrive at a stage a little early, whereas others tend to be a bit late. Some develop very rapidly for a year or two and then slow down; others are just the opposite. Unless your child is exceptionally tardy (if he is still not walking at age two, for example), you shouldn't be overly concerned.

Basically, what we are trying to say is that you should temper whatever understanding you gain from this book with a little old-fashioned common sense. Your own observations of your child will naturally form the basis out of which other insights will grow, and for the most part you should trust them. What we are offering you are guidelines, not prescriptions or literal predictions.

We have chosen to refer to all children not as *he* but as *he* and *she* in alternation. Actually, it would have been possible to assign a *he* to one entire sign, a *she* to the next, especially since the beautifully symmetrical astrological system already does this. Fire signs (Aries, Leo, Sagittarius) and air signs (Gemini, Libra, Aquarius) are considered positive, or "masculine," whereas earth signs (Taurus, Virgo, Capricorn) and water signs (Cancer, Scorpio, Pisces) are considered negative, or "feminine." The reason for this is that the positive signs have traits in common, such as outgoingness, exuberance, and an active interest in expressing themselves to others. In contrast, the negative signs tend to be more receptive, introverted, and concentrated. But the labels *masculine* and *feminine* for *positive* and *negative* unfortunately contribute to a sexist bias. Outgoing girls and introverted boys are not only a common occurrence, they are a natural one—which is as it should be, since boys and girls are equally distributed among the positive and negative signs. Therefore, we have decided to use *he* and *she* alternately within each sign; although it may sound odd to unaccustomed ears, this seems the fairest solution to the problem.

Sun Sign, Moon Sign, and Rising Sign

"What's your sign?" Since the middle of the 1960s this question has become about as familiar and predictable a query upon first introduction to a person as the many other politely cautious attempts we use as aids in sizing each other up—inquiries about one's job, one's age, one's marital status or family background, and what part of town one lives in. There is nothing intrinsically wrong with these social warmers, unless they are abused for snobbish or egotistical ends. In fact, they are useful tools for helping us focus our first impressions about each other; they give name and structure to what would otherwise be formless feelings and unconscious stirrings. And interestingly, even if you know nothing else about astrology, you are very likely to know the answer when someone asks you what your sign is.

Unfortunately, one of the things that currently gives astrology a bad name is the fact that your answer invariably pigeonholes you; it focuses you all right, but only too neatly into one of only twelve possible categories, as though you were exactly like one-twelfth of the human race, as though you had over 350 million doubles (at this writing), with 7 million new copies of you being added each year. Even if your questioner has a mind that is open enough not to oversimplify you and make unwarranted assumptions, even if he has asked the question in order to compare the astrological hypotheses with the well-formed impressions he already has about you, the potential for his understanding of you has nonetheless been reduced by this one-in-twelve classification.

Of course, you are an adult. Presumably you have developed enough self-knowledge that your new friend's overgeneralized perception of you won't influence your opinion of yourself or alter your ability to express yourself in all your fullness. However, a child is more vulnerable, and the damage an adult's conceptual fencing-in can wreak on a seedling self-image is considerable.

But isn't that what this book is about? We offer you twelve personality descriptions, corresponding to the twelve signs of the zodiac; don't we intend for you to assign one of them to your child according to his or her birthday?

Actually what we intend is for you to look up *three* of these descriptions for your child.

There are three distinct, though somewhat overlapping, reference points—the *sun sign*, the *moon sign*, and the *rising sign*—from which basis you can begin to understand your child. When these reference points are blended together, you have a much more complete picture of your child's personality and how it is projected. It's a little like perceiving something in three dimensions instead of one. A fairly accurate description of your child can thus be narrowed down to 1 in 364 possible three-sign combinations (from Aries-Aries-Aries, Aries-Aries-Taurus, all the way to Pisces-Pisces-Pisces). Further, if the meanings of sun sign, moon sign, and rising sign can be kept distinct—which is admittedly quite difficult, especially in describing a child—the three-sign blend is 1 in 1,728 (for example, Aries sun, Taurus moon, Sagittarius rising versus Taurus sun, Aries moon, Gemini rising, and so on).

In this chapter we will discuss the meaning of the sun sign, moon sign, and rising sign and illustrate how they can be blended together into a whole picture. There are, of course, astrological considerations other than these three reference points that can contribute to an even more complete description of your child, and it is possible that one of these factors is so significant that it overshadows the three-sign blend. (We mention one such possibility on page 13.) But the simple combination of sun, moon, and rising signs is generally so descriptive of the essential personality of most of us that parents who know nothing else about their child's astrological makeup should have with this blend an insight into who their child is, what her fundamental motivations are, and in what directions she is heading.

The Sun Sign

When anyone asks you what your child's sign is, they are really inquiring about the sun sign—that is, the sign in the yearly twelve-sign cycle the sun was in when he or she was born, as seen from the orbiting earth.

The sun is the center of our solar system—*our* center. It is the star without whose radiant energy there would be no life. Astrologically, the sun represents the vital spirit, or driving force within your child; it is his or her inner sense of purpose, the conscious reason for living. Your child's sun sign describes the particular way in which this driving force and sense of purpose are expressed. The sun also represents your child's identity tag, his or her essential core self; it symbolizes the child's recognition of him or herself as an individual distinct from all other individuals. Your child's sun sign describes how he or she expresses this core self. For example, if your daughter's sun sign is Aries, she should express herself dynamically and impulsively; she will be bright and eager, sometimes loud and active, and she will always be looking for novel ways to assert herself. On the other hand, if her sun sign is Taurus, we would expect that she would be more cautious in her self-expression, preferring familiar and comfortable methods of operating to the exploration of uncharted territory.

Alas, it's not so simple! Consider two five-year-olds, Noah and Jake, both with Taurus sun. In fact, they were born on the same day—Jake ten hours after Noah. Noah seems characteristically Taurus: He is easygoing, and he moves slowly and deliberately; he prefers quiet play, and he doesn't like to go away from home too often. Even when he is in the company of noisy, rambunctious children, he remains patient and calm; hardly anything can ruffle him. In contrast, Jake is always on the go; he becomes restless and nervous when he can't go outside to run with his friends or play over at their house. Noah has difficulty sharing his toys with other children. Jake, on the other hand, will occasionally loan out one of his toys and then forget all about it. Noah wants his mother to stay close to him whenever they go out, but Jake seems to prefer other children. Noah can take direction easily, whereas Jake loves to defy adults.

When we look beyond the sun sign, we can better understand the differences between these two children. Noah's moon sign is Capricorn, and his rising sign is Cancer—two signs that reinforce the Taurus concern for security and sameness. Jake's moon has gone into the next sign, Aquarius, and he has Sagittarius rising; the emphasis of these two signs is on personal independence combined with convivial social interaction.

When we explore only the surface behavior, Noah seems like a Taurus and Jake doesn't. But when we look more closely, we find that they do have quite a bit in common. Both boys are extremely stubborn, though Jake expresses this trait verbally by offering his inflexible opinions to whomever will listen. Also, when confronted with a problem that interests them, both boys will persevere determinedly until it is solved: Noah will plod away at it with deep, even brooding concentration, whereas Jake will attack it again from a fresh angle when one approach fails.

Your child's sun sign describes the way he or she expresses an inner light. With all children the sun sign indicates a basic orientation, the inner meaning that underlies their behavior. But as we will see, the moon sign and the rising sign have additional information to offer.

Note: If you are unsure of your child's sun sign, or if he was born between the eighteenth and the twenty-third of the month, you can resolve any doubt by referring to the listing in Appendix A.

The Moon Sign

Your child's moon sign is the sign in the monthly twelve-sign cycle that the moon was passing through at the time of birth. It takes about two and a half days for the moon to move through one sign.

Astrologically, the moon represents your child's response to life, the adjustment of his inner sense of purpose (the sun) to the necessities of the world. Children's adjustment characteristically goes through phases: Sometimes it seems that their responses are aligned with their self-concept, but at other times they will be at odds with themselves as they balance what they want with what others want of them. The moon also represents a child's gut connection with his or her mother, a sense of oneness with family and the past, which endures long after the umbilical cord is severed. Furthermore, the moon symbolizes the shifting tides of emotion that children so easily display. It represents your child's natural instincts, habits stemming from the most fundamental unconscious being and attachment to and memories of infancy.

Jonathan's moon sign, for instance, is a description of the special way he responds to the world and expresses his feelings. It indicates his natural way of being, how he is when he's not consciously asserting his identity. It also suggests the traits he might habitually exhibit, or fall back on, in times of stress. In other words, when he is very tired, ill, or frustrated, the characteristics of his moon sign may be more evident than at other times.

Thus, a child with a Sagittarius moon might respond to you good-naturedly and exuberantly, and even if she doesn't initiate humor herself, she will probably laugh at your jokes. In addition, she may be quite impatient with slight frustrations, and when she is tired, she may characteristically start senseless arguments with you. In contrast, a child with Capricorn moon would be able to postpone the satisfaction of his desires for long periods, and he might be the only calm one in the family when the car's radiator hose springs a leak fifty miles from home on a Sunday afternoon. But he probably won't express his feelings very well, and when he is tired or ill he might be prone to gloom.

Note: Refer to the listing in Appendix A to discover your child's moon sign.

Combining the Sun and the Moon

The sun represents your child's conscious self-assertion, which is a slowly developing phenomenon. In contrast, the moon symbolizes instinctual responses to the world. Thus, it would seem that the moon alone ought to describe your child as a baby. Indeed, many astrologers feel that the moon sign is overwhelmingly prominent until a child is about seven years old.

Unfortunately for this notion, we have observed both sun-sign and moon-sign manifestations in the young children we know. Some babies even behave according to their sun sign, which seems very strange, since they have no clear conception of themselves as separate entities. Perhaps the problem lies with our definition of *self* as the emotions thoughts, sensations, and behavior that emanate from a single body distinct from other bodies. It could very well be that a baby identifies with the world in general. When your son exhibits the characteristics of his sun sign, he is asserting this general identity. In other words, whereas his moon sign represents his natural gut reactions to stimuli, the sun sign describes the way he actively makes demands upon the universe, even when, in infancy, that universe appears inseparable from himself. As he grows into greater awareness of his separateness from others, his sun sign behavior becomes more recognizably conscious and purposeful. In any event, even when the behavior of a young child seems instinctual, we cannot disregard his sun sign.

Nonetheless, children generally tend to express their moon sign more freely than adults do. There is considerable social pressure on us grown-ups to keep our emotions out of sight. Children are not expected to observe such restraint. This is another reason, besides the slow development of solar self-awareness as well as other factors in the birth chart, that the sun sign is not at first apparent in some children.

How can children's expression of their moon-sign responsiveness be distinguished from their assertion of their sun sign? Familiarizing yourself with sun- and moon-sign traits once you have identified those signs will help, but it is not possible to distinguish sun-sign expression from moon-sign expression in every instance. Nor is it really necessary, for that matter. It is often easier to see a child in terms of a final blend than to analyze him or her into component parts.

Remember that sun-sign and moon-sign characteristics often seem to reinforce each other, but they are just as often mutually contradictory. You may read in the "Childsigns" section that your Pisces sun–Capricorn moon baby will want to suck for long periods because he is a Pisces and then learn that he will be finished sucking in fifteen minutes because he is a Capricorn. Or that your Leo sun–Virgo moon child should be warm and exuberant because she is a Leo and reserved because she is a Virgo. Try to remember that our sign descriptions delineate the possibilities; they are inclinations, not rigid patterns that your child is fated to exhibit. Just as more than one sign is important in everyone's astrological makeup, there are contradictory tendencies within each of us. Ultimately you will have to use your own powers of observation—and common sense—to recognize the ways in which these tendencies are displayed in real behavior.

Sun and moon, assertion of identity and instinctive responses, join together in your child in making up a fundamental character. When you blend in this very special style of interacting with people—described by the rising sign—you should have insight into his or her whole personality.

The Rising Sign

Your child's rising sign is the sign in the daily twelve-sign cycle that, as the earth was spinning, was coming up on the eastern horizon of the place of birth at the time of birth. It may take from less than a half hour to over three hours for one sign to cross the horizon.

A child born the same day as your child and in the same place but at a slightly different time may have a different rising sign. Likewise, a child born the same day and at the same time but in a different place could very well have a different rising sign. Your child's rising sign is very specific and personal; it describes his particular signature in the world. It indicates the first impression he makes on other people, how he initially comes across to them, his outer personality and mannerisms, even his physical appearance. It describes a distinctive style of relating to others, how he projects his sun-moon character in interactions with you, his siblings, friends, and anyone else he encounters.

For example, if your daughter's rising sign is Aquarius, she is likely to come across to people as a bright and socially aware child, and she will project her basic character (described by her sun and moon signs) in a friendly though at times rebellious manner. If her rising sign is Pisces, she will probably come across as dreamy and quite vulnerable to being hurt, and she will project her basic character in a quiet, sensitive manner.

Note: Refer to the tables in Appendix B to discover your child's rising sign.

Putting It All Together

We have examined how inadequate the sun sign is in describing your child's total personality in our discussion of Noah and Jake (pages 9-10). Also we have cast doubt on the speculation of many astrologers that the moon sign would outweigh the sun sign in portraying your child, for we have observed the sun shining prominently in the behavior of many babies. Finally, we have stated that the role of the rising sign is limited to describing the way a child typically projects his fundamental sun–moon characteristics in interactions with people.

The point, of course, is that no single sign will do a child justice (unless he's a "triple"— see page 14). You will need to blend these three reference points together to see the whole picture. The blend will be so specific to your child that if you meet another child with that blend (a rare occurrence), you will probably be astounded by the striking similarities between them.

How do we merge three signs into a coherent picture? Theoretically, the sun sign and moon sign have about equal weight, the sun sign describing your child's active behavior and the moon sign his reactions. The rising sign should be given slightly less weight; it describes an outer, less fundamental personality, and it may indicate how others tend to view your child before they really get to know him.

In actual practice it's usually not so simple and neat to separate these functions, and again, it's the blend that matters. A comparison that may sound funny can help to demonstrate this: If you liken your child's personality to a cake, the sun sign and moon sign are the basic ingredients and the rising sign is the particular seasoning that gives the cake its own special flavor. When you eat the cake, you can't distinguish egg, butter, flour, salt, sugar, or nutmeg. But obviously children are more complex than baked goods. The point we are making is that you should consider all three signs important—even when you can't identify the function of each in your child's personality.

There may be traits your child exhibits that are not described by either the sun sign, the moon sign, or the rising sign, and you may need to have an astrologer interpret the entire birth chart in order to understand the relevance of these traits in the child's overall personality. The reason for this is that occasionally another factor may make sun, moon, and rising signs relatively unimportant. Three-year-old Marjorie has sun in Libra, moon in Sagittarius, and Aries rising. She is quite polite with adults and considerate with other children (Libra), but the fiery enthusiasm you might expect from Sagittarius and Aries is conspicuously missing. So is the typical Libra smile. Marjorie's most striking trait is her deadpan expression and her serious outlook. But when we examine her birth chart, we can immediately identify the powerful planetary focus that corresponds to her sobriety. Such considerations are beyond the scope of this book; but rest assured, it is extremely rare that the blend of sun, moon, and rising signs misses the mark completely.

Doubles and Triples

More than a third of all children are "doubles"—that is, two of the three signs in the blend are the same. For example, a child with Aries sun, Aries moon, and Taurus rising is a "double Aries."

Naturally the sign that is double is strongly emphasized, with the third sign exerting only a moderating influence. A child with the sun and moon in the same sign (that is, self-assertion and emotional reactions expressed the same way) is likely to display the characteristics of that sign wholeheartedly and powerfully. But that child may have little internal check on herself because even more than most children she tends to be heedless of consequences. On the other hand, such a child may hardly ever be at odds with herself.

A child with the same sun and rising sign (that is, self-assertion and special style of interacting are expressed the same way) would probably want to be in the limelight a great deal, and you may have to contend with seemingly never-ending insistence on your full attention. On the other hand, this child is likely to become quite secure in his identity early in life.

A child with the same moon and rising sign (that is, emotional reactions and special style of interacting are expressed the same way) and may be quite sensitive to the surrounding environment and may become upset if tension is perceived around him. On the other hand, these children may have a great deal of compassion. At least, you won't be wondering what they're feeling inside.

About one child in thirty is a "triple"—that is, the sun, moon, and rising signs are all the same. You can be sure that such children will express that sign very intensely, for their self-assertion, emotional reactions, and special style of interacting are all in concert. They come the closest to being a pure type (but again, you would have to look at an entire birth chart to understand traits not described under the tripled sign). They will tend to experience life in this singular way. But no sign is more valuable than any other. Each one is only a single dimension in the twelve-fold spectrum, so each has within it the potential for growth. If your child's sun, moon, and rising signs are all the same, you can be sure that he or she will express that one dimension to its fullest extent. Your task will be to help modify the excesses of that sign and gather some experience in other realms.

PART TWO:
Childsigns

Under the name of each sign we have included the approximate span of time the sun was in that sign. For exact date and time of sun-sign change, see Appendix A.

The descriptions in Part Two apply to moon sign and rising sign also.

♈

Aries

(SUN SIGN, MARCH 21–APRIL 20)

*Peter paid no attention to Grandfather's words. Boys like him are
not afraid of wolves.*

Prokofiev, Peter and the Wolf

Aries is number one, and children of this sign strive to keep it that way. With their strong, active bodies and bright, alert minds, this is never very difficult for them, but when the newness of a challenge fades away, so may your Aries. Fun and excitement are what the Aries child seeks, and for want of anything better he'll create his own.

The Aries child is willing to try anything and usually does so with an enthusiasm bordering on hyperactivity. Impulsiveness is the key to the Aries temperament, whether it's the energy that keeps their bodies in constant motion every waking moment, the emotional needs that drive them to grab for a toy or scream in rage at a domineering adult, or the courageous spirit that makes them natural leaders in the eyes of other children. It will be hard to get these children to settle down for bedtime and even harder to keep them out of scuffles.

One of the inevitable consequences of their restless, hard-driving activity that will undoubtedly trouble parents is their proclivity for accidents, most likely blows to the head, cuts, and burns. Parents should be reassured to know, however, that the characteristic Aries crash is matched by the proverbial Aries bounce—their often vigorous constitution and capacity to heal themselves. In any case, parents should try to avoid undermining their child's self-confidence through overprotection and worrying. Caution can and should be taught to Aries children but always with the tether long enough for them to spend their abundant energy.

The Aries impulsiveness may lead the child off other cliffs as well. When, with disarming candor, the four-year-old Aries tells you that you're a "goddamn hynee poopooperson," you may blanch at the bluntness of such a frontal attack. But when she throws her arms around you and tells you how completely she loves you, you should know that it comes from the same fresh source—the unreflecting simplicity of the Aries self-expression.

Of course, you say, but all children behave this way. And this is in some measure true; it's just that there is a sense in which Aries grown-ups are children, too. Their concerns will change, but their manner of approaching them will always have the infuriating self-centeredness yet endearing innocence of the child.

Patience, an attribute ordinarily in short supply in young children, will be especially scarce in an Aries. "But I want it," he'll insist over and over again, and, even in the later, more reasonable ages, that will be the only justification he considers necessary for the immediate satisfaction of his desire. His determination may be formidable, so the magic wand of distraction may not be much help here. You had better be prepared for considerable fiery agitation until some practicable solution is found.

You may find your Aries children particularly demanding at certain ages, especially at those points in the growth cycle when demands are strong and definite but abilities lag way behind. Eighteen months was a trying age for Norah and her parents: "Tay-ba, ta-ay-ba!" she would cry repeatedly as she pointed to the dining table, her way of insisting on being lifted up to stand on it precariously for the umpteenth time that day (because, foolishly, her parents had allowed it *once*). And firm though they seemed to be in other areas of their life, one of them simply had to remain there by her side for whatever length of time it pleased her to be up there as she anticked about, delighted to have gotten her way once again. Parents who can endure these frustrating periods will be rewarded by the growing competence and self-confidence they will undoubtedly observe in their child.

Aries shares with the other fire signs (Leo and Sagittarius) an intense need to express itself; and with Aries children this trait emerges as self-assertion, which may be revealed in the early years as simple aggression and in the later, more peer-oriented ages as competitiveness for praise. Positive reinforcement, rather than scolding and lecturing, seems to work best with such children. Adults are far better advised to encourage them to excel in competitive sports and games than to try to suppress such unrestrainable energy, for it will only reemerge in some less acceptable form, such as beating up the cat. With Aries, spring bursts forth upon the land, the creative spark is lit, and nothing can hold it back, so you might as well welcome it in—or out, as the case may be.

Aries is so full of positive energy that parents need not worry that their Aries child will be dominated by another child (except, perhaps, another Aries), for he is likely to be leading every adventure or at least be competing for the leadership. Many other children will be drawn to one who is so sure of himself, who is so ready to take on even adult adversaries at times, and who takes the initiative in assigning roles and materials to all the others in a playgroup. Daring, spontaneity, and decisiveness are a few of the qualities the Aries child possesses in full measure; however, their effect on other people can occasionally be abrasive. Aries will inevitably have to contend with the bruised egos and offended sensibilities of some playmates, especially if these include an older child, who may see no idol in this pushy upstart.

Adults may be able to help these children in a fundamentally important way if they can encourage them to practice receptivity in any form. Since motion is so important to Aries children, try to help them develop their attention to the movement around them by observation games you both can play, such as looking, with ears closed, at an open space (a street corner, a construction site, out the window) and describing the subtle actions you can detect. Learning to cooperate is part of it, too. With younger or less verbal children, you might try creating a Play-Doh Noah's Ark together—anything where you don't have to be working on the same object at the same time but where group effort in creating something is an enjoyable necessity.

Indeed, creativity is quite central to the Aries being, whether it is something artistic or just some activity or event that the child has set in motion. Yet she may not be at all interested in the outcome of her initial thrust and may be quite willing to leave a project just as it has gotten going or others are warming up to it. This tendency is easy to gloss over in the young child, for whom the intrinsic interest of working with new materials is justifiably more important than a finished product. But it can get to be a problem as your child grows up, leaving trails of uncompleted schoolwork, creative projects, or business ideas in her wake.

Astrology gives parents the insight to know how to help their Aries children to learn the value of following through on their enthusiastic beginnings. It will not be easy, for this goes in the opposite direction of the Aries jet stream. But if you can gently encourage them to think through the consequences of their acts and their effect on others, you will have given them a start in building some of the social muscles that can be invaluable to their success in later life.

Your Aries children may seem to be brimming over with promise and talent, and indeed, there is a sense in which this sign is all potential. But with just a little help they will develop into creative, well-functioning, and mature beings who can not only put themselves forth with spirit but receive the offerings of others with grace.

The Evolving Aries

BIRTH TO ONE YEAR

Even before he is born, the Aries baby makes his presence known with his restless kicking and poking, and his emergence into the world may be noisy. This baby expresses his needs and desires quite clearly; parents will soon grow accustomed to his vigorous thrashing of arms and legs in anger. He basically seems impatient to be up and doing, and his rage is really a result of his frustration at the slowness of development. Indeed, he may hurry it along: Some Aries babies pull themselves to standing at seven months, grabbing onto the furniture in a premature effort to walk, and may actually be walking on their own as early as nine months. Initially it may be very difficult to get your crib bouncer and rattle banger to sleep, but you will probably be inspired by her vigor while she is awake and humbled by her courageous comebacks after her repeated falls on the nose. Aries infants are just so happy to be in the world at last that you can't help but share in their delight.

ONE-YEAR-OLDS

With the new independence that walking allows, the Aries child's basic individual disposition emerges: She is determined to prevail over others. Not only does she repeat her insistent demands over and over, but she is not likely to obey your no-no as she turns the knobs on the stove or climbs the bookshelves. You can remove the knobs temporarily, but physical restraint may often be necessary to prevent her from harming herself. Unfortunately, outright thwarting is likely to bring on a good old-fashioned sit-down head-banging temper tantrum, particularly with the eighteen-month-old Aries. It may be possible to prevent such outbursts if you provide her with sufficient action toys on which to spend her energy—for example, push and pull toys, balls, a rocking horse, a toy hammer.

TWO-YEAR-OLDS

At two, Aries children often know their own mind, and in six months they will probably not even show much of the indecisiveness characteristic of the two-and-a-half-year-old. Some Aries children may even have "decided" that it's high time they were out of diapers and have taken measures to correct the situation. Their growing command of language helps them in their effort to assert their will, but the sly parent can make use of it, too, to control them with cajolery and humor. When, at two and a half, they resist getting dressed, as well as all other routines, try giving them some choice in the matter: "Do you want to wear a red shirt or an orange shirt?"

Aries at two is a daring explorer; if sent to nursery school at this age, he will probably surprise everyone with his independence of his parents from the very first day as he marches in to see what it's all about. However, he may be quite aggressive in the inevitable combat over toys, perhaps so much so that other kids won't play with him. But, of course, he shouldn't be blamed for this—it's more an expression of his immaturity than anything else. The wise adult should try instead to reroute him and provide him with substitutions as much as possible. Praise for his physical feats works wonders.

THREE-YEAR-OLDS

Aries loves to be first, and there is no better way to get your balking Aries three to stop roughhousing and go to the bathroom when it's clear she has to than to start off in that direction yourself and say, tauntingly, "Me first!" It works every time. Their growing physical competence makes Aries children obsessed with sheer power and might; even Aries girls at this age may enjoy watching backhoes and bulldozers, later imitating them, with full sound effects, in their play with wagons or trikes. They are really fun to be with at this age, and their exuberance can now be channeled into play with other children. However, you might as well accept that it will probably be competitive play and gear your supervision to preventing the more physical forms of aggression where necessary. Remember that they may tire very quickly, especially at three and a half, and, fatigued, they may regress to belligerent hell raisers.

FOUR-YEAR-OLDS

The intrepid Aries four seems ready for anything and impatient to usurp the adult's power and authority. Parents should be circumspect in giving directions to their Aries child and should probably avoid head-on collisions with him; his response may vary from insolent rudeness to kicking, spitting, biting, and obscenely threatening far worse. Such rampages may sometimes need to be met with physical punishment, but parents should not spank too frequently. Aggression harshly squelched with further aggression will emerge in other ways—she may break her toys, for example, or take out her hostility on a sibling. And, convinced that naughtiness can be "paid for" with a spanking, the child may not learn self-control, a much-needed lesson for an Aries.

Parents are not the only brunt of their Aries child's cheekiness; he can now be a far more effective tease and general nuisance to his older brother or sister. Basically he needs an outlet for working off his aggression: Outdoor play equipment or the privilege of using a workbench with real tools might be just the answer.

FIVE-YEAR-OLDS

Parents who have by now grown used to the bellicosity of their impassioned Aries child are likely to be amazed by the peacefulness that descends on their household when she becomes five. She is definitely easier to live with at this age and may even independently assume the faithful execution of chores she couldn't have been trusted with previously. Moreover, these duties are sure to be performed with considerable speed, even with rush and bustle.

The Aries child may seem to be running or climbing constantly, and he will need to replenish his abundant energy by gulping and gobbling his food. Mealtimes may be nothing more than pit stops for his racing engine. Anything parents can do to slow him down—from interesting conversation to foods that require a great deal of active cutting and chewing—will do their Aries whirlwind a world of good.

The Aries five will be better able to express her aggression verbally and may sometimes pretend naughtiness in order to pull your leg. Some Aries children may be controlling belligerent urges with great difficulty, however, and may be plagued by nightmares in which *they* are the victims of these urges. These fears can usually be worked out in active play.

If you give sufficient acclaim to the newly acquired skills of your Aries child and award new privileges for acceptable behavior, his high spirits and fresh approach to the world he is conquering may make you feel vigorous and new yourself.

♉

TAURUS

(SUN SIGN, APRIL 21–MAY 21)

Isn't it funny
How a bear likes honey?
Buzz! Buzz! Buzz!
I wonder why he does?
Then he climbed a little further . . . and a little further . . . and
then just a little further. By that time he had thought of another
song.
It's a very funny thought that, if Bears were Bees,
They'd build their nests at the bottom of trees.
And that being so (if the Bees were Bears),
We shouldn't have to climb up all these stairs.

A. A. Milne, Winnie-the-Pooh

If you want to understand the unique value of your Taurus child, just think of the earth, how it supports all living things yet itself never seems to move; how it endures no matter what is wreaked upon it, yet when finally it ruptures (as in an earthquake), how slow it is to mend, how we take it for granted because it is so much the basis for everything.

It is sometimes difficult for parents to appreciate these little bull calves, for they tend to move and think so slowly that they're apt to seem almost dimwitted. Indeed, their steadfast attachment to the tried-and-true can exasperate, perhaps even bore, more quickly paced adults as they exhaust their store of interesting games, playmates, or even foods they think the Taurus child will like.

It is not that he doesn't like these things, in fact he *loves* them, but only on his own terms. We know of one boy who for years would eat *nothing* but hamburgers for dinner. At Thanksgiving, out would come the splendid turkey—and Jeremy's hamburger. Food will be so much enjoyed that it can even become a problem if the chosen fare happens to be candy and desserts (which is highly likely of these sweethearts); and Taureans are known for the quantities they can methodically set about to pack away. With the Taurus, as with any individual, it is important not to thwart him in his natural affinities and predispositions, only to direct and channel as wisely as possible. Thus, you might provide such children with a wealth of nourishing foods, using honey and dried fruits for sweeteners as necessary. They may actually need food more than most in order to build the strong, stocky body the Taurus is famous for. And of course, you can suggest moderation when necessary. Actually, if they are provided with enough activities they like—and especially with steady love and affection from you—overeating should not be too much of a problem.

Getting these children to partake of sufficient fresh air and exercise may be a more weighty undertaking. The Taurus child can be so pleasure-loving, so relaxed in her chosen comforts, that the motor within those little legs and arms may have trouble getting started. In fact, she may seem downright lazy. She knows what she likes, she likes what she knows, and she resists any change in the status quo. The key here is to find the one or more activities she can truly respond to and let her stick with these.

Taurus is an eminently physical sign; it is only the initial impetus that's lacking. Tricycles may be much loved by three- to four-year-olds, for they can sit and watch the world roll by while they get exercise at the same time. Competitive games, or anything in which the child has to take a risk, will be far less liked. Building with blocks—especially if you can set them up outdoors—may be a perfect pastime for such children, for they share with the other earth signs (Virgo and Capricorn) a steadfast need to see the tangible results of their labors. Sand play, especially if a little water is added to make the sand the consistency of mud, will provide hours of sensually creative enjoyment.

This affinity for the material and the concrete shows itself in several ways. Taurus children are characteristically deeply attached to the here-and-now world of physical sensations. When new ideas are presented to them, they need to have them explained in concrete, down-to-earth terms, preferably with some sense of their practical applications. They will be greatly thrown off balance by a parental life-style that involves many changes of residence or inconsistencies of approach. More than most children, they require a high degree of sameness and constancy in their day-to-day lives, and when they are threatened, they may become emotionally grasping and possessive, both of their caretakers and of their personal possessions. They'll hoard toys away, selfishly clinging to what is theirs. But when significant changes must occur in the family's life, parents can help the child to adapt simply by being aware of how difficult it will be for him and protectively easing his way. Taurus children won't break under the strain: Strength is one of their most salient qualities. But it's kinder not to force the issue.

Given the security they need, these children will be some of the most affectionate and loving you could ask for, patiently supporting you in times of personal stress (as long as it doesn't threaten them), devoted and loyal friends. All they ask in return is that they be loved and valued. They need a good deal of cuddling and holding and the firm knowledge that you're there for them. Once satisfied, there's no one who can be more deeply content. In fact, their unquestioning acceptance of others can make Taurus children almost magnetic to people who are less secure. They won't get upset easily, patiently enduring the emotional changes that others act out against them.

But unfeeling they are not: When the spade has hit rock bottom, watch out, for there's great power hidden beneath that thick surface, and once it upheaves, things may never be the same again. They can hold a grudge forever—no one is better at it—and, as in other areas, once their minds are set, it can be a Herculean labor to change them. This does not mean, of course, that sensitive parents should live in fear of turning their child against them. All relationships of any depth have their natural ups and downs. Parents can, however, encourage these children gently, lovingly, in whatever way they can, to express their emotions and let them go so that they can be done with. As ever with these basic character traits, this will not be easy—it may seem like trying to move a mountain—and you will have to exercise a great deal of patience yourself in this matter. But just as the seasons change in their own sweet time, so will your slow and steady Taurus.

Because they are so attuned to the earth, Taurus children should respond well to nature, feeling uplifted and deeply centered by its rough-cut beauty. If you live in the country, life with Taurus children should be relatively easy, for this is their natural habitat, but if the city is your home, do make use of the parks for daily leisurely walks if possible. Most people with this sign are fond of animals, so acquiring a dog as a pet may be just the answer for providing your four- or five-year-old Taurus child with some steady loving companionship as well as a reason to exercise out of doors.

A final anecdote may help to illustrate the fixity of purpose and great stubbornness that is typical of Taurus children. A four-year-old friend of ours allowed himself to be encouraged by his enthusiastic mother to join a children's dance class, but when the big day finally arrived and he was brought into the new group of active, eager children, he determinedly announced, "I'm not going to do this. I'll watch." Ever since, week after week, month after month, Virgil faithfully returns to the "class," where he sways to the music with obvious enjoyment and agreeably sits or lies in the center of the floor as the other children dance around him.

The sign of Taurus supplies a kind of energy that is essential to all of us—the strength to see things through—and children of this sign, if helped to come out of themselves a bit more, will increasingly lend their support to others as they mature. Appreciating beauty and creating it wherever they are, these young treasures can provide the valued foundation upon which all else rests.

The Evolving Taurus

BIRTH TO ONE YEAR

The Taurus baby may be quite peaceful in the womb, enter the world rather sluggishly, and, having regarded it briefly, fall asleep within fifteen minutes. When he's frustrated, which is seldom, he typically prefers to whimper softly rather than cry. When he does get upset and bellow loudly, he is more likely to become rigid than to kick and flail. He is easily soothed on these occasions with breast or bottle or with a little warm cuddling.

A Taurus infant will probably be remarkably regular with her feedings (she eats everything), and clocks could be set according to her sleep periods. Parents of such a content, self-contained child may be the envy of the neighbors, but they may be worried about the languorous pace of her development. While the neighbor's kid is fingering, grasping, and shaking rattles, the Taurus child may be intently watching the beads strung across her crib. While others are starting to creep, she may still be sitting and smiling and looking and listening. In fact, some Taurus babies *never* creep; they just sit around until they are ready to stand. Even if a Taurus doesn't walk until eighteen months, he is soaking up large globs of the world through his senses. He loves the feel of things, not only the food he squishes in his hands and smears on his face, but his soft blanket, his stuffed animal, and you when you hold him lovingly.

ONE-YEAR-OLDS

When the Taurus child does finally begin to walk, she is likely to be carrying with her a security blanket or some other dearly treasured object. By their first birthday Taurus children will probably have revealed their warmly affectionate nature, which is directed not only toward you—kissing is a favorite pastime—but toward the teddy bear, the caterpillar pull toy, and the high chair as well. Your Taurus typically enjoys the outdoors immensely, especially from the seat of the moving stroller. Just tell him it's time for a walk, and he should submit without fussing—almost without moving—to being bundled into his snowsuit. Encouraging him to use his legs may be a bit more difficult, however, and when he finally does use them, try not to be impatient with his plodding amble; he was not made to hurry but to savor each step in life with resolute thoroughness.

The predictable regularity of this sign enables many eighteen-month-old Taureans to be toilet trained. You'd better keep an eye on them, though, since their artistic appreciation of color and texture may manifest itself in a gala episode of stool smearing.

TWO-YEAR-OLDS

If you prefer keeping your bed to yourself, the Taurus is one child you probably shouldn't allow to snuggle up with you after she wakes up frightened in the middle of the night. This sensuous little cuddler may soon become attached to this delight, and it will become a rigid practice that will take years for you to convince her to relinquish.

The difficult, ritualistic age of two and a half will probably be especially hard for the Taurus, not to mention his parents. If you don't serve him exactly the same lunch each day, for example, he may stamp his feet, become rigid, and bawl vehemently. The possessiveness typical of the age is more marked in the sign of Taurus. These children will probably keep very careful track of all their toys, and all must be within easy reach. Though they are likely to play best with other children in their own home, they may be quite incapable of giving up control of a single belonging. Those Taureans who still aren't completely toilet trained may now be very reluctant to give up their bowel movements, especially since they can't trust their parents to take good care of them—the bowel movements, that is—and it may take all your wit to erode their intransigence.

THREE-YEAR-OLDS

The toilet-training problems of the Taurus are likely to be cleared up by this age, but there may be an occasional accident because he doesn't like any interruptions from his intensely concentrated play. Taurus threes are now more capable of playing with other children than formerly, but they are more likely to enjoy quiet interaction with one or two other children than the clamor of a large group. Give them some Play-Doh, fingerpaints, or colored paper, paste, and child scissors and they may play contentedly for long periods.

You may become irritated with your Taurus offspring, however, when you need to get someplace with her quickly; it appears that the more you hurry her, the longer it takes. Unfortunately, that may be more than an appearance. The swiftest course to your goal may be simply to take your time. Taurus threes are capable of such deep concentration that they are likely to miss out on exciting events: When one young boy we know was visiting Yellowstone National Park with his family, he became so engrossed in his play with his toy cars in the dirt that he couldn't be persuaded to watch the eruption of Old Faithful.

FOUR-YEAR-OLDS

By now your Taurus has probably given up that security blanket (actually, many have stored it away long before), but a stuffed animal may have taken its place. The Taurus four is still more of a follower in social situations than a leader, but her involvement is definitely more active now. The boasting that is characteristic of the age is likely to be expressed by Taurus children with regard to the size and amount of their possessions. This possessiveness extends to their friends, too. All four-year-olds can be very jealous, but since Taurus children tend to invest their affection in only a few special friends, the jealousy can be rather acute. The usefulness of such a child's focused attention should now be evident as she spends hours learning how to lace her shoes until the technique is mastered. Her concentrated play with clay, fingerpaints, and complicated Lego sets should be encouraged as well as any experimentation she may do with musical instruments or with singing, for music is one of the things Taurus loves best.

FIVE-YEAR-OLDS

Do not startle your Taurus five by a sudden change in routine, because he may become quite flustered and out of sorts: The characteristics of the age and of the sign are mutually reinforcing, and the result is a child who is unusually down-to-earth, home centered, and conservative. Now your Taurus child will make every effort to comply with your wishes and regulations instead of dragging her feet in passive resistance (although she may not hear you if she's deeply involved in some project). Do not abuse her good intentions, however, by trying to transform her into a speed demon; you should know her basic nature by now. Taurus children may need extra time on kindergarten mornings for dressing themselves and eating breakfast. Just remember that what goes along with this deliberateness is persistence; Taureans do not easily give up when practicing a new skill, and manifold new skills for them to master will be introduced when they enter first grade.

♊

Gemini

(SUN SIGN, MAY 21–JUNE 21)

> *"If a Flyer goes very fast, I should like to be one," Tootle answered. "I love to go fast. Watch me."*
> *He raced all around the roundhouse.*
> *"Good! Good!" said Bill. "You must study Whistle Blowing, Puffing Loudly When Starting, Stopping for a Red Flag Waving, and Pulling the Diner without Spilling the Soup.*
> *"But most of all you must study Staying on the Rails No Matter What. Remember, you can't be a Flyer unless you get 100A+ in Staying on the Rails."*
>
> Gertrude Crampton, Tootle

We suspect that the main problem the parents of Gemini children will complain of is simply keeping up with them, for these little birds can usually outtalk, outrun, and even outthink almost everybody else. They may exhaust with amazing rapidity the panoply of games and materials you provide for them, jabbering your ear off as they flutter from one thing to the next; they may well evade your most clever attempts at discipline; and when at last they come to rest, it will be with the fizzle and clink of a short-circuited electrical system.

No doubt this is the extreme, but it does give a sense of the high pitch of energy that most Geminis thrive on. These children will function best when doing several things at once. They will feel most centered when their hands are occupied as well as their brains: With ease your Gemini can simultaneously work a puzzle, listen to a record, talk aloud to herself, and pay attention to a conversation going on at the other side of the room.

In fact, the expansion of language will be a constant preoccupation. Even before age two, she may be explaining the rules of the household to her dolls in many-word sentences accompanied by enthusiastic gesticulation, reciting several nursery rhymes in a row in animated soliloquy, "reading" to herself from memory the storybooks you've been reading to her, and even counting to eight. But there is a danger that she will overextend herself, for her restless curiosity often leads her to attempt so much that she either withers in frustration or blows herself out in a frenzied excess of nervous excitement. Parents must be attentive to the ways of their little thinkers—when they themselves have a moment to reflect, that is—lest these children spend themselves too fast. If you can get them to slow down for periodic rest and refueling and can, as much as possible, keep them to one track until any one thing is completed, you will have gone a long way toward making your Tootles (the little engine of the children's book they so much resemble) into the Flyers they can someday be.

Geminis may find it more difficult to concentrate, to give sustained attention, than other children, and this could be an irritation to you or the nursery school teacher, who must follow their path of toys not put away and passionate interests quickly discarded. Though they should learn to pick up after themselves, do not be too upset by their discursions. Remember that the Gemini's characteristic method of understanding the world is to examine cursorily many details at once and then organize them into a coherent pattern.

The task of helping your Gemini to focus his diversified interests may seem at times like trying to confine the wind, for it really seems to go against his essential nature. You can be reassured, however, that these children may accept guidance more readily than most. They don't really know what they want (this is definitely not a child to whom you should offer choices as a technique for handling), and they'll be interested in anything you have to teach them. But most of all, even from an unusually early age, they'll be children you can reason with. Gemini shares with the other air signs (Libra and Aquarius) a conscious need for communication with others, and you can make use of this highway to their minds whenever you need to steer them in some better direction.

In fact, mind is what the sign of Gemini is all about, and a good percentage of children with this sign will have a particularly intellectual sort of intelligence. They'll want to understand the relationships between things. Books and puzzles will be high on the list of best-loved, most-used learning tools, and Gemini children may also have a precocious interest in symbolic systems, such as the alphabet and numbers. They may be drawn to intelligent adults or older children, for they seek out anyone who can teach them something, craving new information the way some children crave candy. With some Gemini preschoolers, nascent intellect may not be so evident, but even these highly active children, physically into everything, will more likely be in pursuit of some object of their curiosity than activity for its own sake.

With their characteristically slight, alert, wiry little bodies, they will probably be fast (and early) talkers as well as fast movers. It's important to give attention and respect to the Gemini child's need to express herself verbally, hard as it may be for the typically harried parent. If you aren't comfortable with constant verbal give-and-take, do at least set aside time each day to converse with her. Even as early as age three, you might play question-and-answer games together. Or try to collaborate in composing a poem; this stellar twin loves to have a partner in her mental shenanigans. Or ask her to tell *you* a story.

One thing is certain, the Gemini child will often be able to make you laugh. Bright and cheerful as the breeze, he can see the humor in everything, and there is no better monkey than he when it comes to mimicking people. Yet there is a problem with this that may hinder him in later life, and you should be aware of it in order to help him with it now: His rapport with the rational side of life may blind him to its feeling side. Not being very emotional himself, he may be somewhat insensitive to this dimension in others. Conscious of this, the parent or teacher can try to encourage him toward greater awareness of others' emotional needs.

The Gemini's own moods will be highly changeable, and it is a cliché of this sign that in this child you'll have several different people rolled up into one. When she becomes discouraged or angry—or downright impossible from your point of view—it should be relatively easy to distract her and thus lead her in the direction you want (that is, if she hasn't already long ago outsmarted you). Variety is the only staple of her diet—whether it's to be found in food, in friends, in books and toys, or in places—and she'll be impatient with anything less.

The ready adaptability of the Gemini child is not only a necessary mode of existence for him, it can be a boon to you, for you'll be able to take him traveling, visiting, or on short excursions with ease. In fact, one of your parental tasks will be to provide an interesting environment for him. You may have to spend some thought and energy on this when he's an infant and very young toddler, but after that you should be able to teach him to turn himself on.

You'll have to learn to be tolerant of scientific experiments on the living-room rug and obstacle courses in the kitchen, but the alternative is boredom, which to invoke on the Gemini child is equal to the cruelest, harshest punishment. On the other hand, the mother of one Gemini girl we know was so successful at providing this needed stimulation (she worked in a children's book publishing house) that she overheard her four-and-a-half-year-old daughter say to her sister one morning, "Gina, I just had a terrible dream: I woke up Christmas morning, and the only things under the tree were books and records!"

But take a hint from your Gemini's mercurial ways and don't take these words too seriously. Like multiband receiver sets, these children can literally pick up on everything. With even the sparest materials at their disposal they'll use their able wit to see the inherent connections between things, and they'll beam their insights back to you in stimulating profusion.

The Evolving Gemini

BIRTH TO ONE YEAR

Typically, the restive Gemini infant is highly excitable and unusually alert, even from birth. He may awaken at the slightest noise, and even during sleep you may find him squirming. You probably won't be able to depend on the hour of his awakening or on the amount of his food intake; variability is a keynote for Gemini children. If you are trying to program them to a more definite schedule, however, you might try rocking them or carrying them on your shoulder when they fuss, for they love distraction. In fact, when your lithe little six-month-old Gemini is twisting and rolling all over the changing table, a trait common to most babies this age, you may be able to calm her down by talking with her spiritedly about any adult concern with which you're currently preoccupied; the delighted, eloquent babbling of syllables with which she responds may so much resemble real conversation that it will almost convince you she understands perfectly and has already given the matter considerable thought. Or you might try handing her some object, but you'd better have a series of other objects to back it up, for after she has deftly probed it with her fingers, shaken it, and banged it around a few times, she is likely to become bored with it and drop it. Gemini babies will probably be irritable if they run out of things to do. So if you've exhausted your repertoire of baubles, try putting your Gemini in a bounce chair; the constant motion will soothe her.

ONE-YEAR-OLDS

Once the Gemini toddler has independent mobility, it is likely to be even more difficult to get him to sleep than it is for other one-year-olds. The world is just too interesting, and he can't seem to get enough of looking into every little thing. Most Geminis are very nimble on their new legs. One eighteen-month-old of our acquaintance, Micah, was always climbing up onto the dining table, no matter how many times his mother tried to get him to stop. Unfortunately, he often fell, but he never hurt himself enough to forego the excitement of an encore.

Probably the greatest thrill for a Gemini, though, is the acquisition of language. At the time of her first birthday she is no doubt daily augmenting her vocabulary with great numbers of new words. In the course of a year you will probably be amazed at how rapidly her jargon begins to resemble the English you speak, especially if you spend a good deal of time talking with her, for she can only learn what she's exposed to.

This brings us back to the initial problem we posed about the Gemini toddler: How do you get him to sleep? Try instituting a nightly ritual of quietly reading two picture books to him in a rocking chair; at the end of the second book turn the light out and sing a little as you rock. It may work—if he's sufficiently tired. If not, he'll sing right along with you, a companion in arms.

TWO-YEAR-OLDS

You may encounter some difficulty with your Gemini two with regard to toilet training, especially since the times of her movements are likely to be unpredictable. It may be easier if she socializes with other children who are already trained, since Geminis are such great imitators. You should also encourage her to report to you whenever she feels the urge (it may help if you report to her when *you* feel the urge); this will probably better enable her to control her eliminations, just as language has given her control over so many other areas of her life.

The ambivalence so characteristic of the difficult age of two and a half may be particularly marked with Geminis. Do not bother them with choices, for they can become utterly impossible with their vacillations. Just inform them of the day's itinerary, be sure to offer them second chances when they resist your directives, and distract them from their screaming fits with matter-of-fact conversation.

THREE-YEAR-OLDS

Your Gemini at this sociable age may be introducing others at nursery school to the good sense of sharing toys and taking turns. In fact, since he is characteristically capable of seeing both sides of an issue, he may take the role of referee, helping two friends resolve their dispute.

Language, the forte of Geminis, is the medium through which you can control their unacceptable behavior. Reason usually works with children of this sign, but distraction is still an effective technique. When you see resistance building up to your rational and moderate request, ask her if she thinks it will rain tomorrow or point out how much longer the icicles are today than they were yesterday.

Discipline problems may be almost negligible if the Gemini three is provided with riddle books, puzzles, and an occasional educational television program. At three and a half he may show a faltering of his verbal agility, and some Geminis may even develop temporary stuttering. This leveling period could be a useful occasion for parents to realize that they may have been expecting too much maturity from the linguistically precocious Gemini. Underneath the finesse with speech may lie an unrecognized emotional insecurity; if you can be sensitive to more than just the face value of his words, you may help him allay the fears typical of this age.

FOUR-YEAR-OLDS

The Gemini four is likely to boast about her ability to count and to "write." In fact, she may very well be able to print her own name and can probably count a good many objects while pointing to them. Also she can no doubt talk circles around anyone, including you, and you may become quite vexed with her nagging inquisitiveness, her endless chain of whys. Gemini fours seem to have a knack for clowning with language, and at an age where verbal silliness prevails, they amuse with their rhymes and amaze with their coinages. Some Geminis enjoy "lying," however, and rather than get upset about an essentially harmless developmental stage, you might try winking at them while you disarm them with an even taller tale.

FIVE-YEAR-OLDS

One way to channel your garrulous Gemini five's incessant chatter is through supervised play with a tape recorder. Both of you will probably be delighted when you hear his witty juxtapositions and offhand insights played back in his own version of a radio talk show. Or maybe you would enjoy viewing your little anchorman delivering the six o'clock news live through a window cut out of a large box. Most Geminis of this age are capable of engaging in a penetrating discussion with an adult and can sufficiently deal with such abstract concepts as fairness and honesty that now may be a good time to help them develop a mature ethical sense. Exceptions to rules will likely perplex them, however (five is a particularly literal age), so you'd best have logical explanations handy for all your ad hoc directives.

♋

Cancer

(SUN SIGN, JUNE 22–JULY 23)

When Bobby got close to the hedge the first time, Momo's face appeared and said, "Hi, Bobby!" Although Bobby wanted to be there, he felt so uncomfortable that he hid behind his grandmother.

When Bobby got close to the hedge the next time, Momo's face appeared again and said, "How do you feel today, Bobby?" And although Bobby wanted to be there, he felt so uncomfortable that he closed his eyes.

When Bobby got close to the hedge the next time, Momo's face appeared again and said, "Your nickname is apricot, Bobby!" And though Bobby wanted to be there, he felt so uncomfortable that he covered his face with Grandmother's hand.

When Momo said next time, "Oh, Bobby, you look like a big boy today!" Bobby wanted to see her. He kept his eyes open. Sure enough, right there, smiling eyes in Momo's face were looking straight at him! And Bobby smiled right back.

Taro Yashima, The Youngest One

Many parents secretly cringe in embarrassment and disapproval when their young child clings to them in fear of strangers who are in fact acting kindly enough in their attempts to amuse the little one. We want our offspring to respond to others in a friendly manner, as we have learned to do, perhaps not recognizing that we ourselves may not always really feel as open and sociable as we choose to believe. Cancer children manifest this behavior more consistently than most, and parents will simply have to learn to appreciate its significance if they want to raise a happy child.

Cancer's keynote is feeling, and with that goes an intuitive sensitivity to all possibly threatening situations. Soft yet serious looking, these children sense early and well where their security lies—close by their mother's side and within the protective walls of home. Just like the crab, whose hard outer shell protects its soft underbelly, their vulnerability is very real to them, and they'll never expose it until they're sure of the response. Their intuitions are often right, so adults who aren't affected by such things themselves could afford to trust them.

These children will flower, however, in the presence of their home and family, and you will be amazed later on to discover how many details they vividly remember from early childhood. (One four-year-old friend of ours announced in all gravity one day, after a particularly rewarding afternoon with her grandmother, "I'll never forget this as long as I live—not even if I live to be eighteen!") They'll collect and treasure memories in the same way that they'll preserve all objects that are old and that have sentimental value, such as the dress-up clothes and jewelry you hand down to them or the seashells you gathered together one summer. They may truly prefer the dusty one-eyed teddy bear that you found in the attic to the new and brightly colored Winnie-the-Pooh you just purchased, and their preferences, of course, should be respected. From their collection of treasures they'll lovingly assign certain items as gifts to this family member or that, feeling reassured in the sense this gives them of a connection to their loved ones. More than with children of other signs, it is said that a happy home life and a good relationship with their parents almost guarantees a secure and well-adjusted Cancer adult.

But, as with all things "good," there is an underside to this, a negative to the positive that fills out the whole. Cancer children do need a little gentle help from people they trust in order to overcome their natural timidity and fear of insecurity. They will grow by facing the new as well as by absorbing the old, and not everything in life can be so carefully insured as they would have it. Their own changing and unpredictable moods are as unstabilizing to them as the insensitive, perhaps critical responses they may be afraid to receive from others, and they are capable of inexplicable shifts into crabby bad tempers and silent bottlenecks as a result.

But wise and informed parents can help them invaluably if they can guide them toward a conscious understanding of these fluctuating emotions. Mere release of emotion in a torrent of tears may not be sufficient for Cancers truly to let go of feelings; for some this may come all too easily and may not really resolve anything. Parents will have the long, hard job of trying to teach them to gain some perspective on themselves—a task that may sometimes seem as impossible as trying to stop the tide at full swell. More so than most children, Cancer young ones see everything in terms of their private feelings, and they share with the other water signs (Scorpio and Pisces) a deep need to respond to the world emotionally. They'll want to brood in some secret place they have, but in due course they should be encouraged to brighten up and return to the fold.

It may go without saying, but unless this drawing out is attempted with respect and understanding, you may have a compliant but still deeply resentful crab on your hands. They'll be more perceptive of the feeling tone behind your words than you may realize, so you'd better be sure of it yourself. When the emotions of a Cancer are thwarted, they plunge right to her stomach, and parents may find themselves having to deal with a spate of bellyaches or related gastrointestinal upsets instead. Similarly, if the atmosphere is a tense one, don't expect your Cancer sponge to remain dry of her surroundings. At difficult moments you can always try giving her a bath or setting her up with some water play, for this is her natural medium, the place where she can always reestablish her peaceful center.

Pregnant with feelings, Cancer children are also the perfect little parents to their dolls, siblings, and even friends. They'll solicitously change their diapers, feed them, and protect them. In a pinch you can always depend on the Cancer boy or girl among your children to look after the other ones, but don't fall back on this too often; natural as this is for them, they, too, must have their full measure of carefree childhood dependency. Even without this kind of responsibility, they'll have a tendency to overworry, allowing their rich imagination to reveal to them all possible kinds of harm that could befall their loved ones, and they can get quite upset over this. However, in happier frames of mind they'll be thoughtful, helpful, and extremely affectionate.

Cancer children are deeply receptive to fairy tales, as well as to music. They love to weave dreamy webs of romance around themselves in the form of reassuring cocoons. Possessing the innate capacity to resonate fully with all the vibratory dimensions of emotion, they can nonetheless transmute this wealth of feeling into practical, homespun terms. Thus, you'll one day be amused to find your Cancer child soothing her family of dolls with her own version of "Snow White and the Seven Dwarfs," her own beguiling lullabyes. And who knows, someday you may be the proud parent of a widely respected creative artist.

By now it should be clear that these tender moon children need never be treated roughly or be severely scolded in order to get the message across that you disapprove of some behavior. They will feel your disappointment in them the way that water reflects light, and because they need you so badly, they will usually come around on their own. If you offer them ungrudgingly the security and love they need, they, like the watchful, reflecting moon, will generously return to others all they have received from you and more.

The Evolving Cancer

BIRTH TO ONE YEAR

The Cancer baby typically has a very changeable disposition. For a half hour or so she may be utterly consumed by fretful crying; then an hour may go by while she lies silent, emitting an occasional gurgle but mostly just soaking up impressions of her new world. You probably won't be able to predict the onset of her next crying jag, and once you've eliminated hunger and the gas bubble, you may not have any idea why she is so upset. It seems that Cancers are more under the sway of mysterious visceral pangs than are most infants. Also they often seem quite homesick for the security of the womb, and for this reason you may be able to soothe them by holding them close, stroking them, and gently rocking them. Some of your Cancer's brightest moments are likely to be when you are bathing him; perhaps the buoyancy and massage of the sloshing water brings back pleasant memories. He probably will be in no great hurry over the usual developmental milestones, which thrust him further from his prenatal haven, and he may at first withdraw from such new experiences as solid foods or an unfamiliar person's visit. But he'll slowly adapt as he comes to learn that you can really be trusted to return from the bathroom and that his home is a stable, relatively unchanging nest.

ONE-YEAR-OLDS

The newfound ability to walk gives the Cancer child a sense of independence she may not have realized up to now how much she really did need. Now she can meander around—and begin to control—the environment that is so important to her. Her exploration is typically directed toward finding special private niches for herself in the house. She may be most content playing in some corner of her room surrounded by walls of pillows, her toy chest, and assorted chairs. This will be her "home," and you'd better have an invitation before you disturb its sanctity.

Cancer toddlers usually display considerable affection toward their toys, and there may be one they're especially fond of, without which they won't be able to sleep. They may also enjoy putting toys inside containers, where they'll be "safe." This child's concern for his belongings often extends to many other objects in the household, and he may be helpful in small ways as you straighten things up.

Your Cancer is now learning to talk, but don't expect to understand all the causes of his bad moods; he may not know what's wrong himself. You shouldn't rule out jealousy of the new baby just because he seems so cherishing of her. His emotions are probably quite mixed—his fear of feing displaced in the family may compete with his happiness about the family's enlargement—and you should watch that his loving embrace of the baby isn't a bit too snug.

TWO-YEAR-OLDS

The ambivalent feelings of the Cancer child toward his other siblings may well have been resolved by the time he is two. Now he is more likely to be friendly and protective toward them. In fact, Cancer twos may already be developing a tremendous loyalty to their family and concern for their welfare (which is actually an extension of the personal insecurity that is characteristic of this age), and they may worry that any visiting guests will upset the domestic routine. A Cancer two is typically very shy with an unfamiliar adult and should be allowed to soak up the stranger's presence without being forced to interact. Eventually, if the adult throws only an occasional warm glance or lighthearted remark toward her, she may hospitably accept him into her domain. You should never let your worries about what others may think pressure you into forcing your Cancer two to relate to a stranger—including "Santa Claus."

At two and a half her attachment to the familiar may wax to unmanageable proportions, and she may respond to your rearrangement of the furniture with a series of bad-tempered outbursts alternating with whimpering, finger-sucking reviews of her infancy. Activities that bring the entire family together will usually help assuage her peevishness, and these occasions are likely to become her earliest memories.

THREE-YEAR-OLDS

By his third birthday the Cancer child may at times still insist on getting into his parents' bed after waking from a disturbing dream, but he is generally much less insecure. He is not likely to be especially outgoing, however, and sometimes prefers quiet play by himself to the more active social scene at the nursery school. His clannishness may come to encompass the teacher and kids at school, too, so you'd better think twice before you transfer him. He is likely to be very susceptible to the environment, so don't be surprised if you have difficulty fathoming him after he has spent a particularly grueling day at school.

Cancers have active imaginations, and you probably should indulge any invisible personage who comes to befriend your child, accompanying her everywhere. "He" will go away soon enough of "his" own accord, but in the meantime your child will be comforted by the companionship.

FOUR-YEAR-OLDS

At this age your Cancer child will probably be bragging about *you* to all her friends. Don't be too quick, out of some misplaced sense of modesty, to disabuse her of the notion that you're so great; her exaggerations about her family will actually help her enlarge her world beyond it, for this is her way of attempting to increase her stature among her playmates. Cancer fours are likely to be assets in any group of children, since they can empathetically soothe the wounded egos of those unfortunates ostracized from the tribal in-groups typical of this age.

The ebb and flow of their moods may still be perplexing to adults, however: Cancer-moon Jeff, a very casual acquaintance, was one of the children we drove in our nursery school car pool. He rarely spoke with us and often seemed withdrawn during the entire long ride. But when we arrived at school, he, not our daughter, would regularly snuggle up and kiss us good-bye.

FIVE-YEAR-OLDS

By now you may be able to appreciate your Cancer child's phenomenal memory as he recalls the very words you used three years before when you scolded him for running across the street or reminisces about his third Christmas, when grandma visited for a week. Unfortunately, during this characteristically conservative age, he may not be very open to new ideas. He may also be swallowing your philosophical outlook all too unquestioningly; that, too, is typical of the age, but Cancer children are far more tenacious than most about concepts acquired at this time. If you don't wish your child to grow into an adult who clings too dearly to outmoded ideas, a reactionary whose mind is an indomitable bulwark against fresh approaches to problems, try playing devil's advocate with your own beliefs and avoid unnecessary preaching.

Don't be surprised if your Cancer five stews about you when you go out for the evening; the motherly role is appropriate for this sign. She only stews because you are so dear to her. Her ability to nurture may surprise you someday when you feel you must soften the impact on her of some family adversity: She will probably be the one consoling you.

♌
Leo
(SUN SIGN, JULY 24–AUGUST 23)

"Rabbit," they said. "Oh, you wonderful rabbit! What in the world did you talk to the tawny, scrawny, hungry, terrible lion about?"

The fat little rabbit jumped up in the air and said, "Oh, my goodness! We had such a good time with that nice, jolly lion that I guess we forgot to talk about anything at all!"

And before the big animals could say one word, the tawny lion came skipping up the path. He had a basket of berries for the fat rabbit sisters, and a string of fish for the fat rabbit brothers, and a big bunch of daisies for the fat rabbit himself.

"I came for supper," he said, shaking paws all around.

Kathryn Jackson, Tawny Scrawny Lion

Leo children can be lovable indeed, with their sunny spirits and optimistic natures that warm all those close to them. In fact, it may be difficult for their parents to feel anything but the greatest pride in such glowing offspring, for, during the preschool years at least, we parents are anxious to have these fruits of our devoted labors shine for us. With his characteristically strong, forceful physique well-balanced by graceful good posture, your Leo child will be courageous and proud, king of the beasties, born leader of the playgroup. He'll approach all things with an innate sense of dignified yet playful exuberance and will rarely, if ever, become depressed or worried over matters that would make less confident children feel insecure.

Yet there is one thing that parents of Leo children may have to deal with if they want to send their young stars into even higher orbits. Used to your loyal love, expecting the unquestioning support of their rightfully impressed followers, Leo children can become so full of themselves that there is little room for anyone other than their adoring entourage. Flourishing in the limelight, they are quite capable of creating dramatic emotional scenes in order to recapture center stage if it has been momentarily lost.

How you deal with these tendencies in your young prince or princess will probably have a significant effect on the child's later bearing. But words of caution are in order: The needs of the Leo personality, as with all the other signs, run deep, and trying to discipline this raw energy may seem as unnatural as turning off the sun. For example, two-year-old Katy is an absolute delight, and her mother loves her dearly. But Katy is so attached to her mother's enjoyment of her antics that she simply can't tolerate solitude or any inattention on her mother's part. In fact, it's gotten to the point where her mother actually has to lock herself in the bathroom to get a few minutes away from her demanding daughter, a situation that causes unhappiness all around.

So if you don't want to have an adorable dictator on your hands eventually, it's desirable to try to teach Leo children some regard for others as well as for themselves. This doesn't mean that you should try to curb their high, bright spirits. Harsh criticism or ridicule could really hurt them, for their pride is vital to them. Without it they can forget their own real virtues and shrivel to the status of a purrless kitten.

Besides, just as they thrive on self-respect, they also need to respect their parents as their primary role models. Coveting the crown themselves, Leo children will look to you, their king or queen, for the present, for guidance; so whatever you can do to manifest yourself as a wise being who treats everyone with benevolence and consideration will set an example for them that they can absorb as they do the rays of the sun. (In fact, it's helpful to remember—whenever those bossy, attention-demanding ways get to be too much for you—that Leos have a great affinity with that other ruler: the sun. Its penetrating warmth will generally calm them, bringing them back to a state of centered equilibrium.) And if your Leo child is certain of your love, she will strive wholeheartedly not to disappoint your expectations of her.

Since Leos share with the other fire signs (Sagittarius and Aries) an intense need to express themselves, these well-endowed children may show an unusual degree of inspired creativity in their general play. They may prefer to produce their artwork on the largest possible scale, and you might consider the inexpensive purchase of a large role of butcher paper (this can be done through your grocer) to serve as a ground upon which they can create vistas or civilizations or worlds. They radiate an instinctive sense of organization, which is also part of their leadership ability, and with their flair for the dramatic, you may find even your four-year-old lion cub directing (and starring in) a play of Peter Pan and the pirates. Leo boys and girls will adore dress-up clothes (with their elegant artistic sense, they'll appreciate the more beautiful among them), so don't stint on this play material if you can help it.

But again, though you can expect to find them at the enthusiastic hub of any group of children, do be aware that some young Leos may lapse into being bullies if they do not get their way. Power will be a central focus for them their whole life long, so they need to be taught from an early age the right sources of it. Overbearing superiority may influence enemies, but it doesn't win friends.

This should not be too difficult for Leo children to learn, however. Since they so much desire the respect of others, they recognize early that honesty and a basic sense of fairness earn them this right. Boasting and showing off work for them in the early years, but since these techniques can't command the essential *self*-respect, they'll (hopefully) be discarded.

But most Leo children actually maintain their power over others not through bullying but through their generous affection. They literally love their following and any child in their sphere of influence will be treated with warmth and kindness. Their tendencies to arrogance, furthermore, are usually more than compensated for by their unbounded capacity for magnanimous love. It may be safe to say that no one can love you like a Leo child. Even when he's disappointed, he doesn't become bitter, and if he fundamentally trusts and respects you, he'll forgive you completely no matter how angry you've made him in an argument. You'll find this love a mainstay, returning to it for replenishment whenever you need it.

Leos shine most of all for their immediate family. Quintessential children, they bask in the positive vibrations they feel from their near dear. Their deep attachment to their own kin can be so great that they may have trouble emotionally leaving the supportive embrace of home for the wider world of unknown elements. Helped with this by informed, conscious adults, Leo children can learn to expand their talent of giving love to their family and to themselves into a gift of love for all.

Leos are determined to enjoy themselves to the fullest extent, but since they cannot live for themselves alone, they want everybody to enjoy life with them. Even as young children, they have a way of making any get-together lively and fun, and just observing their zest for life is enough to make every experience with them a festival.

The Evolving Leo

BIRTH TO ONE YEAR

The Leo baby, more than other infants, is the center of the household. Most Leos regulate themselves to a fairly fixed schedule rather quickly, which is fortunate because it will probably be impossible to ignore your Leo baby when he wants something: He is likely to scream with despotic authority. Most of the demands are for company, for there is probably nothing Leo babies love more than a convivial atmosphere. They especially enjoy visitors who like babies, and they will bask in the attentions of grandpa, Aunt Ruth, or your kitchykooing neighbor. Any adult or older child who makes funny faces or is fluent in baby talk will probably be regarded with lusty chortles. It may be difficult, however, for the visitor to resume the adult conversation, since the Leo baby's appetite for interaction is likely to be close to insatiable. And you may have to be hardhearted (and unhearing) after returning your nine-month-old to the crib at the conclusion of her wee-hour feeding; she probably won't understand why you can't join her in some after-dinner fun and games.

Leo babies really flourish in front of an appreciative audience and will gladly give many repeat performances of grabbing their feet, using the crib rail to pull themselves up, saying "mama," or whatever developmental milestone they have mastered.

ONE-YEAR-OLDS

Though he may insist that you keep him company when he is enthroned in his high chair, your Leo toddler will probably want to feed himself. Mealtimes can become very difficult if you don't go along with him on this. But if you prepare for these festive occasions by spreading out newspapers on the floor and if you serve him wholesome foods he can dip his fingers into, you'll find it hard to restrain your laughter as your little epicure attacks his banquet in grand style.

A Leo child can become quite impossible if you dare assault his dignity by removing a knife or your visitor's glasses from his hands, and he may try to frighten you back to your place with a colossal tantrum. Though you shouldn't give in to such a display, you might try offering a more acceptable toy or doing something silly to make him laugh. If that doesn't work, affection might—anything to help him save face.

Your Leo may call you back quite a few times after you've said goodnight, and you may find it hard to be gracious about this after a full day of her constant demands. Leaving the door slightly ajar so that she can enjoy a small shaft of living-room light and the sounds of your evening good fellowship may help her relax into sleep.

TWO-YEAR-OLDS

Leo twos usually respond well to toilet training, provided they are given enough latitude. Supply them with a potty chair, which they can manage without your help, and without waxing ecstatic, appreciate their performance.

Your Leo two may at first deeply resent being upstaged by the entrance of a new brother or sister, but if you give him some important responsibility in the baby's care, such as fetching diapers or wiping up spit-ups, and if you show your appreciation with frequent praise, you may eventually be remarking to friends how you wouldn't be able to get along without his help. With time, your child care burdens may be greatly alleviated: Your Leo will be keeping the baby entertained, and as a consequence he will need your devoted attention far less frequently. Already at this age Leos have a lively theatrical ability, and their exuberant imitation of you and other adults is bound to delight you.

Leo twos are generally very proud of any new articles of clothing, and you may meet considerable resistance when you petition yours to remove her new shoes before she goes to bed. Almost all children become somewhat imperious at two and a half, but you may conclude that not even Napoleon could compare with your Leo when her every haughty word seems to have the authority of fiat. There will probably be fewer tantrums if you let her choose in those instances where the outcome of her choice doesn't matter to you. Instead of "It's bedtime now," try saying, "Which story shall I read you before you get into bed?"

THREE-YEAR-OLDS

You may by now think your house will never be silent again as your Leo enthusiastically voices his deafening dog yaps and cat yowls. In fact, since he derives so much merriment from acting, you should never be at a loss for ways of playing with him. Just say, "Let's pretend . . . " and the play will begin.

Probably one of the greatest problems Leo threes need to contend with is loneliness, but they are usually mature enough by now to handle the responsibility of a pet, particularly a puppy, which might well result in a relationship that will enliven every adventure for the next several years.

Your Leo at three and a half may attempt to control you by threatening the withdrawal of her love. Don't be frightened by an "I don't love you," and certainly don't retaliate with a counterwithdrawal, which can be very damaging to her morale. Your child is likely to be somewhat insecure at this age (hence her intensified need to assert her will over yours), and in order to gain reassurance she may repeatedly ask you if you love her. Do reassure her.

FOUR-YEAR-OLDS

At least according to him, no child can outdo your swaggering Leo four. And his exaggerations may be more believed than those of other kids his age because they are delivered with such hearty self-confidence. His great prestige with his playmates enables his say-so at the nursery school to have nearly as much weight as the teacher's. Back at home your Leo will still have a knack for capturing your attention. (After drawing out the performance of his slapstick gags as long as visiting adults are willing to listen, Ian brings storybooks to his mother and repeatedly interrupts her attempts to socialize by pointing to pictures and eagerly calling out at the top of his voice, "And look at *this* one!")

If you want to get your Leo four to eat more heartily, you might tell her that it's the only way she'll get big. Preoccupied with growth, she may forget how small she still is and try to boss her older brother or sister.

FIVE-YEAR-OLDS

You may very well be able to control your Leo five's naughtiness by eliciting a promise from him. Or express your displeasure (with his actions, not with him) in a heart-to-heart talk; he is quite likely to want to do everything to make you proud of him. If you want his participation in the household chores, try making a game out of them. And delegate to him as much jurisdiction over these areas as you possibly can; he is likely to strive hard not to disappoint you.

Be careful not to express your opinions too forcefully in front of a Leo five; she is prone to adopt them as her own and hold on to them all too rigidly. In any case, you will always appreciate your Leo child's wholehearted enjoyment of things as well as her self-assured composure.

♍

Virgo

(SUN SIGN, AUGUST 24–SEPTEMBER 23)

"Your ears are too big for you, and your nose is a way too big for you. And your skin is much, MUCH *too big for you. It's baggy and saggy. You should call yourself Saggy-Baggy!"*

Sooki sighed. His pants did *look pretty wrinkled.*

"I'd be glad to improve myself," he said, "but I don't know how to go about it. What shall I do?"

"I can't tell you. I never saw anything like you all my life!" replied the parrot.

The little elephant tried to smooth out his skin. He rubbed it with his trunk. That did no good.

He pulled up his pants legs—but they fell right back into dozens of wrinkles.

It was very disappointing, and the parrot's saucy laugh didn't help a bit.

K. & B. Jackson, **The Saggy Baggy Elephant**

Virgo children often have a hard time being understood by more outgoing types. They are imbued with a natural reserve that can make getting close to them seem laboriously difficult. Rather than feeling immediately at ease the way you would with some children, you might rightly get the impression that you're being scrutinized, assessed inside and out, and tentatively classified until further behavior puts you into a different category. At the very least, you'll pick up that there's no open highway to knowing these sensitive creatures but only a circuitously winding inward path.

Painfully shy are these cautious little beings. Where some children might take the occasion of a casual "How are you?" to tell you everything they ate for breakfast, how their father banged his knee, a complete inventory of their toys, and what their mother said when their sister spilled her milk, Virgo children will typically answer in monosyllabic mumbles. That is, unless you have found them in a talkative mood—more likely after they know you well—when they can yap your head off with an outpouring of their attentive, busy minds.

But unfortunately, Virgos often perceive themselves as not being liked or highly regarded, and, in their intense and sincere modesty about themselves, they more or less accept this as a general fact of life. To a small degree this may be a self-fulfilling prophecy because, not putting themselves forward sufficiently, they may not evoke in others the respect they deserve. However, more often than not, people really do accept them for what they are—the quiet doers of this world—and it is actually their constant *self*-criticism and high standards that make them feel restricted.

The obvious role for the parent or teacher here is to help these children learn to be easier on themselves. This is one group of children for whom reassurance and encouragement are definitely needed on an ongoing basis. They may sometimes give up on a task even before it's attempted, worried that they are inadequate to it. Get them to *try* to figure out how to work that buckle or lace their shoes, even if these things can't be done properly the first few times. Learning through trying is what counts, not perfect results, and they can be taught to concentrate on the process rather than on the end product. With your uncritical support, they may gain in self-confidence. However, it must be remembered that the striving after perfection is essential to the Virgo nature, so your efforts to help them loosen up can begin to seem as futile as convincing the Internal Revenue Service to forget its paperwork. Try not to get discouraged yourself.

Another way you can help these children acquire confidence in what they *can* do is by getting them to help with chores. This may sound peculiar, because everyone knows how children *hate* to do chores. But these conscientious beavers really thrive on them, preferably when it means genuine assistance to poor harried you and not just some meaningless ritual. They can learn to set the table when you're really busy with dinner, find you the proper tools when you're fixing the lamp, or diaper the baby when your hands are full of flour. Sharing with the other earth signs (Capricorn and Taurus) a steadfast need to see the tangible results of their labors, they have the gift of losing themselves in the act of helping others, and their affinity for hard work and careful attention to detail make them real and valuable assistants.

Detail, in fact, is one of the Virgo hallmarks. Children of this sign are incredibly observant, and even the young ones will want to have every fact of a situation—relevant and irrelevant—told to them before they feel satisfied that they've received the information properly. As you leave to go out for an evening, you may have to take some extra time to explain who you and mommy are going to see, what part of town it's in and which route you expect to take, who else will be there, what you plan to do if it snows and which umbrella you're going to take and why, what you're going to tell the host if you're late, and how much you plan to tip the cab driver. After that you may leave your child playing happily with the baby-sitter, reason—if not punctuality—having at last prevailed. It is almost as if the details themselves are all-important to the Virgo child, far more so than the overall meaning they may have in any larger sense. Busy little squirrels, they'll collect minutiae like acorns, storing them away into this hole and that.

It's a cliché of the Virgo temperament that people of this sign are neat and tidy; yet one always knows at least a few whose whole approach to life seems to spell M-E-S-S! Actually, as one Virgo mother of a Virgo boy described it to us, it's really just an organized chaos. What looks to the casual observer like a bedroom in complete dishevelment is to the Virgo child a meaningful concatenation of pockets of . . . well, *things*. Parents had best learn not to clean a Virgo child's room without permission—or, better still, supervision. One mother discovered the hard way—by provoking copious tears—that she had better henceforth respect the sanctity of her daughter's collection of paper scraps, each with its own little scribble. No one knew what they meant but Stacy—and she wasn't telling.

With all this concentration on the raw data of life, you would think that these children would get a little overwrought at times. And indeed, nervous tension is a common ailment, with intestinal upsets the frequent result. Characteristically slender and high-strung, with cool, chiseled features, Virgo people seem to have the task in life of digesting for all of us the food of experience. Health, therefore, plays a major role in their orientation to life, whether it's the proper balance that comes from attention to good diet or the overattention to the state of their bodies that can lead to debilitating hypochondria.

Extreme worry and fretfulness are the concomitants of such nervous tension, to which even children are prone: From the moment that three-year-old Aaron was told he would be taken to the Well Baby Clinic in a few days to get his shot, he became very quiet. This was highly unusual for this little chatterbox, but his mother counted her blessings and didn't question it further. Came the scheduled appointment for the injection, he went to his fate in ashen silence, though all around him children were screaming and crying in distress. Aaron, unique among all others, was smiling in relief as he emerged from the medical office. "They didn't shoot me!" he told his mother happily.

When Virgo children you know seem particularly burdened by the countless cares they so readily take on their little shoulders, try setting them up with crayons and paper, maybe some measuring cups or cookie cutters for their sandbox, or, best of all, a real hammer and nails (for the threes and up). The medium in which they can best express themselves and find inner peace is a tangible yet creative one. They are the makers among us, the craftsmen who shape the earth into usable form. Steer them in this natural direction, and Virgo children will be healthy, well-regulated, and reasonably content.

The Evolving Virgo

BIRTH TO ONE YEAR

The typical Virgo infant is a poor sleeper: It may take a very long stint of cradle rocking to get her to succumb to needed slumber, and a creaky closet door or the barking of a dog several houses away is likely to rouse her. The first three months with a Virgo baby may be quite taxing: Many may be colicky, and some bottle-fed Virgos are quite prone to allergies. Even after this fretful period, your Virgo may not smile and coo as much as the baby next door; she just seems to observe everything carefully—suspiciously, you might think—and may resist with angry fussing your efforts to play with her hands and feet. And if you let a stranger intrude himself too closely to her, you may have to deal with her distress for half an hour. It's as though she wants to figure out the world completely before she gets involved in it. But a Virgo needs and craves as much stimulation as any other baby; it's just that you should give her some time to warm up.

Virgos generally like things they can manipulate, and they will make good use of crib pullers, knockers, bells, and beads. They will also enjoy your talking to them, and you may be able to overcome some of your Virgo's resistance to the foods you're trying to get past his discriminating palate by beguiling him with a lively conversation. It also may help if you let him wield a teething biscuit while you feed him; you will probably be amused to see the delicate way he licks it all over before putting it into his mouth.

ONE-YEAR-OLDS

Even when he's upset, your Virgo toddler may not like being held; he just seems to squirm and fidget. He may also be quite ticklish, a quality Uncle Ed may be tempted to exploit to get him to lighten up with some exuberant giggles. There are methods that are gentler and in the long run more successful for developing the sociability of Virgo children, however. Most Virgos are extremely interested in language, specifically in learning the names of things. They will probably love your reading a book to them, especially if you let them turn the pages, and they will often be aware of subtle distinctions in the pictures. "Word books," with a multitude of objects on a double-page spread, may be a particular delight.

Your Virgo toddler will probably enjoy exploring cupboards and closets throughout the house and may select a few places to store her little treasures—extra bottle nipples, barrettes, plastic bracelets, and discarded jar lids.

These children may develop severe constipation if you apply too much pressure in toilet training at this age. Virgos are quite capable of feeling considerable humiliation and shame, and they may become very upset that they can't meet your expectations of them.

TWO-YEAR-OLDS

Since Virgo twos know where things belong and like to help put them away, your toilet-training efforts may be more auspicious now—provided you put more emphasis on praise for their successes than on disappointment over their accidents. Some Virgos at this age may insist on being fed because they are disgusted with the messes that result from their ineptitude with eating utensils. This is even more likely to happen if you allow yourself to become overly upset with flecks of gravy on the tablecloth or ketchup moustaches.

At two and a half your Virgo may pay more scrupulous attention to petty rituals than other children his age. Your irritation with his querulousness will probably be less frequent if you endeavor to keep these rituals as simple as possible. Virgos are likely to find even the tiniest choice agonizing, so your days with them will be smoother if you announce an itemized schedule in advance.

You should give some thought toward making your Virgo's room a stimulating environment, for she may prefer to stay in it for long periods. Virgos love toys that demand finger dexterity and their talent for discrimination—for example, lacing cards, puzzles, or sorting boxes.

THREE-YEAR-OLDS

Many Virgo threes may need to talk to themselves for an hour or more before they can get off to sleep; it may be that they are trying to organize and digest their many experiences of the day. Not much is likely to escape these perspicacious observers, but if they don't have some regulating order in their life, they may become nervous and tense. Learning to tell time may be beyond many at this age, but you can start them toward that goal by mentioning the hour whenever any routine activity is begun. However, it will take a while for them fully to comprehend duration, especially periods longer than a day, and you probably should not give them too much advance warning of a change in activity: They may become apprehensive, and the present would be spoiled.

Your Virgo three is old enough to attend nursery school, and the exposure to a group will be good for him, but he should not be heavily pressured to participate actively with the group. He will probably feel more comfortable with the teacher than with the other children, but at three and a half he may form one or two close friendships. Privacy is very dear to Virgos, however, and at this age they may still be quite content in solitary play with connect-the-dot drawings, intricate Lego sets, dollhouse furnishings, and little boxes with drawers to store costume jewelry, pebbles, or odds and ends.

FOUR-YEAR-OLDS

Your Virgo four may be very squeamish about the meals the rest of the family wolfs down; she may cringe at even well-cooked onions and can turn nearly green at the thought of clams in the spaghetti sauce. If you take a hard line on this, her dislikes may become permanent. It's probably better if you offer nutritionally well-balanced but simpler fare—at least for her—until her curiosity prompts her to taste something new. However, at this age her persnicketiness about the way her sandwich is cut, though indicating the beginnings of an independent aesthetic sense, may actually be a stalling tactic. When you find you are getting annoyed with the persistent whys of your Virgo four, try to ask yourself whether information or mere attention is being sought. Remember that Virgos are sincerely interested in matters that may seem like trifles to your undiscerning mind.

At nursery school your Virgo will probably enjoy keeping a notebook in which he can paste pictures of cars, animals, or other meaningful items. He works best independently and in a deliberate, methodical manner, but he will probably accept the teacher's help on occasion.

FIVE-YEAR-OLDS

When you reprimand a Virgo five, she may drop her eyes and remain silent, and you can be sure that your criticisms have cut quite deeply. Some Virgos, however, cry bitterly with their hurt feelings. Some may even have considerable fear of being called bad. If you engage these children in a *discussion* instead of a stern lecture, they may correct their aberrant behavior and take comfort in your trust in them at the same time.

Virgos should probably be encouraged to undertake a collection of some sort at this age; it will develop their talent for classifying.

Your Virgo five may by now be an able and incessant talker and may have completely memorized many-verse songs with great ease and pleasure. If you can't resist singing along, take care that you, too, know all the lyrics perfectly; he can become very exasperated with you—even furious to the point of tears—for messing up his song.

♎

Libra

(SUN SIGN, SEPTEMBER 24–OCTOBER 23)

The Owl and the Pussy-cat went to sea
  In a beautiful pea-green boat:
They took some honey, and plenty of money
  Wrapped up in a five-pound note.
The Owl looked up to the stars above,
  And sang to a small guitar,
"O lovely Pussy, O Pussy, my love,
  What a beautiful Pussy you are,
          You are,
          You are!
What a beautiful Pussy you are!"
          Edward Lear, The Owl and the Pussy-cat

Making themselves liked by both kids and adults is one problem Libra children probably won't have, though their concern with this will be lifelong. They'll seem to be amenable to any suggestion and will have laudable good manners, they'll be full of thoughtful little gestures and will enjoy giving gifts, they'll know just how to smile back at their grandmother when she straightens their collar and how to make a younger guest feel comfortable and welcome. Yet charming, considerate, and otherwise buoyantly confident five-year-old Melanie smilingly asks her playmate over and over again as she's saying good-bye, "Do you like me? Do you like me?"

Libra means relationship, the balance between self and other. Even as children, Libras are sensitively attuned to what their friends and family want and need. Generally cheerful themselves, calm, attractive, and poised, they have the knack of bringing out the best in others and seem to act almost like magnets for people's good feelings. These children may be especially highly regarded by adults, who'll find that strong discipline is rarely needed due to their well-tempered behavior. Adults will also appreciate their good manners: Our friend Dickie is always being invited over to visit by his playmates' parents, especially at mealtimes, when the adults hope he'll set a good example for their own little ruffians with his polite please-and-thank-you's.

Just observe: Your Libra child will be the social mediator of any group. She will, as she grows older, gain increasing adeptness at being able to explain one family member to another and vice versa, and until she masters this skill, she will be distinctly uncomfortable with any discord around her. "Mama, don't! Papa, don't!" she may implore both of you as you argue mildly over who will do the laundry this week. In fact, Libra children truly hate ill feelings and will seem noticeably unsettled until some resolution is achieved.

Eminently social beings, they will feel most at home in cooperative ventures of all kinds, and their talk will be liberally sprinkled with "C'mon, let's. . . . " They are not solitary players; in fact, some may avoid this as much as possible, and you may regretfully remark to yourself how other children can amuse themselves whereas your Libra seems to be so much at loose ends without a playmate. But it is really that they are not making use of their talent—their gift—to bring people together in a social setting where all energies can be harmonized. Nothing gives them greater pleasure than presiding over a well-appointed tea party of dolls and other nicely behaved guests.

But by the same token, these able politicians can't bear for anyone to think badly of them, and their readiness to shrink from a conflict may be their greatest problem. "If only he would not say yes every time I ask him to do something," complained one mother, "I'd be better able to deal with his actual resistance. At least I would know right then and there that I had to do it myself instead of finding out an hour later, when it's still not done." Libras just love to please, and they will accommodate themselves with seeming pliability rather than stand up to you in open combat.

Interestingly, this softness at the surface often conceals a firm inner determination to have their own way. And, being masterful diplomats, they usually get it, though others may not fully realize what's going on. Sometimes their will is simply to be left in peace, for Libra children are pleasure-loving creatures, happier at rest in the sway of a summer hammock than sweating and toiling beside you in the garden. But other times they will have a strong idea of the way things should be done; it's just that their promotion of it will be sugar coated and quite palatable. For example, even after you think you've said no, absolutely and for the last time, so that you can get on with your work, the sweet appeal of a Libra's "Daddy, could you play with me?" may melt you into a forgetful jellyfish. Like able generals, they'll manage to realize their purposes by means of you, their unwitting minion.

Yet for all their sweetly proportioned (and well-disguised) strength, Libra children characteristically have a woefully hard time making up their minds. All too aware of the alternatives life offers, they can easily swing like pendulums between this possibility and that, never choosing and therefore never acting. Ask our Libra-rising daughter whether she wants to go for a walk or stay home and read a book and she'll say, "I want to go out *and* stay home, *boaf.*"

By recognizing and understanding their natural tendencies, you may be able to help these compulsive jugglers find the courage to assert themselves without constraint. While minimizing the number of choices you throw in their laps, you can encourage them to follow through on the activities they do embark on. If he insists on arranging the toys in his room himself but never gets farther than the rocking horse, you can help him to see that if it's really so hard to decide whether the tail points toward the window or toward the door, perhaps it really doesn't matter anyway. Though getting this idea across to a Libra can seem as impossible as stopping the world from spinning, it's reassuring to remember that since they share with the other air signs (Aquarius and Gemini) a conscious need for communication with others, they will, sooner or later, be reasonably responsive to your words of advice.

In fact, reasonableness is one of Libra's cardinal virtues. These children make wonderful arbitrators in disputes between their friends and seem to possess a sense of fairness quite beyond their years. One father told us that even during his daughter's moments of peak brattiness, she can always be brought around by appealing to that instinct in her. For example, when once, at the age of two and a half, she acted slyly intransigent about keeping a toy for herself that really belonged to the nursery school, he had only to ask her how she would feel if another child kept one of her things. She instantly saw the light and bravely and proudly returned the toy the next day.

Finally, just as all things must be balanced in order for Libras to feel comfortable, so their surroundings, too, must have a certain beauty of composition. Libra children of all ages will show some inclination toward this, whether it's the collecting of small pieces of fabric for the decoration of their room, the voicing of a strong interest in the clothes they wear, or the evidence they show of an advanced architectural sense in their elaborate block constructions. (Whether or not one color "matches to" another color is a matter of great interest to three-year-old Phoebe.) Most of them will likewise show an affinity for all the arts, and most should respond well to concerts of all kinds. Don't hesitate to play your adult collection of records for them; they're sure to appreciate the more soothing ones, especially at bedtime, when a little auditory reassurance that you're somewhere in the house with them can be a great aid in their getting off to sleep.

But most of all, Libra children will need to have the feeling that all their activities, all their relationships, all the fields in which they move are imbued with harmony and equilibrium. If they aren't, Libras will gracefully endeavor to make them so.

The Evolving Libra

BIRTH TO ONE YEAR

Within his first couple of weeks your Libra baby may introduce you to his smile—subtle, playing over his face as he falls asleep after nursing or a bottle. You may be told by parents not so blessed that this is merely a reflexive grimace caused by the passing of gas, but at two months there should be no doubt about the pleasing expression that will grace your home for many years to come.

Many Libras smile and splash around happily in the bath or smile and smack their lips at the first taste of solid foods, but all are likely to smile when people make a fuss over them. In fact, their smiling glances, cooing, gurgling, babbling, and laughter are likely to evoke from you feelings you never thought you had. Unfortunately, your Libra infant may become distressed when she is left to her own devices for more than a few minutes, and she may cry furiously or—after the age of six months—employ her charms to get you involved with her again. This may be a severe problem between that age, when she begins to understand her separateness from other people, and nine or ten months, when she can crawl along after them. On the other hand, she may sit contentedly smiling at and stroking a mirror for long periods. But she may like it even more if you join her, so that she can delight in the paradox of having both you and your mirror image with which to play.

ONE-YEAR-OLDS

Your Libra toddler at age one may not wish to feed himself, not because he can't but out of a desire for give-and-take with you. It is probably best if you continue feeding him and take comfort that at least he is eating; in a few months he will insist on holding the spoon himself but may eat next to nothing.

Libra toddlers may have a great feeling for color and should be provided with crayons and paper; although they may not be able to do much more than bang the one on the other, they will probably enjoy the process and even admire the result. You should participate in this play, not only to keep the art materials from being eaten, but to demonstrate, help, appreciate, and see what you can do when you let yourself go.

At eighteen months your Libra child may dance to music in charming imitation of adults or older children. Games involving hiding and reappearing—for example, peekaboo—may continue to be favorites.

TWO-YEAR-OLDS

Your affectionate Libra two will probably very much want your approval. If you don't treat occasional accidents as major failures, her toilet training should proceed easily, almost as though it had all been settled in an amicable agreement between the two of you. She may inform you of her calls to nature for the next year or two, however, and may seem to be asking for your permission.

Libra twos hate loneliness above all things, and they may resist your abandoning them at bedtime by calling you back for another kiss or a glass of water.

Many are ready for a closely supervised nursery school or playgroup at this time. At first your Libra's play with another child may be somewhat primitive—tittering, friendly screaming, or touching each other—but at two and a half, play involving the sharing of a toy is possible. Libra-moon Ariel approaches our daughter each morning at nursery school and suggests a new activity. Whereas many children her age are still grabbing for whatever is held in another's hands, then losing interest in the booty seized, Ariel seems to have mastered play etiquette and rarely requires teacher intervention.

But home life with your Libra two-and-a-half may not be so pleasant. The decision-making difficulties typical of this age are especially acute with Libras. It is usually better not to add to their agonized wavering by posing too many choices for them.

It can be a great pleasure to watch a Libra develop his aesthetic sensibilities with finger-paints, poster paints, and water colors. He may also like to experiment with color and form on a pegboard or by arranging large wooden beads on a string.

THREE-YEAR-OLDS

Light and shadow may fascinate your Libra three, and he will probably love to learn how to make shadow figures with his hands. Their interest in pattern causes some Libra threes to enjoy looking at the starry sky, and they may even learn to recognize a couple of the brighter constellations, particularly Orion or the Big Dipper, with your help.

At nursery school Libra threes may not only respond to a "Good morning," but may sometimes be heard to initiate the greeting. They may also politely ask permission of another child before handling his toy. And it is always a boon to a harried teacher to have a Libra or two in the group, for they can often arbitrate in squabbles more easily than he or she could.

You should remember, though, that the equilibrium of your Libra is probably very delicate, especially at the age of three and a half. She may feel the need to rebel against her own characteristically complaisant nature in order to right the balance between her own needs and those of others, and you will naturally be the brunt of her confused anger. Yet she probably needs your love now more than ever, and if you lose your temper, she may cry heartrendingly until you've come to a reconciliation.

FOUR-YEAR-OLDS

Though your sociable, cooperative Libra four may flourish in adult-organized group activity, he will probably not be able to function well in unsupervised play with more than one child at a time. It is as though his amicable companionship with one friend must be balanced against a cruel rejection of another. Furthermore, he tends to feel an overriding concern for what other kids think of him and can't withstand the social pressure of "You're Noah's friend? Then I don't like you."

Libra fours are usually willing to comply with rules that seem sensible to them, but they sometimes need to test an adult's determination to enforce them. Your child may not be able to resist arguing with you at times, and you should try not to become too offended by her foot stomping and provocative grimaces. Conversation often works better than direct collision; if that fails, temporary isolation is almost always an effective disciplinary measure.

When it comes to drawing, coloring, and painting, Libra fours are usually quite proud of their products, and your admiration will be very encouraging to them. Their visual sensory awareness can be developed if you take frequent walks with them and discuss what you see; they may especially enjoy trying to see animals, faces, or objects in cloud shapes.

FIVE-YEAR-OLDS

Libra fives are often adept at gracious courtesies and tact. However, they are likely to be preoccupied with the impression they are making on a guest and can become extremely angry with you if you are so uncouth as to spoil it with an untidy fact or two. If you use a little tact yourself when you have to break the unpleasant news that that bottle of perfume is really yours and was not meant to be offered as a gift to anyone, the perplexed guest may give it back without your child making a fuss.

Five is an outstandingly obedient age, and many Libra children ask their parents' permission for nearly everything and request supervision frequently. However, they may also have fairly strong ideas about how a thing should be done: Coming home from a first ballet class, where she did everything correctly, Savitri secretly confided to her mother, "Next time I'm going to show the teacher how *I* do it!"

♏

Scorpio

(SUN SIGN, OCTOBER 24–NOVEMBER 22)

"Rapunzel, Rapunzel! let down thine hair."

Then she let the hair down, and the King's son climbed up, but instead of his dearest Rapunzel he found the witch looking at him with wicked glittering eyes.

"Aha!" cried she, mocking him, "you came for your darling, but the sweet bird sits no longer in the nest, and sings no more; the cat has got her, and will scratch out your eyes as well! Rapunzel is lost to you; you will see her no more." . . .

So he wandered several years in misery until at last he came to the desert place where Rapunzel lived with her twin-children that she had borne, a boy and a girl. At first he heard a voice that he thought he knew, and when he reached the place from which it seemed to come, Rapunzel knew him, and fell on his neck and wept. And when her tears touched his eyes, they became clear again, and he could see with them as well as ever.

Jacob and Wilhelm Grimm, Rapunzel

Scorpio is, by definition, one of the most subtle and mysterious signs of the zodiac, and Scorpio children may be rather hard for their parents and even themselves to fathom. Their fuel is a high-octane emotional intensity that's stored deep within them, hidden until needed for personal use. Their frequently quiet demeanor conceals powerful feelings that can, and do, erupt volcanically in periodic expressions of pent-up hurt and hurtfulness. Frightening as this sometimes strikes more delicate souls, it is helpful to know that rather than being merely destructive, these discharges are usually regenerating for the child, especially if handled with acceptance and understanding by you.

One mother told us of the time she and her three-and-a-half-year-old Scorpio daughter were reenacting *Amahl and the Night Visitors*, which they had recently seen on stage. One was to be the crippled child, the other the mother, and according to the remembered scenario they were to fall crying into each other's arms. But at this point, to everyone's surprise, her daughter actually broke down into uncontrollable sobs, with no other provocation, it seemed, than empathetic feeling for the sad story. The daughter saw no need to explain, and when her tears were dried, she resumed the playacting as if nothing had happened.

Atypical as it may seem of what we usually think of as a happily carefree childhood, these children actually thrive on intensity. They're really not interested in things that don't have meaning, and their lifelong concern will be to go to the roots of any problem, including those within themselves. They have an innate intuitive grasp of psychological complexity, and you may sometimes feel that they know what you are thinking even before you do. "What, mama?" he may inquire as you sit there absorbed in some memory or quandary. How you explain your most private self to a two-year-old is your problem, but be reassured that on some level somewhere he understands. You may even find that these children can easily absorb the stress of your own unavoidable conflicts with your spouse. Indeed, the profound love you'll receive from your Scorpio child—as if he knows you from the inside—is only the luscious fruit of one of the deepest relationships you may ever have in your life. There's nothing superficial about this bond, in which sadness and joy, heights and depths, are inextricably fused.

But the underside to this is that these children may sometimes become obsessed with negative emotions, secretly scheming to enjoy a "cruel revenge" on anyone who has wounded them. As one four-year-old eloquently put it, "I hate my ookle sister. She is ugly, disgraceful, horrible, and sputchen. She keeps asking for trouble, and I'm gonna put her in jail, and then I'm gonna drive a car in the jail and run her over until she's broken into sixty pieces."

The birth of a new sibling is one loaded situation that parents should do their utmost to relieve, preferably by preparing the child well in advance, letting him share in the excitement, and eventually including him in the new responsibilities, perhaps with some sphere of special authority mapped out just for him.

Unfortunately, the Scorpio child's capacity for focused emotion occasionally makes him vulnerable to being hurt by more fickle friends than he. Slow to warm up to people, he usually holds onto the friends he finally does choose with great loyalty and possessiveness. He just can't see how Angelo could like Otis when Otis is such a wishy-washy pest, for even at an early age he possesses remarkable powers of discernment. And he may go through crises of rejection that not even you can really help him with.

Although Scorpios share with the other water signs (Pisces and Cancer) a deep need to respond to the world emotionally, they unconsciously tend to contain, then condense, these feelings until they've become an obstructive mass of ice. Unless such children are given a rewarding start in life, they may someday attempt to use this cold, hard edge against others, though they are the ones who may ultimately suffer. Trying to help them find a gentler means of release may not be easy, for it's rather like channeling the flow of a geyser, but your understanding tolerance of their necessary mode of being is vital to their sense of self-worth.

It may shock some parents to hear this, but whatever small dose of sadomasochism may be latent in each one of us is probably greatest in Scorpios. It certainly doesn't have to come out in a destructive form, but it is in evidence if you look. Our Scorpio daughter loves her doctor kit, and she especially enjoys using the toy hypodermic needle on her "patients." Although we've repeatedly demonstrated the way most shots are administered, she insists on preparing her victims with these soothing words: "This is really going to hurt *a lot*."

Conscious of this tendency in your children, you can learn not to be overly disturbed when you see the intense loves and hates of which they are capable. Emotional extremes are part of what gives Scorpios their strength, and there will always be a certain heaviness about them. Even their bodies can convey this, for many of them are built with a certain compactness that suggests concentrated power and strength. What they urgently need from you is help in expressing their forceful energy, either through wild and rough physical play and sports or through imaginative play in which aggression is permissible—toy soldiers, a witch's costume, or perhaps a castle with a fire-breathing dragon chained up in a dungeon.

In fact, imagination is a prime outlet for the deep-running Scorpio waters. Fairy tales may provide profound answers to the enigmas Scorpios unconsciously resonate with, so don't ignore these in your attempts to raise your child according to the latest, most enlightened techniques. There are highly spiritual messages buried in their simple words. We find that our daughter loves the Greek myths, classic fairy tales, and stories from the Bible every bit as much as she does today's childhood fare.

Another forte of the Scorpio child is puzzles of all kinds, especially complicated ones that are as interesting to take apart as they are to put back together again. These children are blessed with a sense of determination and a capacity for self-discipline that will make them successful at all kinds of hard work in the future, and you might as well make use of this now to get them to help you recover that lost, overdue library book or figure out just how to unravel that tangled mass of yarn the cat left behind.

Most Scorpio children should avidly respond to the nature projects they may be exposed to in nursery school or that you provide for them at home. An ant farm, a rabbit or hamster (especially if the birth process can be witnessed), or the nursing back to health of a fallen baby bird may be both fascinating and informative to them. Indeed, their many penetrating questions about the secrets of nature may leave you pondering things freshly for some time to come.

The Evolving Scorpio

BIRTH TO ONE YEAR

Your Scorpio baby's first exhalation may be a yowl of anguished intensity that will earn her a good Apgar score and make the obstetrician say he hopes you don't have close neighbors. For the next few years you may as well expect that rousing her from peaceful slumber is likely to bring on a harrowing fit. You will very soon learn to respect this child's persistence: If she wants to be held, she is not likely to stop crying until you pick her up, and you will not be able to pull the wool over her eyes by taking her off the breast before she is ready or giving her a water bottle if she wants milk. In general the response to stimulation of Scorpio infants is quite strong; they want to know their world sensitively and keenly.

You may notice your baby's extraordinary alertness when he is less than two weeks old and feel compassion for his strenuous efforts to focus his eyes. Once he can focus, he would much rather stare trancelike at the crib mobile, it seems, than reach for it. And whereas the baby next door grabs the rattle, knocks it around a little, and drops it, he characteristically prefers to explore it slowly and thoughtfully with his sensual caresses.

Scorpios are generally slow to warm up to new stimuli, as you may discover when you introduce yours to her first bath and she vigorously kicks and screams. But if you don't try to overwhelm her resistance with too much pressure, she will probably come to passionately love playing in water.

ONE-YEAR-OLDS

Your Scorpio toddler will very likely scream with delight when he roughhouses with you or chases after a ball you throw, and this activity will probably be effective in siphoning off energy that might otherwise be applied to activities you don't condone. One important lesson Scorpios must learn in life is how to overcome temptation, but you shouldn't expect your one-year-old to be able to resist seeing how far he can cast your wineglasses; the transferring of valuable objects to high shelves or locked cabinets may obviate constant, futile, and tiresome confrontations.

Scorpio toddlers are usually shy with adult visitors they don't know well, and they will need time to size up the new baby-sitter you have chosen for them.

In spite of your best efforts to enthuse her, your Scorpio toddler may not be interested in many of the toys you have bought; instead she may become so deeply engrossed in only one or two of them that she plays with nothing else. She may carry certain little objects, such as barrettes or plastic-tipped safety pins, wherever she goes. She is likely to show extreme pertinacity in learning a new skill, such as twisting the lid off a container. But when she is fatigued, she may respond to failure by kicking or throwing the object that is frustrating her, after which she may scream with rage.

Do not be surprised if your Scorpio toddler balks at your toilet-training efforts: If she seems content with that warm feeling she gets from the load in her diapers, you should probably postpone your efforts for a few months.

TWO-YEAR-OLDS

Scorpio twos often show a precocious interest in the birth process; in the company of a pregnant visitor one such child enthusiastically exclaimed in one of her earliest complete sentences: "Baby in-a belly come out-a va-GI-na!"

You may discover your Scorpio is able to amuse himself for extremely long periods, especially if you first give him your undivided attention for about half an hour. Scorpio twos typically become very attached to routines—more so than many of their contemporaries—and their demand for repetition (the same record over and over, the same bedtime story every night) may drive you nearly insane.

Your Scorpio may now play well with an older child, but you should take care that she doesn't become overly attached, for when the older child becomes bored with her relative incompetence, she's likely to suffer greatly over the rejection.

THREE-YEAR-OLDS

Your Scorpio three is probably able to form strong and affectionate relationships with children his own age, provided that he can be the dominant partner. You can often pull Scorpio threes out of a dark mood by telling them a secret or mentioning that there is a surprise in the next room.

These children are usually quite fond of wearing costumes composed of cast-off adult clothes and pieces of pretty fabric, and you may be tickled to see them in this garb portraying you as they explain the do's and don'ts of life to their dolls.

They are usually quite interested in family relationships; a Scorpio three seeing deer run across the highway or a new puppy at a friend's house may ask, "But where is its mother and its father?" These children are usually quite affectionate and loving with both parents, but their expressions of their feelings may be subtle: One Scorpio three whose parents were trying to teach him French asked, "How do you say, 'A boy loves his mother and father'?" Nonetheless, these strong attachments are subject to sharp reversals, and you may occasionally be stung with, "I wish you would die!"

Many Scorpio threes are bothered by frequent dreams of monsters or wolves; if you can reassure them that they are really safe at home with you, they can generally go back to sleep with ease.

FOUR-YEAR-OLDS

Your tough and resourceful Scorpio four may display extremes of behavior: Either he is an angel, good-naturedly and diligently executing errands you assign him, or he is impossible, answering your appeals to him with cutting rudeness. At nursery school he is more an observer than an active participant, but when he undertakes a task, he is likely to work persistently until it is completed. Scorpio fours do not enter friendships easily, but the few they have may be so intense that separation at the end of the day may be difficult.

Your Scorpio four may ask you many questions about sex, and it is best if you answer them succinctly, supplying precisely the information she requests. She may be fascinated with a realistic plastic model man and model woman, which would probably satisfy her curiosity better than your explanations.

FIVE-YEAR-OLDS

Your Scorpio five may be much more modest than he was formerly; whatever goes on in the bathroom will probably be his private affair from now on. When he is angry with you, he is not so likely to scream insults or threats as he did at four; now he can double-whammy you with a haughty, withering look, and you may have to help him release his feelings so that they don't become frozen in a long-term grudge. Some Scorpio fives are inclined to be somewhat bossy with other children, constantly admonishing them to obey rules.

Your Scorpio may love to stand around quietly soaking up adult gossip, and—beware!—she probably understands more than you think. A few may seem inordinately interested in the grisly details of someone's misfortune. This fascination is really an expression of the Scorpio's passionate appetite for the nitty-gritty side of life, a resolve to experience the world to its most profound dimension. When one worried mother asked her Scorpio-moon daughter why she insisted on jumping into puddles, leaping from boulder to boulder, and hanging over bridge rails when they went out for a leisurely walk together, five-year-old Gina replied, "Oh, I just love to live dangerously."

↑

Sagittarius
(SUN SIGN, NOVEMBER 23–DECEMBER 21)

Jack's last trip up the beanstalk had made him and his mother rich beyond measure because of the sackful of fabulous diamonds and rubies he had managed to haul back with him. But, dangerous though it was, the time came when he began to itch for just one more adventure. So out he set again, up the beanstalk, higher . . . and higher . . . and higher.

"Jack and the Beanstalk"

The outgoing nature of the Sagittarius is proverbial, and the Sagittarius child goes out in every way possible. As parents you may find this exuberance alternately gratifying and disturbing, but you'll always be amazed at the whirling fireball you're living with.

These children are natural-born explorers whose drive to experience everything life offers is actually the result of their desire to understand it. The world is their school, and they are constantly learning its lessons through their bodies, their hearts, and their minds—in fact, the more fronts they're bombarded on the better, as far as they're concerned. They may make mistakes in their perpetually active experimentation with people and with things, but, more so than other children, they're likely to learn and grow from them.

Because Sagittarians share with the other fire signs (Aries and Leo) an intense need to express themselves, physical, emotional, and mental energy are all in abundance in these children. Most will have a natural aptitude for athletics or at least be generally well coordinated, with especially strong legs and thighs. Although they may be unnervingly gutsy about seeing just how far their bodies can take them, you'll probably learn to trust their judgment, or if not, at least you'll learn in time the incredible resilience with which they are capable of bouncing back if they have incurred an injury.

It would be wise to abet these energetic foals' love of freedom in every way your good sense permits, for, penned in, they'll strain after it unhappily. Indeed, the abundant Sagittarian energy can get to be a real problem to deal with for both parents and children. Con-

67

stricted, it can become explosive and emotionally self-destructive; but left unfocused, it can expand way out of bounds, with the child's boisterous self-expression and love of excitement causing him to forget all caution as he revs his motor past capacity with no inner regulating mechanism to pace him. Both boys and girls can play too wild, too rough, for their or anyone else's good.

Sagittarius children express this energy also in their characteristically high spirits. Their good humor and usually unperturbed optimism can uplift everyone around them, and if you are of a like mind, you'll always find a willing companion for any potentially fun-filled exploit. Sagittarians make especially good travellers, for they adapt well to changes in routine. This may be one of their chief means of growth, in fact, for they're able to get a great deal out of the ever-changing people and places that come their way.

On the level of feeling, too, they are apt to get out of bounds if not helped with limits by loving adults. As with everything Sagittarius children do, all that natural good cheer sometimes leads to overoptimism, in which their own capabilities are exaggerated and the need to bow to certain realities, such as a reasonable bedtime or consideration for another child's feelings, is ignored. For some, freedom is of the utmost importance, so much so that friendships in which real emotional demands are made of them may be avoided. But overall, they tend to be friendly, with a kind of broad warmth that's quite appealing. Three-year-old Janice, who in other respects has her problems, is nonetheless striking in her grown-up self-assurance as she trots over to shake your hand with a "Hi! I'm Janice!"

These children are likely to flaunt convention in their quest to try the limits of society's laws. They resent constraints, no matter who lays them down, and they're practicing an originality of approach that will take them far in later years. Five-year-old Jon thinks it's really "cool" to wear his sweatshirt inside out and doesn't flinch at his playmates' convention-clinging jibes. He has a terrycloth batman cape-*cum*-hood that he regularly wears to nursery school atop his snowsuit: He looks odd but interesting. He really cares about his appearance, but, even at this age, he seems to feel that it's got to make a statement that truly represents him.

Sagittarius children have quite a potential for being leaders. Though they are open and generally fair with their peers, they are not afraid of asserting themselves. They are often way ahead of everyone else with their adventurous, forward-looking spirit, and they possess a keen natural intelligence that, even if unschooled, will manifest itself in everything they undertake.

Although some Sagittarians are never comfortable in school because of its regimentation, preferring instead to take their education from the world at large, many more become avid students who earn themselves a background of formidable knowledge and intellectual prowess. Friends of ours doubted the picture astrology painted of their daughter, Rachel, when she was still preschool age and inordinately fond of roughhousing outdoors. But they were amazed at her transformation as she entered first grade and learned to read, for her love of learning became a consuming interest; in fact, even on weekends and holidays all she wanted to do was play that she was in school. The fact that these two qualities—physical and intellectual excellence—so easily flow from the same person beautifully expresses the dual symbol of this sign: the prancing, snorting horse below united with the far-seeing archer above, the sound mind in a sound body that leads us closer to the best we are capable of.

However, the overflowing energy of the Sagittarian mind can also easily get out of bounds if not tempered with a kind of realism that is not wholly natural to it. Bright though they are, Sagittarius children may overlook important details in their rush to master the problem they have set for themselves and be on to the next one.

Your child may be marvelously inventive, always popping up with some new inspiration to create a "bonker machine" out of a combination of Tinkertoys and Legos or turn a teacup into an airplane with assorted pieces of string and cardboard. But when the airplane falls apart because he didn't bother to knot the wings in place or the construction collapses because he started it on a bumpy rug, he may get angry and frustrated out of all proportion. He can't accept his failures, but neither is he willing to take the time to go back to investigate the mechanics of what went wrong. He'll never be at a loss for some new challenge to conquer, but he may have some trouble overcoming his own restless urge to see the whole pattern before all the facts are in.

This is one of the points at which parents can help their Sagittarius child once they themselves clearly see the issue. Precisely because of their multiple talents, these children need help with focus and structure. Their wonderful enthusiasm often lacks the realistic touch that can give their projects substance, make them effective. As one mother expressed it, they need both an understanding, free rein and a set of boundaries that lets them know you care.

Finding this delicate balance may be quite a job, for it actually amounts to the larger one of starting your Sagittarius child on the lifelong task of acquiring *self*-restraint. You can best help these children actualize their far-flung dreams if you can get them to follow through on their brilliant conceptions until they see the workable results; to sustain the friendliness of their initial overtures to playmates in enduring give-and-take relationships; to control their restless energy sufficiently to put it to good use. These habits more or less established, your Sagittarius child will be well on the way to becoming an extraordinarily capable adult.

The Evolving Sagittarius

BIRTH TO ONE YEAR

Your Sagittarius baby may enter the world kicking with great agility, almost as though he were impatient to get going. You will probably discover early that this child is difficult to hold; he seems to feel claustrophobic when you cuddle him, and he will squirm and roll so much at six months that it may be difficult for you to diaper him without help. You can be sure that he will practice each new motor skill he learns untiringly; any athlete would be inspired watching his push-ups. Once Sagittarians learn to crawl, keeping them in a playpen is inadvisable and probably impossible. Some even attempt to walk at eight months by standing, lunging forward, and grabbing onto the furniture, and their repeated falls leave them undaunted.

Your Sagittarius infant will probably smile and laugh a great deal, but she may scream with indignant fury when you pick her up to prevent her from crawling in some undesirable direction. Not just her new skills but her first solid foods, her first bath in the big tub, in fact, everything new is likely to fill her with pleasure. You should see to it that she gets at least one good outing a day; her horizons will be widened as she views dogs, pedestrians, and big trucks from her carriage or stroller, and she will thrive on the fresh air.

ONE-YEAR-OLDS

Sagittarius toddlers are characteristically great performers and will avidly milk applause from adults who admire their physical feats. It may be difficult for you to keep up with their frenzied pace as they prance recklessly and noisily all over the house, but you should save your worries for the quiet times, when they may be satisfying their curiosity about your turntable and records.

Sagittarians recognize that physical exploration alone is not sufficient to expand their knowledge, and at this age they rapidly become fluent talkers. Your child may very much enjoy your reading simple storybooks to him, and even if he doesn't understand the story completely, the pictures will fire his imagination.

But at this age he is enlarging his world view more through direct encounters, and the fearless way he approaches strangers may sometimes give you concern. You needn't worry, however, when you take your Sagittarius toddler with you to a friend's house for dinner; he often feels more at home away from home and is so happy to have new experiences that unless he's overly curtailed, he will be an entertaining guest. And when his restless energy has been spent, he is likely to have no trouble falling asleep on a strange bed. By the way, one good way to help him spend that energy at home is to get him a rocking horse.

TWO-YEAR-OLDS

Do not despair that your Sagittarius two will never toilet train herself just because the times of her bowel movements are so unpredictable. And don't attempt to force her to sit on the toilet until she does what you want her to; she will not abide such restraints, and you will be locked into a contest you can never win. On the other hand, if you encourage your voluble two-year-old to report to you when she feels the urge and if you explain how much freer she will be without diapers, you will have her on your side, and the training process will go more smoothly.

Sagittarians at two and a half are generally not as intractable as other children their age, and many can be reasoned out of their outrageous demands. Don't forget distraction as a last resort. These children have a lively sense of humor and will generally guffaw at such incongruities as your fitting their shoes onto their hands. If your Sagittarius enters nursery school at this age, he is likely to walk in without hesitation on the first day. Although it may be difficult for him to sit still, he can usually respect rules once they are explained to him.

THREE-YEAR-OLDS

Your gregarious Sagittarius three will probably be able to form friendships readily, and her capacity for enthusiastic horseplay and high-spirited adventure is likely to make her popular with children of either sex. She is probably not shy with adults either, and they may be amazed at her ability to communicate forthrightly. If you can interest your Sagittarius three in some vigorous dancing or competitive ball playing, she will not be so likely to become fidgety and irritable out of boredom. Also, if you want your balking Sagittarius to come in to dinner, you might try racing her to the table (and letting her win). A few Sagittarius threes have so much energy left over at the end of the day that they are likely to wake up in the wee hours; they may wander around the house, turn on lights, help themselves to snacks, sit on the couch and "read" a book, and finally drop off to sleep there.

FOUR-YEAR-OLDS

Sagittarius fours are quite likely to exaggerate their considerable prowess at running and jumping, and you may conclude that they recognize no limits to their power as they repeatedly venture out of bounds. Many cannot resist the temptation to tease children who can't stand up to them, and some seem to challenge the adult's point of view at every turn. If you respond to your boisterous Sagittarius with a sharp rebuke, he may audaciously mock you, which will force you either to retreat or to escalate your unpleasant conflict. Humor is usually a much better management technique with Sagittarians: Instead of getting angry, make an outrageous joke about their mischief ("Uh-oh, Jill has gone goo-goo again!").

If you must forcefully restrain a Sagittarius four, she may threaten to "run away." She may actually pack up a few special belongings and embark, but her desire not to miss out on her favorite dinner, offhandedly mentioned by you to some other family member, will prompt her to return (probably before she gets out the door). Treat her "homecoming" warmly but casually and don't rub anything in, and she will probably comply with your rules for a while. Actually, Sagittarius fours are stretching themselves in order to find their limits; they want to understand the overall pattern and how they fit into it. Their questions are apt to be a good deal more probing than those of their contemporaries, and you have opportunities with your responses to keep them open in their search for meaning.

Your Sagittarius five probably has a firmer grasp on the necessity of certain rules than she did a year earlier, as you will realize when she dogmatically tells another child to blow his nose, although she never blows her own, no matter how many times you've reminded her. Other five-year-olds may behave more responsibly than your spontaneous Sagittarius, but her roguishness is now more verbal than physical.

Sagittarius fives are labeled smart alecks by some adults who may not appreciate their inquiring approach. Many of their objections to adult directives may have to do with fairness ("It's not fair!"), and though their concept of justice at this age is still self-serving, they are beginning to develop the profound ethical sense the sign is famous for. Actually, your Sagittarius five may be quite respectful of rules whose purpose in the larger scheme of things has been explained (or he may propose a conflicting explanation more suited to his desires). In any event, his questioning of them indicates a freedom of thought that will, in its more mature stages, always seek the underlying principle.

♑

Capricorn

(SUN SIGN, DECEMBER 22–JANUARY 20)

Susie likes to play house. She has a family of dolls. She has a little table and chairs. She has a set of little dishes. And she has a really-truly little electric stove, with a set of little pots and pans!

"Now I must learn to cook!" said Susie, the first time she saw her new little stove.

Annie North Bedford, Susie's New Stove:
The Little Chef's Cookbook

Capricorn children have some important lessons to teach the rest of us—and they'll do it, too, by their steady, quiet example. They are the builders among us, the ones who, taking life seriously, apply themselves and all their resources until a job is done. They can be patient and self-disciplined to an extent far beyond what one ordinarily expects of children—and on some of them the toll of their self-imposed maturity may show itself in a kind of stern, intent frown that, despite its innocence, can be somewhat forbidding.

But come what may, most Capricorn children are determined to pin their sights on whatever is realistically possible. Since they have such a firm hold on that dimension, they are also able to accomplish more than people of other signs, and you'll probably be pleased to see your little mountain goat achieving laudable feats as he ascends the developmental scale, whether it's as the nimblest, sturdiest walker on the block or the ablest talker or the most amazing Play-Doh sculptor.

Capricorn shares with the other earth signs (Taurus and Virgo) a steadfast need to see the practical results of its labors. Don't be parsimonious with your approval, for these children thrive on it more than most, though their self-contained demeanor may not readily betray them. Thorough, careful, persevering, they approach all things cautiously, assess the odds and outline their plan for success, and then work diligently until they've realized their goal. You won't catch *them* napping—unless, of course, it's during their scheduled naptime, for they are generally willing to accept the rules and routines you've laid out for them.

This is one child who, even at an early age, enjoys being given responsibilities. She will especially appreciate being given an area of authority all her own, such as the management of her own wardrobe. She can be taught to fold and put away her clothes and to choose her daily outfits thoughtfully. For not only is she increasingly quite capable of these tasks, but she quietly and without fanfare deeply desires recognition as the able executive she is now on a small scale and will someday likely be in the world at large. If she has recently acquired a younger sibling, you may find her reaching new plateaus in trustworthiness as she conscientiously removes the Tiddlywinks from her baby brother's hand-to-mouth grasp or gently pushes him in the stroller.

However, parents and teachers may have to slow these little social climbers down for their own good. In their willing acceptance of the hard realities of life, Capricorn children may take on so many responsibilities that they may actually become overburdened with concerns. Or they may look and act so relatively mature that adults may come to expect more from them than is really fair to their young spirit. But even if you don't restrict the freedom of these children in any way, they're likely to do it to themselves sooner or later. Somber is the feeling tone that rings in the heart of many of them: They are intimately in touch with the necessity of limits. Unfortunately, many of them may be prone to depression or at least to inexplicable dark moods. They make excellent worriers, perhaps even more so than you; they may silently fret over whether or not they'll get to nursery school on time or how Santa will make it down the chimney.

Regardless of how you handle these serious, concentrated beings, there may be the retrospective sense that their childhood was difficult. They are essentially older than their years, not comfortable with frivolity or freedom or their own unpredictable emotions (although they are known for their own brand of wry, capricious wit, which you'll probably find cropping up to brighten matters from time to time). However, they do hold the promise of ripening into a fine old age. Maturity suits them more than most, and their natural sobriety should be respected. One mother of two daughters lovingly refers to her older, Capricorn child as her "dark one," in contrast to her younger, smiling "light one." She understands the ways of her two utterly different offspring and values each one for her own unique qualities.

Although you can try now and then to lighten up your Capricorn child with good humor and the sense that things really aren't so grave as all that, it is his nature and purpose in life to keep his feet solidly planted on firm ground even as he aspires to new heights. Acknowledging the limits of the possible, he's able to make new possibilities real, but first he must pay due respect to the here and now.

These children do not care very much for fantasy and make-believe, and your enthusiastic efforts to introduce them to fairy tales may leave them cold. But they do respond to toys that have a realness about them—a housekeeping set, for example, or actual hammers and nails that are small-size and lightweight. One Capricorn child we know loves what he calls his "supermarket"—a large appliance-size box that contains real (though now empty) containers of detergent, sugar, cereal, eggs.

There is a tendency of the Capricorn temperament that, with consciousness, you may be able to help them with: They can be awfully hard on themselves, with a precocious conscience that judges them for minor mistakes or makes them intolerant of their own human frailty. Our not-quite-four-year-old friend Caroline may be an illustration of this: Her feeling drawing of herself and baby sister Jennifer shows her crying—says Caroline—because she hit Jennifer in a squabble over a toy. She's giving us through her artwork a picture of how she thinks she should feel and how in fact she probably does feel, though no one could have blamed her, at her gentle age, for a remorseless rendition of her selfish desire for the toy. These are high social instincts, and they're somewhat surprising to find in a child so young. But do try to help your Capricorn keep them in their proper perspective.

It should be reassuring for parents to know that the quality of their relationship with their Capricorn child will have an especially formative impact on him. These children really look up to adults and actively strive to model themselves after them. They're likely to adopt parental outlooks, so if yours is a particularly narrow or pessimistic one, you can be sure that your Capricorn child's will be too. But if you can express warmth and show tolerance for yourself and others, your Capricorn child may likewise loosen up his characteristically rigid hold on things and get more in touch with that part of himself that is the playful kid frolicking on the mountainside. For, above all, what the Capricorn goat seeks and needs is a sense of security—the knowledge that the scenery won't change very much, that the path is dependable (if tough), and that there is an edelweiss waiting for him at the top.

The Evolving Capricorn

BIRTH TO ONE YEAR

Your Capricorn baby may be born with a distinct frown. As one nine-year-old boy remarked to the mother of a Capricorn baby, "I've never seen a baby look so annoyed." Your infant may focus her eyes in less than two weeks, but she will probably furrow her brows at what she sees. It may be a continuing challenge for you to coax a smile out of her. You'll probably see a few hearty smiles, however, when she practices a skill freshly learned.

Capricorn infants are characteristically quite businesslike about sucking at breast or bottle: In about fifteen minutes they are finished, and you won't be able to prolong your tender bonding with them. Also, some never nurse when they are distressed, and a pacifier is likely to soothe them only momentarily. However, when they are free of gas bubbles or when the pain of cutting teeth is relieved with a teething ring, these babies are generally quiet.

Capricorns tend to take the world very seriously, even when they are infants. Their style is to look and listen carefully, to absorb as much as possible before they attempt a new skill, and then to keep at it until it is mastered. In fact, it is humbling to watch their persistence. Your Capricorn baby will probably respond with self-satisfied pleasure to your introducing him to solid foods or a walker or almost anything new; he seems to recognize that he has a lot to learn in life and time is of the essence. Although he may be shy when he is introduced to strangers, he is more likely to watch attentively than to scream in terror.

ONE-YEAR-OLDS

With the expanded scope they gain from learning to walk, Capricorn toddlers seem determined to do the things you do as soon as possible. He'll find it hard to resist using his new ability to find out what's in your desk drawers, no matter how many times you've forbidden it. Nonetheless, your disapproval matters a great deal to him: You may find him rifling through your papers, pulling the letter tabs off your dictionary, and snarling your typewriter ribbon, all the while vehemently reprimanding himself, "No, no, nebber, *nebber* dood it!" Try not to be too harsh with him, for he is in the process of forming his own conscience. In fact, your approval may be more effective in helping him control his impulses; try to delegate little responsibilities to him (taking the laundry out of the drier, for example). It will no doubt amuse you when he assumes domestic duties with his toy vacuum cleaner, following you around the house with vigorous sound effects.

TWO-YEAR-OLDS

It will probably not be difficult to toilet-train your Capricorn two, since the times of her bowel movements are likely to be fairly predictable. She will feel very rewarded when she graduates from diapers, and your praise will reinforce her own sense of accomplishment.

Nobody responds better to "I know you could do better if you tried" than Capricorn children. When they are going through the "first adolescence" of two and a half and their grouchy, self-contradictory refusals to cooperate with you are getting a little unnerving, try saying, "I'll give you another chance," or try counting up to five. As a matter of fact, you may be amazed at their fascination not only with rote counting—that five follows four—but with the relative dimension of numbers as well—that five is greater than four. You can stimulate this interest by providing your Capricorn with an abacus or number scale. Also at this age you might supply him with a table and chair his own size (his "desk"). Music will always give them pleasure, so play your records for them frequently.

When your Capricorn two cautiously eyes the water from a safe distance on his first time at the beach, do not apply too much pressure in your desire to see more childlike abandon in him; needing time to warm up, he must first watch you amusing yourself in the water.

THREE-YEAR-OLDS

Your Capricorn three may seem somewhat withdrawn when he enters nursery school for the first time. He is likely to associate more with the teacher than with the other children, and he will probably feel insecure until he knows what is expected of him. However, once he gets the swing of things, he'll probably become an avid schoolgoer and may actually "find himself" in school. Capricorn threes are most comfortable if the school day is structured with a specified time for each activity. At home, on the other hand, some Capricorns seem content building with blocks or working on puzzles for hours at a time.

Your Capricorn at three and a half may be plagued with many auditory fears. If she seems not to hear you when you speak to her but gets extremely upset when you raise your voice, try whispering. If she awakens at night because of terrifying dreams, you may be able to reassure her in practical terms ("That old monster can't get in through the window screens"). A few Capricorns at this age are so preoccupied with perfection that they may speak extremely slowly, and some malinger, hesitating to participate in any activity lest they fail. This is not too likely, however, unless you are exerting great pressure on them to perform beyond their maturity.

FOUR-YEAR-OLDS

Your Capricorn four is not nearly so apt to brag as are his contemporaries, and what abilities he does claim will probably not be exaggerated. He is also more willing to seek adult guidance than are others his age. He usually puts great effort into anything he attempts and is very out of sorts when other children get something he feels they didn't earn. Capricorn fours characteristically want to know the practical value of any object or activity they are asked to partake in, and they are not too willing to help other children unless there is something in it for them. They construct with clay or Legos very carefully and will make the most out of the least material. Even more than their contemporaries, Capricorn fours are attracted to verisimilitude; if you want to see your child beside herself with intent pleasure for long stretches of time, provide her with toys that are as realistic as possible.

Your Capricorn may be slower in grasping a concept than other four-year-olds, but once she has learned it, she will seldom forget it and will happily apply it whenever she can. If you frequently remark how grown-up her "good" behavior is, you will seldom have to deal with the "bad." Capricorn fours generally learn from their own mistakes: A rainstorm may teach her better than your admonishments to bring her toys inside at the end of the day.

FIVE-YEAR-OLDS

Capricorn fives are generally exemplary in their behavior, but they may police the behavior of their contemporaries too. Other kids may seriously resent your Capricorn's nagging reminders to wipe their feet at the doorway or not to yell indoors, and they will probably plot revenge for his tattling to you about their minor infractions. You can improve his social standing by discouraging his tattling outright, and you might diminish this tendency in him by delegating to him important responsibilities in certain areas and stressing that other matters are not his concern.

Though they usually don't show it, Capricorn fives are very sensitive, so you should be gentle on the rare occasions you need to reprimand them. Your greatest challenge with your all too frequently solemn Capricorn five is certainly not discipline. What she probably needs more than anything is some release, some fun. Most Capricorns have considerable musical talent, and if you expose her to some instruments—maracas, kalimbas, even the piano—she will enjoy herself tremendously and may take up serious music study in the future.

~~~
~~~

Aquarius

(SUN SIGN, JANUARY 21–FEBRUARY 19)

Once upon a time, in a small house deep in the woods, lived a lively family of animals.

There were Miss Kitty and Mr. Pup, Brown Bunny, Little Chick, Poky Turtle, and Tweeter Bird.

Each had his little chest and his little bed and chair, and they took turns cooking on their little kitchen stove.

They got along nicely when it came to sharing toys, being quiet at nap times and keeping the house neat. But they could not agree on food. . . .

Finally they all knew something must be done. They gathered around the fire one cool and cozy evening and talked things over.

Jane Werner, Animal Friends

You may think you have at last found the most effective child-rearing techniques, the smoothest-running routines by which to manage your household, the sanest attitudes toward friends, work, and play—but when an Aquarius child enters your life, you may have to think again. That water bearer isn't tipping over those jugs for nothing—he's consciously upsetting the old order in his attempts to bring on the new.

Your Aquarius child may not give a fig about who's at the top of the heap in the nursery school hierarchy or what the family has "always done." She'll think for herself, and her views may be radical, to say the least. She may not know what she wants before she starts out, but as soon as she encounters an obstacle, she knows.

These children tend to be attracted to whatever is unusual and new. Free-spirited and with minds of their own, absolutely nothing stops them in the early years—neither a closet door that just won't open to their little fingers (they'll scream wildly until help comes) nor the fording of a mountain stream (though everyone knows one-and-a-half-year-olds just don't do such things). Since they share with the other air signs (Gemini and Libra) a conscious need to communicate with others, Aquarius children are likely to grow into masters of ratiocination, arguing with doggedly persistent logic about why they should be allowed a candy bar today. But until this verbal facility is acquired, some Aquarians may be prone to temper tantrums: It's just not in their makeup to take no for an answer.

Your Aquarius may embarrass you with his indifference to all social conventions, so you'd better loosen up on some of your inhibitions, quick. He can be absolutely adamant in getting to his mother's breast when the appetite is upon him, and his timing can be highly unpredictable. That you're standing on line in the market at the time is of no concern to him whatsoever; he may even seem to enjoy seeing the old fuddy-duddies scowl. (You'll learn, as he grows older, that shocking people is one of his talented sidelines.) Aquarius children have keen ears for the orthodox, and they reject it with all their being.

Their highly individualistic approach to things may make living with them somewhat difficult at times, and parents may have to learn to know their place. Although she insists on being helped, four-year-old Tara is convinced that thirty-six-year-old Nancy doesn't know the right way to cut with scissors. "I'll cut it my way," she snaps at her mother. Companionship is permissible; guidance is not. "That's not so" is another favorite retort to simple parental statements. Although one more or less expects this kind of stubborn rejection of authority from young children, with Aquarians it is pretty much a lifelong habit of mind. And though it can pose problems for them when they try to function within the established order, it is also one of their strengths, for their role in life is to open all of us up to new, never-before-thought-of ways of being.

It shouldn't be forgotten, however, that as children, Aquarians still need their parents very much as the constants against which they push away. They would be very lost without you, independent though they may think themselves, and for those times when they do feel needy, they should know that their reliance on you is nothing to feel ashamed of, nor does it truly compromise their freedom. Aquarius-rising Adrienne responds to most of her nursery school teacher's suggestions with shocking retorts, but she becomes anxious whenever the teacher leaves the room, and midafternoon fatigue sometimes provokes her to ask to be held.

Clear-eyed and self-restrained, Aquarius children are really live wires, highly tuned. Like sweeping radar screens, they can pick up vibrations that no one else perceives, and they send them out again in the form of intuitive flashes so sharp they can make your head spin. You may never have noticed that your talkative neighbor yawns repeatedly whenever *you* are talking to *her* until your Aquarius child remarks on it one day.

Although bombarding impressions may sometimes get the best of him, making him seem rather scatterbrained, you will probably find it rewarding to encourage your child's unique abilities. He has a natural inventiveness, which he'll use to concoct highly original constructions, repair broken gismos, or suggest a change in a family routine no one had ever considered to be a problem before.

When Aquarius children turn their receptive antennae toward their peers, you'll be amazed at the advanced social consciousness they seem to possess. Aquarius has the paradoxical nature of being both the most highly individualistic of signs and the most profoundly group oriented. These people deeply seek the improvement of society as a whole, and they understand that it only comes about from the tolerant acceptance of all of its disparate elements.

Sharing comes naturally to children of this sign, and it is of the no-strings-attached variety. They will rarely have screaming fits of "Mine!" when another child approaches their toys. One little girl we know actually has the foresight to go and hide the playthings she really cares about when she knows a friend is coming over. She recognizes that the best way to keep the peace is to remove the source of discord.

Some seem to enjoy the accomplishments of their friends as much as they do their own: "You can do it too," he'll say as he patiently teaches his friend how to hammer nails into the living-room wall.

Your Aquarius child will probably demonstrate a genuine interest in others, with an acute awareness of both their abilities and their frailties, and she's likely to be quite caring and sympathetic in an aloof sort of way. She may be the one child in the group who goes over to stand quietly beside three-year-old Lewis, lending him her silent support, as he cries unconsolably on his first day at nursery school. With no prior example from you, she may know just how to pat other kids on the back or on the head to give them the reassurance she senses they need.

However, while universal love comes easily to many Aquarius children, personal commitment does not. Their individual freedom is so highly valued that they may turn off their emotions so as not to get too deeply involved with any one person or situation. This can get to be a problem in later life, and conscious parents may be able to help now to sensitize their children to this part of themselves. On the other hand, has anyone ever tried to write a romantic symphony for computer? Work on getting them to cultivate their feeling side as much as possible anyway. If nothing else, they can regard it as an exercise in awareness.

In spite of his aloofness, your Aquarius child will probably be highly popular with other children, the result of the keen objective interest he so generously pours forth to all. Fair and unselfish, teamwork is his forte, and he much prefers the group energy to solitary ventures. He is a true democrat, always willing to lend himself to any cooperative action. But his original streak must always express itself, and it may well be in his choice of friends. He'll tend to gravitate, in his own zigzag sort of way, to the one oddball in the group, or perhaps it will be the one child you'd never have chosen as a playmate for him. He knows the regular from the eccentric, and he's got to experiment with the whole vast assortment. Yet the contribution he makes will always be fresh, alive, and necessary.

The Evolving Aquarius

BIRTH TO ONE YEAR

Even before he was born, your Aquarius baby probably had his own idea of a schedule; he may have found the hour you wanted to go to bed ideal for "practicing his bicycling exercises" or "playing his trombone." His debut into the world is likely to be erratic. One mother reported a two-and-a-half-day labor consisting of hard contractions for nine-hour stretches with several-hour calm recesses in between. When at last her Aquarius decided to be born, it was in one powerful burst.

Feeding times for Aquarius infants tend to be irregular. Hours may elapse without a feeding, but the next one may be demanded only a half hour later. You should in no way regard this as deliberate perversity (babies are incapable of such cunning); Aquarius children are just naturally unpredictable. But once your child is past the delicate neonatal period, it wouldn't hurt to begin applying some gentle pressure to regularize her feedings.

Many Aquarius babies pay no heed to the developmental timetables: They may be very speedy crawlers long before they can even sit up by themselves. Or they may stand at six months, be able to walk at ten, but persist in crawling until fourteen months; at that age they may get up suddenly to walk and never crawl again.

Your Aquarius will probably be alert and lively, and even when she's not laughing or smiling, she may have a twinkle in her eye. She is likely to be especially bright when there are lots of people around, and she may interrupt your conversations in order to participate with her own babbling comments.

ONE-YEAR-OLDS

Your Aquarius toddler is likely to be a rugged individualist already, and if you tolerate his autonomy in small matters, you will seldom have to deal with insurrection. He will probably feel pressured if you try to feed him. Let him have the spoon to experiment with, but give him foods he can pick up with his fingers; spread some newspapers on the floor and keep him company—but don't sit too close. Don't fret if he doesn't relish the vegetable you consider essential or if he suddenly dislikes some dish you just spent two hours preparing because he ate it with such gusto last week; if he is provided with wholesome foods, he will balance his own diet over time. When he tries to turn the dish over and stand up in the high chair, assume he is satisfied and end the meal.

Aquarius toddlers are even more curious than most of their "into everything" contemporaries, and with their fine independent spirit they are not very likely to listen to your nay-saying, especially if you overdo it. When your Aquarius child pulls electrical cords out of sockets or investigates the connections in back of the TV set, physically remove her while you say your no and supply her with a rolling pin, a set of measuring spoons, or some other safe "adult" object she's never played with before.

TWO-YEAR-OLDS

After resisting your toilet-training efforts for months, your Aquarius two may suddenly train himself in a day or two once he understands how independent it makes him. He will probably want to be left alone while he sits on the toilet, only calling you back to help him wipe. He may also insist on dressing himself, and you should let him attempt it and tolerate such bizarre results as backward sweaters atop inside-out overalls while you subtly assist in lacing shoes or making certain his coat will open in the front.

At two and a half Aquarius children may show very marked extremes in the contradictory behavior typical of their age: One minute they may insist on absolute control of brushing their teeth, the next minute they may not be able to hold a cup of water for themselves; they may be performing in company excitedly, but a minute later they may hide behind you. You may be faced with quite a few tantrums from your child at this age, and though you should disregard them as much as possible, you might offer her some face-saving affection as they subside. Many of these tantrums can be prevented if you refrain from asking her questions that can be answered with a no.

THREE-YEAR-OLDS

When your Aquarius three demands to be permitted to operate your record player because his six-year-old sister does, you should probably let him—with supervision. But he may also insist on staying up until her nine-o'clock bedtime, and your explanations are not likely to satisfy him. In this case you might allow him a quiet half hour in bed with books or toys before the lights go out.

As a rule, Aquarius threes are rather socially adept, and they may take a leading role in group activities even if they are younger than the other children. They may resolve battles over property by independently suggesting that a toy be shared or that everyone take a turn.

It's probably a good idea to start having serious conversations with your Aquarius three about any subject she may bring up; this habit of open communication will pay off in several years when you really want to know how she plans to overthrow the older generation. You can stimulate the inventive minds of Aquarius threes by asking them to imagine what they might be able to do if they had three hands or two heads.

At three and a half your Aquarius child may emphatically resist all routines, but if you're lucky, he will comply with your directives if you can give him good reasons.

FOUR-YEAR-OLDS

By now your Aquarius child is secure in his conviction that you are not omnipotent, and he may enjoy defying your mandates with such taunts as "You're a dumdum!" Since he probably wishes to see the shocking effect this has on you, you might retort immediately and ludicrously with, "And you're a squirty grapefruit!" The backfired shock may delight him and invoke his good-natured cooperation. When all else fails, temporary isolation is usually an effective disciplinary technique.

Aquarius fours are unusually inventive, and many enjoy building intricate contraptions with Legos or Tinkertoys or playing with toys that have many moving parts. They often prefer to bring their toys to other kids' houses, but you may be aggravated by their humanitarian tendency to leave them there for everyone else to enjoy.

Your Aquarius four is likely to challenge her nursery school teacher as well as you; she just wants to do things her own way. It's best to allow her as much freedom as possible and wait for her requests for assistance. She will generally be interested in novel things and will be very inspired by field trips to local industries, where she can see how things really work. The why questions of Aquarius children can often be answered with simplified scientific explanations.

FIVE-YEAR-OLDS

Your Aquarius five will probably be more cooperative at home than formerly, but he may still need to have the logic of every regulation explained to him. He is above all a free thinker, and he will be far less likely than his contemporaries to swallow adult prejudices. More serious and practical now, he may ingeniously propose such household shortcuts as letting the dog help with the dishwashing by giving him the greasy frying pan before it goes into the soapy water. He will probably love to tinker, and if you have a nonworking alarm clock lying around, be sure to let him take it apart; he may not be able to repair it, but he will be fascinated with the gears and springs for a long time.

Aquarius fives are not likely to have very possessive friendships, since they prefer to remain somewhat emotionally detached. But the friendships they do have will probably be longlasting and mutually rewarding.

♓

Pisces

(SUN SIGN, FEBRUARY 20–MARCH 20)

And in all that brown, the sun went down.
It was evening and the colors began to disappear in the warm dark
night.
*   The kittens fell asleep in the warm dark night with all their*
colors out of sight and as they slept they dreamed their dream—
A wonderful dream . . .
Of a purple land in a pale pink sea
Where apples fell from a golden tree
And then a world of Easter eggs
That danced about on little short legs.
And they dreamed that
A green cat danced with a little pink dog
Till they all disappeared in a soft gray fog.
Margaret Wise Brown, The Color Kittens

Are you looking for your Pisces child? Don't bother to address her—she probably won't hear you. Don't waste your time trying to entice her with appealing foods or toys—she probably doesn't care. But catch the next sun ray to Neptune, and you're sure to find her, dancing on a vapor to the music of her dreams.

If it irritates you that you have trouble getting through to your Pisces child at times, that she acts shy and clinging in the company of others and so vague and confused at home, try to understand it this way: These children are as impressionable as the sea. The slightest breeze ripples them. The merest cloud darkens them. Unknown creatures inhabit their depths, and their boundaries are not their own but rather those of whatever contains them. Receptive to every influence both fair and foul, they are all sensitivity, with no mask or shell to protect them. The only way out for them is inward, and they must retreat in order to replenish themselves for their next yielding encounter with reality.

You will find, if you haven't discovered it already, that Pisces children are exceedingly susceptible to being hurt. Although they share with the other water signs (Cancer and Scorpio) a deep need to respond to the world emotionally, they alone have few, if any, defenses, and many of them show this through a great deal of heartfelt crying. It's as if they just can't cope with negativity in any form, and you may find yourself feeling constrained that you can't scold them or say a justifiedly angry word without fear of wounding them cruelly. But they may get just as upset if you yell at the dog or direct a dirty look at your spouse.

You may be able to help your Pisces by getting him to express his feelings in words. Pisces children are so totally responsive to every shifting current, so devotedly willing to give themselves over to every impression, that they can become deeply gloomy from too much exposure to the world and its inevitable dark side. When forced to deal with reality, they can literally be overcome with the weight of it all. They seek and need some escape from their overwhelming feelings, but they also need practice in clarifying some of the fog. Words are one way that they can gain some much needed distance from their feelings as well as a way of maintaining a bridge of communication to you. Words may serve to focus and contain the Pisces nature, something that may sometimes seem as maddeningly difficult as trying to lure a genie into a bottle. Verbalizing is certainly not the only means of focusing self-expression (painting and playacting are two others), but whatever form it takes, some gentle guidance and encouragement from you may go a long way toward helping your Pisces child master his own confusing personality.

The Pisces child has many gifts to offer in exchange for her unworldly ways. She can be profoundly sympathetic to the plight of others. If her baby brother has a bad fall, she'll compassionately share his pain, gently cuddling him while you bandage him up (even though this same baby brother's birth just a few months before caused her such intense agonies of rejection). Or she may sense when you're feeling out of sorts and try to take measures to make you feel better the way four-year-old Meadow did, who ran up to whisper to her father as he was leaving for work, "Get Mommy a present. She's not feeling well." Similarly, two-year-old Zandra won't eat a bite of her meals until she's sure her parents are provided for.

Soft-spoken, charming, and naturally kind, your Pisces child will shrink from hurting others every bit as much as he can't bear being hurt himself, and his beloved doctor kit will be that of the true healer. He may be interested in massage from a very early age, and not only you but his dolls and the cat will have to be the happy recipients of his ministrations. One little boy we know who watched as a doctor helped his mother deliver his baby sister at home is temporarily embarrassing his parents somewhat with his solicitous desire to deliver every female guest of her abdominal bulge.

Dogs, cats, turtles, parakeets, gerbils, snakes, and lizards may all get doting attention from Pisces children, for their affection for all beings is limitless. You might try giving them the job of feeding the family pet, but don't expect too much from them in terms of daily performance: These heavenly fishes are generally poorly grounded in the practicalities of here-

and-now existence. Their toys, too, may be little played with, for there are far more fascinating dramas going on within themselves.

Their emotions continuously spill out in many forms. Many Pisceans are romantic sentimentalists, and parents may be surprised to hear even very young Pisces children frequently reminiscing about happy moments in the past. They can also form idealized attachments to older children, adults, or even storybook heroes, for many of them deeply need a strong character with whom to identify. Their sense of themselves is too evanescent, too easily influenced by others, for them to have a clear idea of who they really are.

This fact of their nature leads us to a very important word of advice for the adults who care for them: These sensitive chameleons can be very much affected by your critical words or even by your own negative preoccupations or personal anxieties. Although you can't (and shouldn't) utterly transform yourselves to satisfy their needs, you should be aware that any attitude you have toward them is likely to be unquestioningly absorbed. If you tell them they're lazy or uncooperative, you can pretty much bet they will prove you right. But if you emphasize the postive, you may find them growing stronger, nourished by the warmth of your love.

The immense imaginative capacity Pisces children have is also the source of exceptional creative abilities, which you should by all means foster. Dance is often their preeminent talent, for through it they seem to lose themselves, body and soul and music all fusing into one joyous form. People often notice what a wonderful sense of rhythm they possess and how completely unself-conscious they become as they sway and glide in their newfound freedom. In fact, music in every form is the water in which the Pisces fish swims best, and that includes poetry too.

Painting is another favorite, and if you see talent in your child in this area, don't be too ready to assume it's just the ordinary creativity all children display. Many a Pisces child has grown up to be a successful visual artist, communicating through color and form what she may have found impossible to squeeze into words.

Their pervasive impressionability leads some Pisces children to pantomime and drama, in which, perhaps, they manage to resolve their identity problems and at the same time give creative expression to their profound intuitive perceptions. When five-year-old Pisces-moon Greg, usually a passive follower in nursery school, played the part of the prince in an impromptu "production" of "Sleeping Beauty," his latent talent for passionate self-expression fully blossomed. The teacher was impressed to see how totally immersed in the drama he became, how he acted without a hint of self-conscious giggling, taking command of the progress of the action, and even kissed the three-year-old sleeping princess with gusto. You might encourage your Pisces child to discover this wonderful outlet for his essentially reclusive spirit by providing a variety of dress-up clothes—with yourselves as the appreciative audience.

It is the Piscean dilemma to have one foot in this world and the other in the next. And it is both the need and the strength of the Pisces to be able to understand and ultimately to transcend this duality through art. Your love for your Pisces child will be returned one-million-fold, not only to you but to all the world through the empathetic attunement he shows in so many ways.

The Evolving Pisces

BIRTH TO ONE YEAR

It is possible that your Pisces baby will be born screaming—one father reported being able to hear his daughter scream *in utero*—but it is very likely that she will begin to cry heart-rendingly soon afterward. It's as though the stark, bright coldness of the outside world is too great a shock after nine months of watery peace. Her entrance may be considerably less disturbing if you can manage to have dim lighting at the delivery and if you can hold her and cuddle her immediately. Pisces infants are characteristically high-strung and need a lot of soothing. They usually have a terrific sucking need in early infancy, and you should let your Pisces nurse for long periods or provide her with a bottle with a small nipple hole, which you can supplement with a pacifier.

Your Pisces infant is likely to be very empathetic, and if there is another child crying within earshot, he may cry also in seeming commiseration. But he is just as apt to copy laughter, and you may be surprised to hear him cackling with mirth in imitation of your guest's laughing at an adult joke. He may employ this gift for mimickry in learning certain skills: After intently watching another baby pick up objects and put them into a container, he may be able to do it himself.

Your Pisces baby's gurgles at six months may be very musical, and if you imitate *him*, he will be delighted. Try to get the resulting duet on tape.

ONE-YEAR-OLDS

Your Pisces toddler may feel very insecure once she learns how to walk, and she may wish to regress to crawling. She may also fear objects that make loud noises (the vacuum cleaner, for example); the world from her upright posture is very strange and confusing to her. She may embarrass you with her clinging and miserable wailing to be picked up when the toddler offspring of your visitor is bravely scouting around your house. Try not to let social pressure inhibit you from comforting your child; you will foster her independence only if you can provide her enough security now. On the other hand, you should not be manipulated by her emotional theatrics when she wants to play with your photo album or refuses to conclude her ninety-minute bath. Though Pisces toddlers often seem compliant, even submissive, on the surface, they are just as willful as their contemporaries and they can exploit a wide variety of affective attitudes. If they can't charm you, they may shriek in agony, gag and vomit, or turn themselves into catatonic zombies. If you are alarmed by this behavior, they probably will be also, for they may get so carried away that they don't realize they are putting it on. You will need to use discretion in separating real need from make-believe hysterics.

Your Pisces toddler will probably be very affectionate with you, especially when he is tired, and he may plead "sleepy time" in order to enjoy the special closeness of bedtime routines. In order to relax sufficiently for sleep, however, he may need to rock himself in the crib while he sings all the new words he's been learning.

TWO-YEAR-OLDS

The toilet training of your Pisces two may be difficult unless you are vigilant, for if she's deeply involved in her play, she may not realize her urge until the fait accompli. You will have to be ready with a reminder whenever you notice that familiar faraway look on her face.

Pisces twos characteristically retreat from unpleasant situations; when another child socks your Pisces in order to seize his toy, he may be reluctant to fight back, not because he is afraid but because of his distaste for violence. Unfortunately, he may be concealing strong feelings inside, which may emerge as whining and whimpering.

The wild tantrums of your two-and-a-half-year-old Pisces will probably stem more from confusion and insecurity than from anger. Don't perplex him with choices, and try to make your directives more palatable by singing them. In fact, music (your singing, especially) is often an ideal way to calm him down, whether he's crying over some hurt or is unable to resume sleeping after a nightmare.

THREE-YEAR-OLDS

Your Pisces three will probably have as many haunting dreams as a year earlier, but now she will be able to tell you more about them. Actually, she may have trouble distinguishing her sleeping dreams from her reveries while awake, and her imagination will be able to conjure some pretty terrible apparitions in the dark. You can often soothe her by playing along with the fantasy: Just brush the "toads" out of her bed or chase the "snake" away.

The sensitive ears of Pisces threes are often bothered by sounds that you hardly notice, which is one more indication of their natural talent for music. You should remember that your Pisces three's stuffed animals, dolls, or toy figures are probably quite real to him—there may be an invisible brother or walrus as well—and you can often persuade these "guests" in your home to argue on your behalf when you want your child to come to dinner or get ready for bed.

FOUR-YEAR-OLDS

Your Pisces four is likely to imitate his playmates, and he may become unduly influenced by the questionable behavior of another child. You shouldn't attempt to argue him out of this unfortunate attachment; you probably won't convince him, and he is likely to go to his room, shut the door, and sulk the rest of the day. The best help may be to expose him to a person whose influence is stronger but more positive, to whom he can shift his unquestioning devotion.

Pisces children often seem not to be there when you talk to them. Although you may not think your Pisces four is listening to your response to her why question, she is probably absorbing the answer she seeks; it just may not be in the terms you use. At this age Pisces children usually make great intuitive leaps; they seem to be soaking up everything. Unfortunately, they are likely to be quite gullible, and since they tend to confuse reality with what they imagine, they may innocently tell you quite a few whoppers. These stories are often very dramatically narrated and can be quite entertaining. Without being overly mundane, try to help your Pisces four adapt to the real world, perhaps by setting aside special times for fantasy enactments or by encouraging him to draw or paint everything that comes into his head.

FIVE-YEAR-OLDS

Your Pisces five is likely to idealize you, and if you want her not to be severely disappointed in the future, you should consciously try to give her a more realistic image now. On the other hand, like other kids her age, she may not be as open and accessible as she was a year before. In fact, Pisces fives tend to be particularly submerged. Whereas you may feel you never know what's on her mind, she may feel that you wouldn't understand her anyway. If you're finding communication difficult, try easing up on your insistence on the prosaic and occasionally join her on her fantastic excursions.

Many Pisces children escape from the real world they tend to find so humdrum by watching TV for hours on end, which is a shameful waste of their creative imagination. If your Pisces five seems addicted to the tube, you probably should begin regulating his viewing time. You can alleviate his boredom by playing with him. For example, you could both close your eyes and listen, then describe what you've heard to each other. This game will sharpen his powers of auditory discernment, develop his poetic capability with language, and—most important—convince him that the real world is an interesting place too.

PART THREE:
Appendixes

Appendix A:
How to Find Your Child's Sun and Moon Sign

The following pages are a listing for the years 1973 through 1980. It shows the times when the sun and the moon entered each sign.

The days and times that the sun changed signs appear in boldface. All other date and time listings are for the moon changing signs.

All times are eastern times. If your child was born anyplace other than in the eastern time zone, consult Table A–1 to find the number of hours that should be *added to or subtracted from (as indicated)* the times shown in the listings.

We have already adjusted the times in the listings for daylight saving time where appropriate. However, daylight saving time is not observed in Arizona, Hawaii, Michigan, Saskatchewan, and all of Indiana *except* the following twelve counties: Gibson, Jasper, Lake, La Porte, Newton, Pike, Porter, Posey, Spencer, Starke, Vanderburgh, and Warrick. If your child was born in any of these places when daylight saving time was in effect in the rest of the United States and Canada (see Table B-1, page 114), you will have to *subtract 1 more hour* from the times given in the listings.

Example A: Otis was born 5:15 A.M., October 15, 1977, in New York City. We see from the listing that the moon entered Scorpio on October 13 and did not enter the next sign, Sagittarius, until 11:28 A.M. on October 15. Since New York City is in the eastern time zone, we needn't correct this time. Otis's moon sign is Scorpio.

Example B: Louise was born 4:21 A.M., May 21, 1978, in Los Angeles. We see from the listing that the sun entered Gemini at 6:09 A.M. on May 21. But since Los Angeles is in the Pacific time zone, we need to subtract 3 hours from this time (see Table A–1). Thus, the sun entered Gemini at 3:09 A.M. Pacific time. Since Louise was born after that time, her sun sign is Gemini.

Example C: Abigail was born June 28, 1975, at 3:05 A.M. in Phoenix, Arizona. From the listing we see that the moon entered Pisces at 5:34 A.M. on June 28. Arizona is in the mountain time zone. From Table A–1 we see we must subtract 2 hours from this time. Thus, the moon entered Pisces at 3:34 A.M. mountain time. Arizona does not observe daylight saving time. We see from Table B-1 (page 114) that most parts of the United States and Canada were observing daylight saving time on June 28, 1975. Thus, we must subtract an additional hour. The result is 2:34 A.M.—the time the moon entered Pisces in Arizona. Abigail's moon sign is Pisces, since she was born after this time.

Table A–1. Correction for Time Zones Other Than Eastern (in Hours)

Newfoundland Time Zone	+1½
Atlantic Time Zone	+1
Central Time Zone	−1
Mountain Time Zone	−2
Pacific Time Zone	−3
Yukon Time Zone	−4
Alaska-Hawaii Time Zone	−5
Bering Time Zone	−6

1973		Moon Enters	Time	1973		Moon Enters	Time
Jan	3	Capricorn	6:31 am		18	**Pisces**	**2:02 pm***
	5	Aquarius	5:48 pm		19	Libra	12:59 pm
	8	Pisces	3:03 am		21	Scorpio	9:36 pm
	10	Aries	9:58 pm		24	Sagittarius	9:15 am
	12	Taurus	2:25 pm		26	Capricorn	10:04 pm
	14	Gemini	4:42 pm	Mar	1	Aquarius	9:23 am
	16	Cancer	5:39 pm		3	Pisces	5:32 pm
	18	Leo	6:41 pm		5	Aries	10:38 pm
	19	**Aquarius**	**11:49 pm***		8	Taurus	1:51 am
	20	Virgo	9:24 pm		10	Gemini	4:31 am
	23	Libra	3:17 am		12	Cancer	7:30 am
	25	Scorpio	12:53 pm		14	Leo	11:08 am
	28	Sagittarius	1:11 am		16	Virgo	3:43 pm
	30	Capricorn	1:55 pm		18	Libra	9:49 pm
Feb	2	Aquarius	12:56 am		**20**	**Aries**	**1:13 pm***
	4	Pisces	9:23 am		21	Scorpio	6:16 am
	6	Aries	3:29 pm		23	Sagittarius	5:27 pm
	8	Taurus	7:54 pm		26	Capricorn	6:16 am
	10	Gemini	11:11 pm		28	Aquarius	6:13 pm
	13	Cancer	1:45 am		31	Pisces	2:55 am
	15	Leo	4:13 am	Apr	2	Aries	7:49 am
	17	Virgo	7:32 am		4	Taurus	9:59 am

*Boldface type indicates change of the sun sign.

1973	Moon Enters	Time	1973	Moon Enters	Time
6	Gemini	11:12 am	13	Capricorn	9:46 am
8	Cancer	1:05 pm	15	Aquarius	10:15 pm
10	Leo	4:32 pm	18	Pisces	9:08 am
12	Virgo	9:47 pm	20	Aries	5:44 pm
15	Libra	4:50 am	**22**	**Leo**	**7:56 pm***
17	Scorpio	1:52 pm	22	Taurus	11:41 pm
20	**Taurus**	**12:31 am***	25	Gemini	2:59 am
20	Sagittarius	1:02 am	27	Cancer	4:11 am
22	Capricorn	1:50 pm	29	Leo	4:30 am
25	Aquarius	2:22 am	31	Virgo	5:35 am
27	Pisces	12:10 pm	Aug 2	Libra	9:13 am
29	Aries	6:54 pm	4	Scorpio	4:36 pm
May 1	Taurus	9:02 pm	7	Sagittarius	3:37 am
3	Gemini	9:16 pm	9	Capricorn	4:30 pm
5	Cancer	9:36 pm	12	Aquarius	4:53 am
7	Leo	11:37 pm	14	Pisces	3:15 pm
10	Virgo	4:13 am	16	Aries	11:16 pm
12	Libra	11:31 am	19	Taurus	5:14 am
14	Scorpio	9:10 pm	21	Gemini	9:27 am
17	Sagittarius	8:42 am	**23**	**Virgo**	**2:54 am***
19	Capricorn	9:31 pm	23	Cancer	12:08 pm
21	**Gemini**	**12:55 am***	25	Leo	1:50 pm
22	Aquarius	10:18 am	27	Virgo	3:34 pm
24	Pisces	9:06 pm	29	Libra	6:53 pm
27	Aries	4:15 am	Sep 1	Scorpio	1:18 am
29	Taurus	7:28 am	3	Sagittarius	11:25 am
31	Gemini	7:53 am	6	Capricorn	12:02 am
Jun 2	Cancer	7:22 am	8	Aquarius	12:31 pm
4	Leo	7:50 am	10	Pisces	10:41 pm
6	Virgo	10:52 am	13	Aries	5:57 am
8	Libra	5:16 pm	15	Taurus	11:00 am
11	Scorpio	2:52 am	17	Gemini	2:48 pm
13	Sagittarius	2:43 pm	19	Cancer	6:02 pm
16	Capricorn	3:37 am	21	Leo	8:57 pm
18	Aquarius	4:20 pm	**23**	**Libra**	**12:22 am***
21	Pisces	3:29 am	23	Virgo	11:59 pm
21	**Cancer**	**9:01 am***	26	Libra	4:01 am
23	Aries	11:49 am	28	Scorpio	10:19 am
25	Taurus	4:38 pm	30	Sagittarius	7:48 pm
27	Gemini	6:18 pm	Oct 3	Capricorn	8:03 am
29	Cancer	6:09 pm	5	Aquarius	8:49 pm
Jul 1	Leo	5:56 pm	8	Pisces	7:24 am
3	Virgo	7:32 pm	10	Aries	2:29 pm
6	Libra	12:24 am	12	Taurus	6:37 pm
8	Scorpio	9:06 am	14	Gemini	9:09 pm
10	Sagittarius	8:48 pm	16	Cancer	11:29 pm

*Boldface type indicates change of the sun sign.

(Continued)

1973	Moon Enters	Time
19	Leo	2:25 am
21	Virgo	6:19 am
23	**Scorpio**	**9:31 am***
23	Libra	11:29 am
25	Scorpio	6:28 pm
28	Sagittarius	2:58 am
30	Capricorn	2:58 pm
Nov 2	Aquarius	3:59 am
4	Pisces	3:27 pm
6	Aries	11:20 pm
9	Taurus	3:26 am
11	Gemini	5:00 am
13	Cancer	5:47 am
15	Leo	7:20 am
17	Virgo	10:42 am
19	Libra	4:16 pm
22	Scorpio	12:07 am
22	**Sagittarius**	**5:55 am***
24	Sagittarius	10:11 am
26	Capricorn	10:13 pm
29	Aquarius	11:18 am
Dec 1	Pisces	11:33 pm
4	Aries	6:51 am
6	Taurus	2:09 pm
8	Gemini	3:58 pm
10	Cancer	3:52 pm
12	Leo	3:45 pm
14	Virgo	5:21 pm
16	Libra	9:54 pm
19	Scorpio	5:44 am
21	Sagittarius	4:20 pm
21	**Capricorn**	**7:09 pm***
24	Capricorn	4:42 am
26	Aquarius	5:43 pm
29	Pisces	6:10 am
31	Aries	4:35 pm

1974	Moon Enters	Time
Jan 2	Taurus	11:38 pm
5	Gemini	3:00 am
7	Cancer	4:29 am
9	Leo	3:43 am
11	Virgo	3:42 am
13	Libra	6:22 am

*Boldface type indicates change of the sun sign.

96

1974	Moon Enters	Time
15	Scorpio	12:55 pm
17	Sagittarius	11:13 pm
20	**Aquarius**	**6:47 am***
20	Capricorn	11:48 am
23	Aquarius	12:50 am
25	Pisces	1:01 pm
27	Aries	11:32 pm
30	Taurus	7:42 am
Feb 1	Gemini	12:54 pm
3	Cancer	3:06 pm
5	Leo	3:12 pm
7	Virgo	2:52 pm
9	Libra	4:11 pm
11	Scorpio	8:58 pm
14	Sagittarius	6:02 am
16	Capricorn	6:16 pm
18	**Pisces**	**8:59 pm***
19	Aquarius	7:21 am
21	Pisces	7:16 pm
24	Aries	5:13 am
26	Taurus	1:12 pm
28	Gemini	7:11 pm
Mar 2	Cancer	11:00 pm
5	Leo	12:49 am
7	Virgo	1:34 am
9	Libra	2:52 am
11	Scorpio	6:40 am
13	Sagittarius	2:21 pm
16	Capricorn	1:42 am
18	Aquarius	2:39 pm
20	**Aries**	**8:08 pm***
21	Pisces	2:34 am
23	Aries	12:03 pm
25	Taurus	7:10 pm
28	Gemini	12:34 am
30	Cancer	4:40 am
Apr 1	Leo	7:41 am
3	Virgo	9:57 am
5	Libra	12:23 pm
7	Scorpio	4:26 pm
9	Sagittarius	11:28 pm
12	Capricorn	9:57 am
14	Aquarius	10:35 pm
17	Pisces	10:45 am
19	Aries	8:21 pm
20	**Taurus**	**7:20 am***
22	Taurus	2:54 am

1974	Moon Enters	Time	1974	Moon Enters	Time
24	Gemini	7:11 am	30	Capricorn	2:11 pm
26	Cancer	10:18 am	Aug 2	Aquarius	2:47 am
28	Leo	1:04 pm	4	Pisces	3:27 pm
30	Virgo	4:01 pm	7	Aries	3:16 am
May 2	Libra	7:40 pm	9	Taurus	1:13 pm
5	Scorpio	12:44 am	11	Gemini	8:16 pm
7	Sagittarius	8:06 am	13	Cancer	11:49 pm
9	Capricorn	6:16 pm	16	Leo	12:27 am
12	Aquarius	6:35 am	17	Virgo	11:43 pm
14	Pisces	7:04 pm	19	Libra	11:45 pm
17	Aries	5:20 am	22	Scorpio	2:38 am
19	Taurus	12:11 pm	**23**	**Virgo**	**8:29 am***
21	**Gemini**	**6:37 am***	24	Sagittarius	9:35 am
21	Gemini	3:55 pm	26	Capricorn	8:16 pm
23	Cancer	5:46 pm	29	Aquarius	8:53 am
25	Leo	7:13 pm	31	Pisces	9:30 pm
27	Virgo	9:26 pm	Sep 3	Aries	8:59 am
30	Libra	1:16 am	5	Taurus	6:51 pm
Jun 1	Scorpio	7:11 am	8	Gemini	2:37 am
3	Sagittarius	3:22 pm	10	Cancer	7:40 am
6	Capricorn	1:49 am	12	Leo	9:55 am
8	Aquarius	2:03 pm	14	Virgo	10:13 am
11	Pisces	2:44 am	16	Libra	10:18 am
13	Aries	1:53 pm	18	Scorpio	12:15 pm
15	Taurus	9:47 pm	20	Sagittarius	5:47 pm
18	Gemini	1:59 am	23	Capricorn	3:22 am
20	Cancer	3:22 am	**23**	**Libra**	**5:59 am***
21	**Cancer**	**2:38 pm***	25	Aquarius	3:39 pm
22	Leo	3:30 am	28	Pisces	4:15 am
24	Virgo	4:12 am	30	Aries	3:26 pm
26	Libra	6:58 am	Oct 3	Taurus	12:40 am
28	Scorpio	12:41 pm	5	Gemini	8:01 am
30	Sagittarius	9:21 pm	7	Cancer	1:31 pm
Jul 3	Capricorn	8:20 am	9	Leo	5:03 pm
5	Aquarius	8:42 pm	11	Virgo	5:57 pm
8	Pisces	9:26 am	13	Libra	8:11 pm
10	Aries	9:11 pm	15	Scorpio	10:24 pm
13	Taurus	6:22 am	18	Sagittarius	3:15 am
15	Gemini	11:55 am	20	Capricorn	11:45 pm
17	Cancer	1:57 pm	22	Aquarius	11:21 pm
19	Leo	1:44 pm	**23**	**Scorpio**	**3:12 pm***
21	Virgo	1:10 pm	25	Pisces	11:57 am
23	**Leo**	**1:31 am***	27	Aries	10:14 pm
23	Libra	2:20 pm	30	Taurus	7:01 am
25	Scorpio	6:46 pm	Nov 1	Gemini	1:24 pm
28	Sagittarius	3:00 am	3	Cancer	6:02 pm

*Boldface type indicates change of the sun sign.

(Continued)

1974	Moon Enters	Time
5	Leo	9:31 pm
8	Virgo	12:19 am
10	Libra	2:59 am
12	Scorpio	6:24 am
14	Sagittarius	11:39 am
16	Capricorn	7:42 pm
19	Aquarius	6:39 am
21	Pisces	7:12 pm
22	**Sagittarius**	**11:39 am***
24	Aries	6:59 am
26	Taurus	4:05 pm
28	Gemini	9:58 pm
Dec 1	Cancer	1:22 am
3	Leo	3:32 am
5	Virgo	5:41 am
7	Libra	8:43 am
9	Scorpio	1:14 pm
11	Sagittarius	7:35 pm
14	Capricorn	4:04 am
16	Aquarius	2:49 pm
19	Pisces	3:13 am
21	Aries	3:36 pm
22	**Capricorn**	**12:57 am***
24	Taurus	1:45 am
26	Gemini	8:16 am
28	Cancer	11:16 am
30	Leo	12:05 pm

1975	Moon Enters	Time
Jan 1	Virgo	12:33 pm
3	Libra	2:22 pm
5	Scorpio	6:39 pm
8	Sagittarius	1:40 am
10	Capricorn	10:59 am
12	Aquarius	10:04 pm
15	Pisces	10:24 am
17	Aries	11:04 am
20	Taurus	10:22 am
20	**Aquarius**	**11:37 am***
22	Gemini	6:23 pm
24	Cancer	10:21 pm
26	Leo	11:01 pm
28	Virgo	10:14 pm
30	Libra	10:14 pm

1975	Moon Enters	Time
Feb 2	Scorpio	12:54 am
4	Sagittarius	7:11 am
6	Capricorn	4:43 pm
9	Aquarius	4:17 am
11	Pisces	4:46 pm
14	Aries	5:23 am
16	Taurus	5:10 pm
19	**Pisces**	**1:51 am***
19	Gemini	2:35 am
21	Cancer	8:19 am
23	Leo	11:14 am
25	Virgo	10:38 am
27	Libra	9:39 am
Mar 1	Scorpio	10:34 am
3	Sagittarius	3:06 pm
5	Capricorn	11:40 pm
8	Aquarius	11:10 am
10	Pisces	11:50 pm
13	Aries	12:19 pm
15	Taurus	11:53 pm
18	Gemini	9:44 am
20	Cancer	4:49 pm
21	**Aries**	**1:57 am***
22	Leo	8:32 pm
24	Virgo	9:22 pm
26	Libra	8:52 pm
28	Scorpio	9:08 pm
31	Sagittarius	12:10 am
Apr 2	Capricorn	7:09 am
4	Aquarius	5:46 pm
7	Pisces	6:17 am
9	Aries	6:45 pm
12	Taurus	5:54 am
14	Gemini	3:15 pm
16	Cancer	10:28 pm
19	Leo	3:15 am
20	**Taurus**	**1:08 pm***
21	Virgo	5:43 am
23	Libra	6:42 am
25	Scorpio	7:40 am
27	Sagittarius	10:20 am
29	Capricorn	4:09 pm
May 2	Aquarius	1:34 am
4	Pisces	1:35 pm
7	Aries	2:03 am
9	Taurus	1:04 pm

*Boldface type indicates change of the sun sign.

98

1975		Moon Enters	Time	1975		Moon Enters	Time
	11	Gemini	9:45 pm		16	Capricorn	10:26 pm
	14	Cancer	4:08 am		19	Aquarius	8:10 am
	16	Leo	8:39 am		21	Pisces	7:33 pm
	18	Virgo	11:16 am		**23**	**Virgo**	**2:24 pm***
	20	Libra	2:06 pm		24	Aries	8:03 am
	21	**Gemini**	**12:24 pm***		26	Taurus	8:45 pm
	22	Scorpio	4:26 pm		29	Gemini	7:54 am
	24	Sagittarius	7:52 pm		31	Cancer	3:36 pm
	27	Capricorn	1:31 am	Sep	2	Leo	7:09 pm
	29	Aquarius	10:10 am		4	Virgo	7:30 pm
	31	Pisces	9:33 pm		6	Libra	6:38 pm
Jun	3	Aries	10:02 am		8	Scorpio	6:46 pm
	5	Taurus	9:19 pm		10	Sagittarius	9:41 pm
	8	Gemini	5:50 am		13	Capricorn	4:12 am
	10	Cancer	11:22 am		15	Aquarius	1:52 pm
	12	Leo	2:46 pm		18	Pisces	1:32 am
	14	Virgo	5:11 pm		20	Aries	2:08 pm
	16	Libra	7:41 pm		23	Taurus	2:44 am
	18	Scorpio	11:00 pm		**23**	**Libra**	**11:56 am***
	21	Sagittarius	3:35 am		25	Gemini	2:14 pm
	21	**Cancer**	**8:27 pm***		27	Cancer	11:08 pm
	23	Capricorn	9:27 am		30	Leo	4:21 am
	25	Aquarius	6:33 pm	Oct	2	Virgo	6:04 am
	28	Pisces	5:34 am		4	Libra	5:39 am
	30	Aries	6:03 pm		6	Scorpio	5:09 am
Jul	3	Taurus	5:55 am		8	Sagittarius	6:36 am
	5	Gemini	2:59 pm		10	Capricorn	11:29 am
	7	Cancer	8:24 pm		12	Aquarius	8:10 pm
	9	Leo	10:51 pm		15	Pisces	7:41 am
	11	Virgo	11:56 pm		17	Aries	8:21 pm
	14	Libra	1:22 am		20	Taurus	8:44 am
	16	Scorpio	4:24 a.m		22	Gemini	7:52 pm
	18	Sagittarius	9:33 am		**23**	**Scorpio**	**9:07 pm***
	20	Capricorn	4:46 pm		25	Cancer	4:58 am
	23	Aquarius	1:56 am		27	Leo	10:20 am
	23	**Leo**	**7:23 am***		29	Virgo	1:47 pm
	25	Pisces	12:59 pm		31	Libra	2:56 pm
	28	Aries	1:28 am	Nov	2	Scorpio	3:08 pm
	30	Taurus	1:54 pm		4	Sagittarius	4:11 pm
Aug	2	Gemini	12:03 am		6	Capricorn	7:46 pm
	4	Cancer	6:18 am		9	Aquarius	3:00 am
	6	Leo	8:44 am		11	Pisces	1:42 pm
	8	Virgo	8:54 am		14	Aries	2:18 am
	10	Libra	8:52 am		16	Taurus	2:38 pm
	12	Scorpio	10:31 am		19	Gemini	1:15 am
	14	Sagittarius	3:00 pm		21	Cancer	9:37 am

*Boldface type indicates change of the sun sign.

(Continued)

1975	Moon Enters	Time
22	**Sagittarius**	**5:32 pm***
23	Leo	3:49 pm
25	Virgo	8:05 pm
27	Libra	10:48 pm
30	Scorpio	12:37 am
Dec 2	Sagittarius	2:34 am
4	Capricorn	5:59 am
6	Aquarius	12:13 pm
8	Pisces	9:52 pm
11	Aries	10:07 am
13	Taurus	10:40 pm
16	Gemini	9:13 am
18	Cancer	4:50 pm
20	Leo	9:54 pm
22	**Capricorn**	**6:47 am***
23	Virgo	1:28 am
25	Libra	4:28 am
27	Scorpio	7:28 am
29	Sagittarius	10:53 am
31	Capricorn	3:17 pm

1976	Moon Enters	Time
Jan 2	Aquarius	9:34 pm
5	Pisces	6:36 am
7	Aries	6:22 pm
10	Taurus	7:10 am
12	Gemini	6:20 pm
15	Cancer	2:01 am
17	Leo	6:16 am
19	Virgo	8:26 am
20	**Aquarius**	**5:27 pm***
21	Libra	10:11 am
23	Scorpio	12:49 pm
25	Sagittarius	4:52 pm
27	Capricorn	10:25 pm
30	Aquarius	5:35 am
Feb 1	Pisces	2:47 pm
4	Aries	2:18 am
6	Taurus	3:14 pm
9	Gemini	3:17 am
11	Cancer	11:59 am
13	Leo	4:33 pm
15	Virgo	6:00 pm
17	Libra	6:15 pm

1976	Moon Enters	Time
19	**Pisces**	**7:41 am***
19	Scorpio	7:14 pm
21	Sagittarius	10:19 pm
24	Capricorn	3:55 am
26	Aquarius	11:49 am
28	Pisces	9:42 pm
Mar 2	Aries	9:23 am
4	Taurus	10:19 pm
7	Gemini	10:56 am
9	Cancer	8:59 pm
12	Leo	2:56 am
14	Virgo	4:59 am
16	Libra	4:45 am
18	Scorpio	4:18 am
20	Sagittarius	5:34 am
20	**Aries**	**6:50 am***
22	Capricorn	9:49 am
24	Aquarius	5:20 pm
27	Pisces	3:34 am
29	Aries	3:38 pm
Apr 1	Taurus	4:35 am
3	Gemini	5:16 pm
6	Cancer	4:07 am
8	Leo	11:37 am
10	Virgo	3:16 pm
12	Libra	3:55 pm
14	Scorpio	3:15 pm
16	Sagittarius	3:16 pm
18	Capricorn	5:44 pm
19	**Taurus**	**6:04 pm***
20	Aquarius	11:48 pm
23	Pisces	9:28 am
25	Aries	10:37 pm
28	Taurus	11:38 am
May 1	Gemini	12:06 am
3	Cancer	10:54 am
5	Leo	7:10 pm
8	Virgo	12:22 am
10	Libra	2:40 am
12	Scorpio	3:03 am
14	Sagittarius	3:05 am
16	Capricorn	4:32 am
18	Aquarius	9:03 am
20	**Gemini**	**5:22 pm***
20	Pisces	5:27 pm
23	Aries	5:08 am

*Boldface type indicates change of the sun sign.

1976		Moon Enters	Time	1976		Moon Enters	Time
	25	Taurus	6:08 pm		31	Sagittarius	8:29 am
	28	Gemini	6:23 am	Sep	2	Capricorn	12:30 pm
	30	Cancer	4:40 pm		4	Aquarius	6:21 pm
Jun	2	Leo	12:38 am		7	Pisces	2:12 am
	4	Virgo	6:22 am		9	Aries	12:19 pm
	6	Libra	10:00 am		12	Taurus	12:31 am
	8	Scorpio	11:59 am		14	Gemini	1:33 pm
	10	Sagittarius	1:07 pm		17	Cancer	1:07 am
	12	Capricorn	2:46 pm		19	Leo	9:11 am
	14	Aquarius	6:32 pm		21	Virgo	1:17 pm
	17	Pisces	1:44 am		**22**	**Libra**	**5:49 pm***
	19	Aries	12:33 pm		23	Libra	2:28 pm
	21	**Cancer**	**2:25 am***		25	Scorpio	2:34 pm
	22	Taurus	1:22 am		27	Sagittarius	3:22 pm
	24	Gemini	1:37 pm		29	Capricorn	6:14 pm
	26	Cancer	11:30 pm	Oct	1	Aquarius	11:50 pm
	29	Leo	6:40 am		4	Pisces	8:10 am
Jul	1	Virgo	11:47 am		6	Aries	6:50 pm
	3	Libra	3:35 pm		9	Taurus	7:12 am
	5	Scorpio	6:34 pm		11	Gemini	8:15 pm
	7	Sagittarius	9:06 pm		14	Cancer	8:25 am
	9	Capricorn	11:50 pm		16	Leo	5:50 pm
	12	Aquarius	3:54 am		18	Virgo	11:25 pm
	14	Pisces	10:37 am		21	Libra	1:27 am
	16	Aries	8:40 pm		23	Scorpio	1:17 am
	19	Taurus	9:12 am		**23**	**Scorpio**	**2:59 am***
	21	Gemini	9:41 pm		25	Sagittarius	12:49 am
	22	**Leo**	**1:19 pm***		27	Capricorn	1:56 am
	24	Cancer	7:40 am		29	Aquarius	6:06 am
	26	Leo	2:19 pm		31	Pisces	12:54 pm
	28	Virgo	6:24 pm	Nov	2	Aries	11:46 pm
	30	Libra	9:14 pm		5	Taurus	12:24 pm
Aug	1	Scorpio	11:56 pm		8	Gemini	1:22 am
	4	Sagittarius	3:04 am		10	Cancer	1:29 pm
	6	Capricorn	6:55 am		12	Leo	11:37 pm
	8	Aquarius	11:58 am		15	Virgo	6:47 am
	10	Pisces	7:01 pm		17	Libra	10:35 am
	13	Aries	4:50 am		19	Scorpio	11:32 am
	15	Taurus	5:06 pm		21	Sagittarius	11:04 am
	18	Gemini	5:55 am		**21**	**Sagittarius**	**11:22 pm***
	20	Cancer	4:34 pm		23	Capricorn	11:04 am
	22	**Virgo**	**8:19 pm***		25	Aquarius	1:31 pm
	22	Leo	11:31 pm		27	Pisces	7:48 pm
	25	Virgo	3:04 am		30	Aries	6:02 am
	27	Libra	4:42 am	Dec	2	Taurus	6:42 pm
	29	Scorpio	6:06 am		5	Gemini	7:39 am

*Boldface type indicates change of the sun sign.

(Continued)

1976	Moon Enters	Time		1977	Moon Enters	Time
7	Cancer	7:22 pm		6	Libra	1:35 pm
10	Leo	5:13 am		8	Scorpio	3:38 pm
12	Virgo	12:56 pm		10	Sagittarius	3:42 pm
14	Libra	6:14 pm		12	Capricorn	8:40 pm
16	Scorpio	9:02 pm		15	Aquarius	1:01 am
18	Sagittarius	9:55 pm		17	Pisces	7:06 am
20	Capricorn	10:12 pm		19	Aries	3:24 pm
21	**Capricorn**	**12:36 pm***		**20**	**Aries**	**12:43 pm***
22	Aquarius	11:49 pm		22	Taurus	2:06 am
25	Pisces	4:37 am		24	Gemini	2:39 pm
27	Aries	1:32 pm		27	Cancer	3:17 am
30	Taurus	1:44 am		29	Leo	1:41 pm
				31	Virgo	8:26 pm

1977	Moon Enters	Time			Moon Enters	Time
				Apr 2	Libra	11:39 pm
				5	Scorpio	12:40 am
				7	Sagittarius	1:09 am
Jan 1	Gemini	2:43 pm		9	Capricorn	2:41 am
4	Cancer	2:13 am		11	Aquarius	6:25 am
6	Leo	11:21 am		13	Pisces	2:50 pm
8	Virgo	6:24 pm		15	Aries	9:52 pm
10	Libra	11:48 pm		18	Taurus	9:03 am
13	Scorpio	3:45 am		**19**	**Taurus**	**11:58 pm***
15	Sagittarius	6:19 am		20	Gemini	9:38 pm
17	Capricorn	8:03 am		23	Cancer	10:26 am
19	Aquarius	10:13 am		25	Leo	10:44 pm
19	**Aquarius**	**11:16 pm***		28	Virgo	6:53 am
21	Pisces	2:31 pm		30	Libra	11:13 am
23	Aries	10:20 pm		May 2	Scorpio	12:24 pm
26	Taurus	9:42 am		4	Sagittarius	11:59 am
28	Gemini	10:38 pm		6	Capricorn	11:55 am
31	Cancer	10:21 am		8	Aquarius	2:00 pm
Feb 2	Leo	7:12 pm		10	Pisces	7:30 pm
5	Virgo	1:18 am		13	Aries	4:30 am
7	Libra	5:37 am		15	Taurus	4:05 pm
9	Scorpio	9:05 am		18	Gemini	4:51 am
11	Sagittarius	12:12 pm		20	Cancer	5:36 pm
13	Capricorn	3:14 pm		**21**	**Gemini**	**12:15 am***
15	Aquarius	6:45 pm		23	Leo	5:14 am
17	Pisces	11:45 pm		25	Virgo	2:32 pm
18	**Pisces**	**1:32 pm***		27	Libra	8:29 pm
20	Aries	7:23 am		29	Scorpio	10:57 pm
22	Taurus	6:07 pm		31	Sagittarius	10:54 pm
25	Gemini	6:51 am		Jun 2	Capricorn	10:08 pm
27	Cancer	7:03 pm		4	Aquarius	10:44 pm
Mar 2	Leo	4:26 am		7	Pisces	2:36 am
4	Virgo	10:19 am		9	Aries	10:35 am

*Boldface type indicates change of the sun sign.

1977		Moon Enters	Time		1977		Moon Enters	Time
	11	Taurus	9:57 pm			18	Sagittarius	4:29 am
	14	Gemini	10:50 am			20	Capricorn	7:05 am
	16	Cancer	11:29 pm			22	Aquarius	10:13 am
	19	Leo	10:54 am			**22**	**Libra**	**11:30 pm***
	21	**Cancer**	**8:15 am***			24	Pisces	2:30 pm
	21	Virgo	8:30 pm			26	Aries	8:41 pm
	24	Libra	3:36 am			29	Taurus	5:22 am
	26	Scorpio	7:43 am		Oct	1	Gemini	4:34 pm
	28	Sagittarius	9:02 am			4	Cancer	5:10 am
	30	Capricorn	8:49 am			6	Leo	4:58 pm
Jul	2	Aquarius	8:57 am			9	Virgo	1:59 am
	4	Pisces	11:32 am			11	Libra	7:30 am
	6	Aries	6:04 pm			13	Scorpio	10:11 am
	9	Taurus	4:34 am			15	Sagittarius	11:28 am
	11	Gemini	5:16 pm			17	Capricorn	12:51 pm
	14	Cancer	5:50 am			19	Aquarius	3:37 pm
	16	Leo	4:52 pm			21	Pisces	8:27 pm
	19	Virgo	1:59 am			**23**	**Scorpio**	**8:42 am***
	21	Libra	9:10 am			24	Aries	3:35 am
	22	**Leo**	**7:05 pm***			26	Taurus	12:54 pm
	23	Scorpio	2:14 pm			29	Gemini	12:09 am
	25	Sagittarius	5:05 pm			31	Cancer	11:41 am
	27	Capricorn	6:15 pm		Nov	3	Leo	12:04 am
	29	Aquarius	7:05 pm			5	Virgo	10:17 am
	31	Pisces	9:24 pm			7	Libra	4:52 pm
Aug	3	Aries	2:55 am			9	Scorpio	7:43 pm
	5	Taurus	12:19 pm			11	Sagittarius	8:04 pm
	8	Gemini	12:30 am			13	Capricorn	7:51 pm
	10	Cancer	1:05 pm			15	Aquarius	10:01 pm
	12	Leo	11:57 pm			18	Pisces	12:59 am
	15	Virgo	8:26 am			20	Aries	9:14 am
	17	Libra	2:50 pm			**22**	**Sagittarius**	**5:08 am***
	19	Scorpio	7:36 pm			22	Taurus	6:10 pm
	21	Sagittarius	11:03 pm			25	Gemini	5:49 am
	23	**Virgo**	**2:01 am***			27	Cancer	6:21 pm
	24	Capricorn	1:31 am			30	Leo	6:54 am
	26	Aquarius	3:41 am		Dec	2	Virgo	6:06 pm
	28	Pisces	6:47 am			5	Libra	2:18 am
	30	Aries	12:12 pm			7	Scorpio	6:34 am
Sep	1	Taurus	8:52 pm			9	Sagittarius	7:32 am
	4	Gemini	8:28 am			11	Capricorn	6:27 am
	6	Cancer	9:04 pm			13	Aquarius	6:00 am
	9	Leo	8:14 am			15	Pisces	8:10 am
	11	Virgo	4:35 pm			17	Aries	2:12 pm
	13	Libra	10:08 pm			19	Taurus	11:55 pm
	16	Scorpio	1:46 am			**21**	**Capricorn**	**6:24 pm***

*Boldface type indicates change of the sun sign.

(Continued)

103

1977		Moon Enters	Time
	22	Gemini	11:52 am
	25	Cancer	12:30 am
	27	Leo	12:52 pm
	30	Virgo	12:14 am

1978		Moon Enters	Time
Jan	1	Libra	10:32 am
	3	Scorpio	3:36 pm
	5	Sagittarius	6:04 pm
	7	Capricorn	5:55 pm
	9	Aquarius	5:06 pm
	11	Pisces	5:51 pm
	13	Aries	10:06 pm
	16	Taurus	6:31 am
	18	Gemini	6:07 pm
	20	**Aquarius**	**5:05 am***
	21	Cancer	6:51 am
	23	Leo	7:03 pm
	26	Virgo	5:57 am
	28	Libra	3:08 pm
	30	Scorpio	10:04 pm
Feb	2	Sagittarius	2:14 am
	4	Capricorn	3:51 am
	6	Aquarius	4:05 am
	8	Pisces	5:48 am
	10	Aries	7:57 am
	12	Taurus	2:51 pm
	15	Gemini	1:25 am
	17	Cancer	1:56 pm
	18	**Pisces**	**7:22 pm***
	20	Leo	2:10 am
	22	Virgo	12:40 pm
	24	Libra	9:04 pm
	27	Scorpio	3:29 am
Mar	1	Sagittarius	8:03 am
	3	Capricorn	10:59 am
	5	Aquarius	12:51 pm
	7	Pisces	2:46 pm
	9	Aries	6:09 pm
	12	Taurus	2:19 am
	14	Gemini	9:49 am
	16	Cancer	9:50 pm
	19	Leo	10:13 am
	20	**Aries**	**6:34 pm***

1978		Moon Enters	Time
	21	Virgo	8:50 pm
	24	Libra	4:42 am
	26	Scorpio	10:02 am
	28	Sagittarius	1:38 pm
	30	Capricorn	4:24 pm
Apr	1	Aquarius	7:06 pm
	3	Pisces	10:21 pm
	6	Aries	2:52 am
	8	Taurus	9:22 am
	10	Gemini	6:28 pm
	13	Cancer	6:00 am
	15	Leo	6:31 pm
	18	Virgo	5:45 am
	20	**Taurus**	**5:50 am***
	20	Libra	1:54 pm
	22	Scorpio	6:40 pm
	24	Sagittarius	9:01 pm
	26	Capricorn	10:28 pm
	29	Aquarius	12:29 am
May	1	Pisces	5:00 am
	3	Aries	10:28 am
	5	Taurus	5:53 pm
	8	Gemini	3:19 am
	10	Cancer	2:42 pm
	13	Leo	3:18 am
	15	Virgo	3:16 pm
	18	Libra	12:25 am
	20	Scorpio	5:39 am
	21	**Gemini**	**6:09 am***
	22	Sagittarius	7:32 am
	24	Capricorn	7:42 am
	26	Aquarius	8:11 am
	28	Pisces	10:37 am
	30	Aries	3:53 pm
Jun	1	Taurus	11:51 pm
	4	Gemini	9:54 am
	6	Cancer	9:31 pm
	9	Leo	10:08 am
	11	Virgo	10:35 pm
	14	Libra	8:56 am
	16	Scorpio	3:29 pm
	18	Sagittarius	6:02 pm
	20	Capricorn	5:52 pm
	21	**Cancer**	**2:10 am***
	22	Aquarius	5:08 pm
	24	Pisces	5:58 pm

*Boldface type indicates change of the sun sign.

104

1978		Moon Enters	Time	1978		Moon Enters	Time
	26	Aries	9:54 pm	Oct	1	Libra	10:17 am
	29	Taurus	5:22 am		3	Scorpio	5:49 pm
Jul	1	Gemini	3:38 pm		5	Sagittarius	11:07 pm
	4	Cancer	3:34 am		8	Capricorn	2:53 am
	6	Leo	4:14 pm		10	Aquarius	5:43 am
	9	Virgo	4:45 am		12	Pisces	8:13 am
	11	Libra	3:49 pm		14	Aries	11:07 am
	13	Scorpio	11:47 pm		16	Taurus	3:23 pm
	16	Sagittarius	3:50 am		18	Gemini	10:06 pm
	18	Capricorn	4:34 am		21	Cancer	7:53 am
	20	Aquarius	3:42 am		**23**	**Scorpio**	**2:38 pm***
	22	Pisces	3:27 am		23	Leo	8:05 pm
	23	**Leo**	**1:01 am***		26	Virgo	8:32 am
	24	Aries	5:46 am		28	Libra	6:52 pm
	26	Taurus	11:51 am		31	Scorpio	12:53 am
	28	Gemini	9:31 pm	Nov	2	Sagittarius	5:04 am
	31	Cancer	9:29 am		4	Capricorn	7:41 am
Aug	2	Leo	10:11 pm		6	Aquarius	10:04 am
	5	Virgo	10:30 am		8	Pisces	1:07 pm
	7	Libra	9:30 pm		10	Aries	5:12 pm
	10	Scorpio	6:12 am		12	Taurus	10:36 pm
	12	Sagittarius	11:43 am		15	Gemini	5:45 am
	14	Capricorn	2:04 pm		17	Cancer	3:17 pm
	16	Aquarius	2:16 pm		20	Leo	3:10 am
	18	Pisces	2:05 pm		**22**	**Sagittarius**	**11:05 am***
	20	Aries	2:30 pm		22	Virgo	3:58 pm
	22	Taurus	8:06 pm		25	Libra	3:08 am
	23	**Virgo**	**7:58 am***		27	Scorpio	10:39 am
	25	Gemini	4:32 am		29	Sagittarius	2:24 pm
	27	Cancer	4:00 pm	Dec	1	Capricorn	3:45 pm
	30	Leo	4:40 am		3	Aquarius	4:36 pm
Sep	1	Virgo	4:47 pm		5	Pisces	6:37 pm
	4	Libra	3:16 am		8	Aries	10:40 am
	6	Scorpio	11:39 am		10	Taurus	4:51 am
	8	Sagittarius	5:40 pm		12	Gemini	12:55 pm
	10	Capricorn	9:20 pm		14	Cancer	10:50 pm
	12	Aquarius	11:09 pm		17	Leo	10:38 am
	15	Pisces	12:10 am		19	Virgo	11:35 pm
	17	Aries	1:51 am		**22**	**Capricorn**	**12:22 am***
	19	Taurus	5:44 am		22	Libra	11:41 am
	21	Gemini	12:57 pm		24	Scorpio	8:33 pm
	23	**Libra**	**5:26 am***		27	Sagittarius	1:08 am
	23	Cancer	11:32 am		29	Capricorn	2:16 am
	26	Leo	12:02 pm		31	Aquarius	1:54 am
	29	Virgo	12:12 am				

*Boldface type indicates change of the sun sign.

(Continued)

1979	Moon Enters	Time		1979	Moon Enters	Time
Jan 2	Pisces	2:09 am		10	Libra	1:46 pm
4	Aries	4:42 am		12	Scorpio	11:16 pm
6	Taurus	10:18 am		15	Sagittarius	6:19 am
8	Gemini	6:43 pm		17	Capricorn	11:24 am
11	Cancer	5:15 am		19	Aquarius	3:03 pm
13	Leo	5:17 pm		**20**	**Taurus**	**11:36 am***
16	Virgo	6:11 am		21	Pisces	5:42 pm
18	Libra	6:41 pm		23	Aries	7:52 pm
20	**Aquarius**	**11:01 am***		25	Taurus	10:28 pm
21	Scorpio	4:51 am		28	Gemini	2:49 am
23	Sagittarius	11:09 am		30	Cancer	11:12 am
25	Capricorn	1:28 pm		May 2	Leo	9:57 pm
27	Aquarius	1:13 pm		5	Virgo	10:42 am
29	Pisces	12:26 pm		7	Libra	10:48 pm
31	Aries	1:12 pm		10	Scorpio	8:11 am
Feb 2	Taurus	5:04 pm		12	Sagittarius	2:25 pm
5	Gemini	12:34 am		14	Capricorn	6:26 pm
7	Cancer	11:06 am		16	Aquarius	9:26 pm
9	Leo	11:26 pm		19	Pisces	12:19 am
12	Virgo	12:18 pm		21	Aries	3:31 am
15	Libra	12:38 am		**21**	**Gemini**	**11:55 am***
17	Scorpio	11:13 am		23	Taurus	7:21 am
19	**Pisces**	**1:14 am***		25	Gemini	12:29 pm
19	Sagittarius	6:52 pm		27	Cancer	7:51 pm
21	Capricorn	11:01 pm		30	Leo	6:09 am
24	Aquarius	12:13 am		Jun 1	Virgo	6:41 pm
25	Pisces	11:53 pm		4	Libra	7:12 am
27	Aries	11:55 pm		6	Scorpio	5:06 pm
Mar 2	Taurus	2:10 am		8	Sagittarius	11:15 pm
4	Gemini	7:59 am		11	Capricorn	2:24 am
6	Cancer	5:35 pm		13	Aquarius	4:07 am
9	Leo	5:48 am		15	Pisces	5:57 am
11	Virgo	6:43 pm		17	Aries	8:53 am
14	Libra	6:42 am		19	Taurus	1:19 pm
16	Scorpio	4:50 pm		21	Gemini	7:23 pm
19	Sagittarius	12:39 am		**21**	**Cancer**	**7:57 pm***
21	**Aries**	**12:22 am***		24	Cancer	3:25 am
21	Capricorn	5:57 am		26	Leo	1:48 pm
23	Aquarius	8:53 am		29	Virgo	2:15 am
25	Pisces	10:05 am		Jul 1	Libra	3:09 pm
27	Aries	10:48 am		4	Scorpio	1:58 am
29	Taurus	12:37 pm		6	Sagittarius	8:56 am
31	Gemini	5:09 pm		8	Capricorn	12:08 pm
Apr 3	Cancer	1:24 am		10	Aquarius	1:00 pm
5	Leo	12:58 pm		12	Pisces	1:23 pm
8	Virgo	1:53 am		14	Aries	2:58 pm

*Boldface type indicates change of the sun sign.

1979		Moon Enters	Time	1979		Moon Enters	Time
	16	Taurus	6:44 pm		23	Sagittarius	1:10 pm
	19	Gemini	1:00 am		**23**	**Scorpio**	**8:29 pm***
	21	Cancer	9:41 am		25	Capricorn	8:12 pm
	23	**Leo**	**6:49 am***		28	Aquarius	1:17 am
	23	Leo	8:31 pm		30	Pisces	3:30 am
	26	Virgo	9:02 am	Nov	1	Aries	5:10 am
	28	Libra	10:07 pm		3	Taurus	6:17 am
	31	Scorpio	9:47 am		5	Gemini	8:26 am
Aug	2	Sagittarius	6:06 pm		7	Cancer	1:24 pm
	4	Capricorn	10:23 pm		9	Leo	10:15 pm
	6	Aquarius	11:29 pm		12	Virgo	10:21 am
	8	Pisces	11:06 pm		14	Libra	11:17 pm
	10	Aries	11:11 pm		17	Scorpio	10:30 am
	13	Taurus	1:22 am		19	Sagittarius	6:57 pm
	15	Gemini	6:42 am		22	Capricorn	1:02 am
	17	Cancer	3:18 pm		**22**	**Sagittarius**	**4:55 pm***
	20	Leo	2:29 am		24	Aquarius	5:37 am
	22	Virgo	3:12 pm		26	Pisces	9:18 am
	23	**Virgo**	**1:48 pm***		28	Aries	12:17 pm
	25	Libra	4:14 am		30	Taurus	2:55 pm
	27	Scorpio	4:13 pm	Dec	2	Gemini	6:03 pm
	30	Sagittarius	1:40 am		4	Cancer	11:02 pm
Sep	1	Capricorn	7:34 am		7	Leo	7:10 am
	3	Aquarius	10:00 am		9	Virgo	6:33 pm
	5	Pisces	10:04 am		12	Libra	7:30 am
	7	Aries	9:30 am		14	Scorpio	7:09 pm
	9	Taurus	10:13 am		17	Sagittarius	3:37 am
	11	Gemini	1:55 pm		19	Capricorn	8:55 am
	13	Cancer	9:28 pm		21	Aquarius	12:13 pm
	16	Leo	8:26 am		**22**	**Capricorn**	**6:11 am***
	18	Virgo	9:16 pm		23	Pisces	2:51 pm
	21	Libra	10:11 am		25	Aries	5:41 pm
	23	**Libra**	**11:17 am***		27	Taurus	9:08 pm
	23	Scorpio	9:55 pm		30	Gemini	1:33 am
	26	Sagittarius	7:36 am				
	28	Capricorn	2:41 pm	1980		Moon Enters	Time
	30	Aquarius	6:50 pm				
Oct	2	Pisces	8:24 pm	Jan	1	Cancer	7:30 am
	4	Aries	8:29 pm		3	Leo	3:48 pm
	6	Taurus	8:45 pm		6	Virgo	2:49 am
	8	Gemini	11:08 pm		8	Libra	3:39 pm
	11	Cancer	5:10 am		11	Scorpio	3:56 am
	13	Leo	3:12 pm		13	Sagittarius	1:18 pm
	16	Virgo	3:53 am		15	Capricorn	6:52 pm
	18	Libra	4:45 pm		17	Aquarius	9:26 pm
	21	Scorpio	4:03 am				

*Boldface type indicates change of the sun sign.

(Continued)

1980	Moon Enters	Time		1980	Moon Enters	Time
19	Pisces	10:34 pm		24	Virgo	5:13 am
20	**Aquarius**	**4:49 pm***		26	Libra	6:10 pm
21	Aries	11:52 pm		29	Scorpio	7:35 am
24	Taurus	2:32 am	May 1	Sagittarius	6:22 pm
26	Gemini	7:12 am		4	Capricorn	3:15 am
28	Cancer	2:03 pm		6	Aquarius	10:04 am
30	Leo	11:09 pm		8	Pisces	2:34 pm
Feb 2	Virgo	11:22 am		10	Aries	4:45 pm
4	Libra	11:05 pm		12	Taurus	5:25 pm
7	Scorpio	11:47 am		14	Gemini	6:08 pm
9	Sagittarius	10:20 pm		16	Cancer	8:53 pm
12	Capricorn	5:13 am		19	Leo	3:15 am
14	Aquarius	8:20 am		**20**	**Gemini**	**5:43 pm***
16	Pisces	8:55 am		21	Virgo	1:33 pm
18	Aries	8:43 am		24	Libra	2:12 am
19	**Pisces**	**7:03 am***		26	Scorpio	2:37 pm
20	Taurus	9:36 am		29	Sagittarius	1:05 am
22	Gemini	12:59 pm		31	Capricorn	9:15 am
24	Cancer	7:35 pm	Jun 2	Aquarius	3:30 pm
27	Leo	5:11 am		4	Pisces	8:10 pm
29	Virgo	4:54 pm		6	Aries	11:24 pm
Mar 3	Libra	5:41 am		9	Taurus	1:30 am
5	Scorpio	6:23 pm		11	Gemini	3:23 am
8	Sagittarius	5:39 am		13	Cancer	6:30 am
10	Capricorn	2:03 pm		15	Leo	12:23 pm
12	Aquarius	6:46 pm		17	Virgo	9:48 pm
14	Pisces	8:11 pm		20	Libra	9:56 am
16	Aries	7:42 pm		**21**	**Cancer**	**1:48 am***
18	Taurus	7:14 pm		22	Scorpio	10:27 pm
20	**Aries**	**6:11 am***		25	Sagittarius	9:02 am
20	Gemini	8:48 pm		27	Capricorn	4:47 pm
23	Cancer	1:56 am		29	Aquarius	10:04 pm
25	Leo	10:59 am	Jul 2	Pisces	1:49 am
27	Virgo	10:53 pm		4	Aries	4:47 am
30	Libra	11:49 am		6	Taurus	7:31 am
Apr 2	Scorpio	12:22 am		8	Gemini	10:34 am
4	Sagittarius	11:35 am		10	Cancer	2:45 pm
6	Capricorn	8:43 pm		12	Leo	9:03 pm
9	Aquarius	3:00 am		15	Virgo	8:12 am
11	Pisces	6:07 am		17	Libra	5:56 pm
13	Aries	6:41 am		20	Scorpio	6:34 am
15	Taurus	6:11 am		**22**	**Leo**	**12:43 pm***
17	Gemini	6:42 am		22	Sagittarius	5:43 pm
19	Cancer	10:12 am		25	Capricorn	1:45 am
19	**Taurus**	**5:24 pm***		27	Aquarius	6:35 am
21	Leo	5:53 pm		29	Pisces	9:11 am

*Boldface type indicates change of the sun sign.

1980		Moon Enters	Time		1980		Moon Enters	Time
	31	Aries	10:54 am			19	Pisces	3:32 pm
Aug	2	Taurus	12:56 pm			21	Aries	4:44 pm
	4	Gemini	4:10 pm			**23**	**Scorpio**	**2:19 am***
	6	Cancer	9:13 pm			23	Taurus	3:56 pm
	9	Leo	4:24 am			25	Gemini	3:18 pm
	11	Virgo	1:55 pm			27	Cancer	4:01 pm
	14	Libra	1:33 am			29	Leo	9:39 pm
	16	Scorpio	2:16 pm		Nov	1	Virgo	7:19 am
	19	Sagittarius	2:08 am			3	Libra	7:32 pm
	21	Capricorn	11:12 am			6	Scorpio	8:20 am
	22	**Virgo**	**7:42 pm***			8	Sagittarius	8:26 pm
	23	Aquarius	4:33 pm			11	Capricorn	7:16 am
	25	Pisces	6:44 pm			13	Aquarius	4:11 pm
	27	Aries	7:12 pm			15	Pisces	10:22 pm
	29	Taurus	7:42 pm			18	Aries	1:22 am
	31	Gemini	9:51 pm			20	Taurus	1:52 am
Sep	3	Cancer	2:40 am			**21**	**Sagittarius**	**10:42 pm***
	5	Leo	10:23 am			22	Gemini	1:28 am
	7	Virgo	8:32 pm			24	Cancer	2:19 am
	10	Libra	8:23 am			26	Leo	6:24 am
	12	Scorpio	9:07 pm			28	Virgo	2:38 pm
	15	Sagittarius	9:29 am		Dec	1	Libra	2:14 am
	17	Capricorn	7:46 pm			3	Scorpio	3:01 pm
	20	Aquarius	2:31 am			6	Sagittarius	2:58 am
	22	Pisces	5:28 am			8	Capricorn	1:13 pm
	22	**Libra**	**5:10 pm***			10	Aquarius	9:37 pm
	24	Aries	5:38 am			13	Pisces	4:04 am
	26	Taurus	4:54 am			15	Aries	8:22 am
	28	Gemini	5:22 am			17	Taurus	10:37 am
	30	Cancer	8:47 am			19	Gemini	11:40 am
Oct	2	Leo	3:58 pm			**21**	**Capricorn**	**11:57 am***
	5	Virgo	2:20 am			21	Cancer	1:04 pm
	7	Libra	2:31 pm			23	Leo	4:34 pm
	10	Scorpio	3:16 am			25	Virgo	11:33 pm
	12	Sagittarius	3:38 pm			28	Libra	10:06 am
	15	Capricorn	2:37 am			30	Scorpio	10:37 pm
	17	Aquarius	10:54 am					

*Boldface type indicates change of the sun sign.

Appendix B:
How to Find Your Child's Rising Sign

The following simple tables enable you to find your child's rising sign accurately but without the rigorous conversions and interpolations astrologers generally use.*

Step 1

Your child's time of birth may need to be translated to standard time. Consult Table B–1 to determine whether or not your child was born when daylight saving time was in effect. If it was in effect, *subtract 1 hour* from the recorded time of birth to find the standard time. If daylight saving time was not in effect, leave the recorded time alone (it's standard time already).

Note: Disregard this step if your child was born in Arizona, Hawaii, Michigan, or Saskatchewan. Also disregard this step if your child was born in any part of Indiana other than the following counties: Gibson, Jasper, Lake, La Porte, Newton, Pike, Porter, Posey, Spencer, Starke, Vanderburgh, or Warrick.

Example A: Kenneth was born August 17, 1977, at 3:31 P.M. in Phoenix, Arizona. Since he was born in Arizona, we know that his recorded birth time was already standard time and we can disregard this step.

Example B: Lisa was born November 2, 1979, at 12:38 A.M. in Coeur d'Alene, Idaho. From Table B–1 we see that daylight saving time was not in effect, so we know that 12:38 A.M. was standard time.

Example C: Lenny was born February 26, 1975, at 7:38 A.M. in Grand Junction, Colorado.

---

*You can use these tables to find your own—or anyone's—rising sign as well, within 4 minutes of accuracy. But since Table B–1 covers only the years 1973 through 1980, you may need to check with local authorities to find out whether or not daylight saving time was in effect. Consider the result from Step 1 the adjusted standard time (AST) and disregard Step 2.

From Table B–1 we see that daylight saving time was in effect, so we must subtract 1 hour from the recorded birthtime. Lenny's birthtime as expressed in standard time was 6:38 A.M.

Example D: Debby was born June 3, 1976, at 10:15 A.M. in New York, New York. From Table B–1 we see that daylight saving time was in effect, so we must subtract 1 hour from the recorded birthtime. Debby's birthtime as expressed in standard time was 9:15 A.M.

Step 2

Because of the variability in the number of days in a year (that is, leap years versus common years), you must adjust the standard time of your child's birth in order to account for year irregularity. Refer to Table B–2 under the year for your child's birth and *add* the number of minutes given there to the standard time (which you determined in Step 1). The result is the *adjusted standard time* (AST).

Example A: 1977 was Kenneth's birth year. From Table B–2 we see that 3 minutes must be added to the 3:31 P.M. standard time. The result is 3:34 P.M., the AST.

Example B: 1979 was Lisa's birth year. From Table B–2 we see that 1 minute must be added to the 12:38 A.M. standard time. The result is 12:39 A.M., the AST.

Example C: 1975 was Lenny's birth year. From Table B–2 we see that 1 minute must be added to the 6:38 A.M. standard time. The result is 6:39 A.M., the AST.

Example D: Debby was born in 1976, after March 1. From Table B–2 we see that 4 minutes must be added to the 9:15 A.M. standard time. The result is 9:19 A.M., the AST.

Step 3

Now refer to Table B–3 and read to the right of your child's birthday until you find the closest time *before* your child's AST. (If your child was born in the wee hours, you may have to refer to the previous day in order to find the closest time before AST.) Write this time down. Then read up to the head of the column, where you will find your child's approximate rising sign.

You can consider this sign the correct rising sign and disregard Steps 4 and 5 *if* (*a*) your child's AST is more than 20 minutes later than the closest time before it in Table B–3 and more than 20 minutes earlier than the closest time after it, *and* (*b*) your child's birthplace was in northern California, Colorado, Connecticut, Delaware, District of Columbia, Illinois, eastern Iowa, Maryland, western Massachusetts, eastern Missouri, northwestern Nevada, New Jersey, eastern New York, eastern Pennsylvania, Rhode Island, southern Vermont, eastern Virginia, southeastern Wisconsin, or southeastern Wyoming. If both these conditions are *not* met—or if you are in doubt—you should proceed to Step 4.

Note: Occasionally two times are given for the same sign on the same day. One time is just after midnight at the beginning of the day; the other is just before midnight at the end of the day.

Example A: From Table B–3 we see that on August 17, 1:24 P.M. is the closest time before Kenneth's 3:34 P.M. AST. We write this time down. It corresponds to Sagittarius rising. Since the birthplace is in Arizona (not one of the exempted locations in the preceding list), we must go on to Step 4 to check this result.

Example B: Table B–3 supplies no time on November 2 before Lisa's 12:39 A.M. AST. We must use the latest time given for the previous day, November 1, and that is 10:16 P.M. We write this time down. It corresponds to Leo rising. Since the birthplace is in Idaho, we must go on to Step 4 to check this result.

Example C: From Table B–3 we see that on February 26, 6:27 A.M. is the closest time before Lenny's 6:39 A.M. AST. We write this time down. It corresponds to Pisces rising. Even though the birthplace was in Colorado, we will need to proceed to Step 4 to check our result because there is less than 20 minutes between his AST and 6:27 A.M.

Example D: From Table B–3 we see that on June 3, 8:14 A.M. is the closest time before Debby's 9:19 A.M. AST. We write this time down. It corresponds to Leo rising. Since her AST is more than 20 minutes after 8:14 A.M. *and* more than 20 minutes before 10:45 A.M. (the closest time after Debby's AST that is given in Table B–3 for June 3), *and* since New York City is in eastern New York State, we can be certain that Leo is the correct rising sign.

Unless your child's birthtime meets the exemptions spelled out in Step 3 (see Example D), you must consider the rising sign you found in that step as only approximate. Your child's birthplace is an important factor also, and when you take it into account in Steps 4 and 5, you will either verify the rising sign you found in Table B–3 or find a new one.

Step 4

In Table B–4, find the large city closest to your child's birthplace. Read to the right until you come to the column that corresponds to the approximate rising sign determined from Step 3. The number of minutes given there must be *added to or subtracted from (as indicated)* the time in Table B–3 that corresponds to the approximate rising sign—that is, the time you wrote down in Step 3.

If the result of the addition or subtraction is earlier than your child's AST, go on to Step 5a. If the result is later, go on to Step 5b.

Example A: Reading to the right from Phoenix, Arizona, to the Sagittarius column, we see that 11 minutes must be added to 1:24 P.M. (which corresponds to Sagittarius on August 17 in

Table B–3). The result is 1:35 P.M. Since that time is earlier than 3:34 P.M., Kenneth's AST, we go on to Step 5a.

Example B: Reading to the right from Coeur d'Alene, Idaho, to the Leo column, we see that 37 minutes must be subtracted from 10:16 P.M. (which corresponds to Leo on November 1 in Table B–3). The result is 9:39 P.M. Since that time is earlier than 12:39 A.M., Lisa's AST, we go on to Step 5a.

Example C: Reading to the right from Grand Junction, Colorado, to the Pisces column, we see that 13 minutes must be added to 6:27 A.M. (which corresponds to Pisces on February 26 in Table B–3). The result is 6:40 A.M., which is later than Lenny's 6:39 A.M. AST. Thus, we must go on to Step 5b.

Step 5a

Go back to Table B–3 and read to the right of your child's birthday to the closest time *after* your child's AST. (If your child was born late at night, you may have to refer to the next day for the closest time after AST.) Write this time down. Then refer again to Table B–4. Read to the column that corresponds to the rising sign *after* the approximate rising sign you found in Step 3. For example, if the approximate rising sign determined in Step 3 is Gemini, read to the Cancer column. (If the approximate rising sign is Pisces, go to the Aries column.) The number of minutes given there must be *added to or subtracted from (as indicated)* the new time you just wrote down from Table B–3.

If the result is later than the AST, the approximate rising sign is correct. If it is earlier, the following rising sign is probably the correct one: Consider it the new approximate rising sign and repeat Step 5a, writing down from Table B–3 the next closest time after the AST.

Example A: Reading Table B–3 for August 17, we see that 3:45 P.M. is the closest time after Kenneth's 3:34 P.M. AST. We write this new time down. Then reading Table B–4 from Phoenix to the column that corresponds to Capricorn rising (the sign after Sagittarius), we see that 8 minutes should be added to the time we just wrote down. The result is 3:53 P.M., which is later than Kenneth's AST. Thus, we are certain that Kenneth has Sagittarius rising.

Example B: Reading Table B–3 for November 2, we see that 12:48 A.M. is the closest time after Lisa's 12:39 A.M. AST. We write this new time down. Then reading Table B–4 from Coeur d'Alene to the Virgo column (since Virgo is the sign after Leo), we see that 25 minutes should be subtracted from the time we just wrote down. The result is 12:23 A.M., which is earlier than Lisa's AST. We must consider Virgo the new approximate rising sign and repeat Step 5a. We write down the next closest time after the AST in Table B–3 for November 2, which is 3:19 A.M. Reading from Coeur d'Alene to the next column to the right (Libra) in Table B–4, we see that 13 minutes should be subtracted from this new time. The result is 3:06 A.M., which is later than Lisa's AST. Thus, we know that Virgo is her correct rising sign.

Step 5b

Go back to Table B–3 and find the time that *precedes* the time you wrote down in Step 3—that is, the *second closest* time before your child's AST. (If your child was born in the early morning, you may have to refer to the previous day for this time.) Write this new time down. Then refer to Table B–4 again. Read to the column that corresponds to the rising sign *before* the approximate rising sign you found in Step 3. For example, if the approximate rising sign is Scorpio, read to the Libra column. (If the approximate rising sign is Aries, go to the Pisces column.) The number of minutes given there must be *added to or subtracted from (as indicated)* the time you just wrote down from Table B–3.

If the result is earlier than the AST, this new rising sign is the correct one. If the result is later, repeat Step 5b, writing down the *next* earlier time from Table B–3, until you are certain.

Example C: Reading Table B–3 for February 26, Lenny's birthday, we see that 5:00 A.M. is the time that precedes 6:27 A.M. By reading Table B–4 from Grand Junction to the column that corresponds to Aquarius rising (the sign before Pisces), we see that 12 minutes must be added to 5:00. The result, 5:12 A.M., is earlier than Lenny's 6:39 A.M. AST. Therefore, we can be certain that Lenny has Aquarius rising.

Table B–1. Duration of Daylight Saving Time in the United States and Canada, 1973–1980

	Daylight Saving Time in Effect	
Birth year	From 2:00 a.m. on	To 1:59 a.m. on
1973	April 29	October 28
1974	January 6	October 27
1975	February 23	October 26
1976	April 25	October 31
1977	April 24	October 30
1978	April 30	October 29
1979	April 29	October 28
1980	April 27	October 26

Table B–2. Adjustment of Standard Time of Birth

Birth year	Add to birthtime
1973	3 minutes
1974	2 minutes
1975	1 minute
1976	
January 1–February 29	0 minutes
March 1–December 31	4 minutes
1977	3 minutes
1978	2 minutes
1979	1 minute
1980	
January 1–February 29	0 minutes
March 1–December 31	4 minutes

Table B–3. Uncorrected Times of Beginning of Rising Signs by Date*

Date	♈ ARI	♉ TAU	♊ GEM	♋ CAN	♌ LEO	♍ VIR	♎ LIB	♏ SCO	♐ SAG	♑ CAP	♒ AQU	♓ PIS
Jan. 1	11:21a	12:33p	2:00p	3:54p	6:16p	8:48p	11:18p	1:53a	4:24a	6:46a	8:41a	10:07a
Jan. 2	11:17a	12:29p	1:56p	3:50p	6:12p	8:44p	11:14p	1:49a	4:20a	6:42a	8:37a	10:03a
Jan. 3	11:13a	12:25p	1:52p	3:46p	6:08p	8:40p	11:10p	1:45a	4:16a	6:38a	8:33a	9:59a
Jan. 4	11:09a	12:21p	1:48p	3:42p	6:04p	8:36p	11:06p	1:41a	4:12a	6:34a	8:29a	9:55a
Jan. 5	11:05a	12:17p	1:44p	3:38p	6:00p	8:32p	11:02p	1:37a	4:08a	6:30a	8:25a	9:51a
Jan. 6	11:01a	12:13p	1:40p	3:34p	5:56p	8:28p	10:58p	1:33a	4:04a	6:26a	8:21a	9:47a
Jan. 7	10:57a	12:09p	1:36p	3:30p	5:52p	8:24p	10:54p	1:29a	4:00a	6:22a	8:17a	9:43a
Jan. 8	10:53a	12:05p	1:32p	3:26p	5:48p	8:20p	10:50p	1:25a	3:56a	6:18a	8:13a	9:39a
Jan. 9	10:49a	12:01p	1:28p	3:22p	5:44p	8:16p	10:46p	1:21a	3:52a	6:14a	8:09a	9:36a
Jan. 10	10:45a	11:57a	1:24p	3:18p	5:40p	8:12p	10:42p	1:17a	3:48a	6:10a	8:05a	9:32a
Jan. 11	10:41a	11:53a	1:20p	3:15p	5:36p	8:08p	10:38p	1:13a	3:44a	6:06a	8:01a	9:28a
Jan. 12	10:37a	11:49a	1:16p	3:11p	5:32p	8:04p	10:34p	1:09a	3:40a	6:02a	7:57a	9:24a
Jan. 13	10:33a	11:45a	1:12p	3:07p	5:28p	8:00p	10:30p	1:05a	3:36a	5:58a	7:53a	9:20a
Jan. 14	10:29a	11:41a	1:08p	3:03p	5:24p	7:56p	10:26p	1:01a	3:32a	5:54a	7:49a	9:16a
Jan. 15	10:25a	11:37a	1:04p	2:59p	5:20p	7:52p	10:22p	12:57a	3:28a	5:50a	7:45a	9:12a
Jan. 16	10:22a	11:34a	1:01p	2:56p	5:17p	7:49p	10:19p	12:53a	3:25a	5:47a	7:42a	9:09a
Jan. 17	10:18a	11:30a	12:57p	2:52p	5:13p	7:45p	10:15p	12:50a	3:21a	5:43a	7:38a	9:05a
Jan. 18	10:14a	11:26a	12:53p	2:48p	5:09p	7:41p	10:11p	12:46a	3:17a	5:39a	7:34a	9:01a
Jan. 19	10:10a	11:22a	12:49p	2:44p	5:05p	7:37p	10:07p	12:42a	3:13a	5:35a	7:30a	8:57a
Jan. 20	10:06a	11:18a	12:45p	2:40p	5:01p	7:33p	10:03p	12:38a	3:09a	5:31a	7:26a	8:53a

a = a.m.; p = p.m.; m = midnight; n = noon
*Table B–3 gives the correct times for 40° north latitude on the standard time meridian.

(Continued)

Table B–3. *Continued*

Date	♈ ARI	♉ TAU	♊ GEM	♋ CAN	♌ LEO	♍ VIR	♎ LIB	♏ SCO	♐ SAG	♑ CAP	♒ AQU	♓ PIS
Jan. 21	10:02a	11:14a	12:41p	2:36p	4:57p	7:29p	9:59p	12:34a	3:05a	5:27a	7:22a	8:49a
Jan. 22	9:58a	11:10a	12:37p	2:32p	4:53p	7:25p	9:55p	12:30a	3:01a	5:23a	7:18a	8:45a
Jan. 23	9:54a	11:06a	12:33p	2:28p	4:49p	7:21p	9:51p	12:26a	2:58a	5:19a	7:14a	8:41a
Jan. 24	9:50a	11:02a	12:29p	2:24p	4:45p	7:17p	9:47p	12:22a	2:54a	5:15a	7:10a	8:37a
Jan. 25	9:46a	10:58a	12:25p	2:20p	4:41p	7:13p	9:43p	12:18a	2:50a	5:11a	7:06a	8:33a
Jan. 26	9:42a	10:54a	12:21p	2:16p	4:37p	7:09p	9:39p	12:14a	2:46a	5:07a	7:02a	8:29a
Jan. 27	9:38a	10:50a	12:17p	2:12p	4:33p	7:05p	9:35p	12:10a	2:42a	5:03a	6:58a	8:25a
Jan. 28	9:34a	10:46a	12:13p	2:08p	4:29p	7:01p	9:32p	12:06a	2:38a	4:59a	6:54a	8:21a
Jan. 29	9:30a	10:42a	12:09p	2:04p	4:25p	6:57p	9:28p	12:02a	2:34a	4:55a	6:50a	8:17a
								11:58p				
Jan. 30	9:26a	10:38a	12:05p	2:00p	4:21p	6:53p	9:24p	11:54p	2:30a	4:51a	6:46a	8:13a
Jan. 31	9:22a	10:34a	12:01p	1:56p	4:17p	6:49p	9:20p	11:50p	2:26a	4:47a	6:42a	8:09a
Feb. 1	9:18a	10:30a	11:57a	1:52p	4:13p	6:45p	9:16p	11:46p	2:22a	4:43a	6:38a	8:05a
Feb. 2	9:14a	10:26a	11:53a	1:48p	4:09p	6:41p	9:12p	11:42p	2:18a	4:39a	6:34a	8:01a
Feb. 3	9:11a	10:23a	11:50a	1:45p	4:06p	6:38p	9:09p	11:39p	2:14a	4:36a	6:31a	7:58a
Feb. 4	9:07a	10:19a	11:46a	1:41p	4:02p	6:34p	9:05p	11:35p	2:11a	4:32a	6:27a	7:54a
Feb. 5	9:03a	10:15a	11:42a	1:37p	3:58p	6:30p	9:01p	11:31p	2:07a	4:28a	6:23a	7:50a
Feb. 6	9:00a	10:11a	11:38a	1:33p	3:54p	6:26p	8:57p	11:27p	2:03a	4:24a	6:19a	7:46a
Feb. 7	8:56a	10:07a	11:34a	1:29p	3:50p	6:22p	8:53p	11:23p	1:59a	4:20a	6:15a	7:42a
Feb. 8	8:52a	10:03a	11:30a	1:25p	3:46p	6:18p	8:49p	11:19p	1:55a	4:16a	6:11a	7:38a
Feb. 9	8:48a	9:59a	11:26a	1:21p	3:42p	6:14p	8:45p	11:15p	1:51a	4:12a	6:07a	7:34a
Feb. 10	8:44a	9:55a	11:22a	1:17p	3:38p	6:10p	8:41p	11:11p	1:47a	4:08a	6:03a	7:30a
Feb. 11	8:40a	9:51a	11:18a	1:13p	3:35p	6:06p	8:37p	11:07p	1:43a	4:04a	5:59a	7:26a
Feb. 12	8:36a	9:47a	11:14a	1:09p	3:31p	6:02p	8:33p	11:03p	1:39a	4:00a	5:55a	7:22a
Feb. 13	8:32a	9:43a	11:10a	1:05p	3:27p	5:58p	8:29p	10:59p	1:35a	3:56a	5:51a	7:18a
Feb. 14	8:28a	9:39a	11:06a	1:01p	3:23p	5:54p	8:25p	10:55p	1:31a	3:52a	5:47a	7:14a
Feb. 15	8:24a	9:35a	11:02a	12:57p	3:19p	5:50p	8:21p	10:51p	1:27a	3:48a	5:43a	7:10a
Feb. 16	8:20a	9:31a	10:58a	12:53p	3:15p	5:46p	8:17p	10:47p	1:23a	3:44a	5:39a	7:06a
Feb. 17	8:16a	9:27a	10:54a	12:49p	3:11p	5:42p	8:13p	10:43p	1:19a	3:40a	5:35a	7:02a
Feb. 18	8:12a	9:23a	10:50a	12:45p	3:07p	5:38p	8:09p	10:39p	1:15a	3:36a	5:31a	6:58a
Feb. 19	8:08a	9:19a	10:46a	12:41p	3:03p	5:34p	8:05p	10:35p	1:11a	3:32a	5:27a	6:54a
Feb. 20	8:05a	9:16a	10:43a	12:38p	3:00p	5:31p	8:02p	10:32p	1:08a	3:29a	5:24a	6:51a
Feb. 21	8:01a	9:12a	10:39a	12:34p	2:56p	5:27p	7:58p	10:28p	1:04a	3:25a	5:20a	6:47a
Feb. 22	7:57a	9:08a	10:35a	12:30p	2:52p	5:23p	7:54p	10:24p	1:00a	3:21a	5:16a	6:43a
Feb. 23	7:53a	9:04a	10:31a	12:26p	2:48p	5:19p	7:50p	10:20p	12:56a	3:17a	5:12a	6:39a
Feb. 24	7:49a	9:01a	10:27a	12:22p	2:44p	5:15p	7:46p	10:16p	12:52a	3:13a	5:08a	6:35a
Feb. 25	7:45a	8:57a	10:23a	12:18p	2:40p	5:11p	7:42p	10:12p	12:48a	3:09a	5:04a	6:31a
Feb. 26	7:41a	8:53a	10:19a	12:14p	2:36p	5:07p	7:38p	10:08p	12:44a	3:05a	5:00a	6:27a
Feb. 27	7:37a	8:49a	10:15a	12:10p	2:32p	5:03p	7:34p	10:04p	12:40a	3:01a	4:56a	6:23a
Feb. 28	7:33a	8:45a	10:11a	12:06p	2:28p	4:59p	7:30p	10:00p	12:36a	2:58a	4:52a	6:19a
Feb. 29	7:29a	8:41a	10:07a	12:02p	2:24p	4:55p	7:26p	9:56p	12:32a	2:54a	4:48a	6:15a
Mar. 1	7:29a	8:41a	10:07a	12:02p	2:24p	4:55p	7:26p	9:56p	12:32a	2:54a	4:48a	6:15a
Mar. 2	7:25a	8:37a	10:03a	11:58a	2:20p	4:51p	7:22p	9:52p	12:28a	2:50a	4:44a	6:11a

a = a.m.; p = p.m.; m = midnight; n = noon

116

Date	♈ ARI	♉ TAU	♊ GEM	♋ CAN	♌ LEO	♍ VIR	♎ LIB	♏ SCO	♐ SAG	♑ CAP	♒ AQU	♓ PIS
Mar. 3	7:21a	8:33a	9:59a	11:54a	2:16p	4:47p	7:18p	9:48p	12:24a	2:46a	4:40a	6:07a
Mar. 4	7:17a	8:29a	9:55a	11:50a	2:12p	4:43p	7:14p	9:44p	12:20a	2:42a	4:36a	6:03a
Mar. 5	7:13a	8:25a	9:51a	11:46a	2:08p	4:39p	7:10p	9:40p	12:16a	2:38a	4:32a	5:59a
Mar. 6	7:09a	8:21a	9:47a	11:42a	2:04p	4:35p	7:06p	9:36p	12:12a	2:34a	4:28a	5:55a
Mar. 7	7:05a	8:17a	9:43a	11:38a	2:00p	4:31p	7:02p	9:32p	12:08a	2:30a	4:24a	5:51a
Mar. 8	7:01a	8:13a	9:39a	11:34a	1:56p	4:27p	6:58p	9:28p	12:04a / 12:00	2:26a	4:20a	5:47a
Mar. 9	6:57a	8:09a	9:35a	11:30a	1:52p	4:23p	6:54p	9:24p	11:56p	2:22a	4:16a	5:43a
Mar. 10	6:54a	8:06a	9:32a	11:27a	1:49p	4:20p	6:51p	9:21p	11:53p	2:18a	4:13a	5:40a
Mar. 11	6:50a	8:02a	9:28a	11:23a	1:45p	4:16p	6:47p	9:17p	11:49p	2:15a	4:09a	5:36a
Mar. 12	6:46a	7:58a	9:24a	11:19a	1:41p	4:12p	6:43p	9:13p	11:45p	2:11a	4:05a	5:32a
Mar. 13	6:42a	7:54a	9:20a	11:15a	1:37p	4:08p	6:39p	9:09p	11:41p	2:07a	4:01a	5:28a
Mar. 14	6:38a	7:50a	9:16a	11:11a	1:33p	4:04p	6:35p	9:05p	11:37p	2:03a	3:57a	5:24a
Mar. 15	6:34a	7:46a	9:12a	11:07a	1:29p	4:00p	6:31p	9:01p	11:33p	1:59a	3:53a	5:20a
Mar. 16	6:30a	7:42a	9:08a	11:03a	1:25p	3:56p	6:27p	8:58p	11:29p	1:55a	3:49a	5:16a
Mar. 17	6:26a	7:38a	9:04a	10:59a	1:21p	3:52p	6:23p	8:54p	11:25p	1:51a	3:45a	5:12a
Mar. 18	6:22a	7:34a	9:01a	10:55a	1:17p	3:48p	6:19p	8:50p	11:21p	1:47a	3:42a	5:08a
Mar. 19	6:18a	7:30a	8:57a	10:51a	1:13p	3:44p	6:15p	8:46p	11:17p	1:43a	3:38a	5:04a
Mar. 20	6:14a	7:26a	8:53a	10:47a	1:09p	3:40p	6:11p	8:42p	11:13p	1:39a	3:34a	5:00a
Mar. 21	6:10a	7:22a	8:49a	10:43a	1:05p	3:36p	6:07p	8:38p	11:09p	1:35a	3:30a	4:56a
Mar. 22	6:06a	7:18a	8:45a	10:39a	1:01p	3:33p	6:03p	8:34p	11:05p	1:31a	3:26a	4:52a
Mar. 23	6:02a	7:14a	8:41a	10:35a	12:57a	3:29p	5:59p	8:30p	11:01p	1:27a	3:22a	4:48a
Mar. 24	5:58a	7:10a	8:37a	10:31a	12:53p	3:25p	5:55p	8:26p	10:57p	1:23a	3:18a	4:44a
Mar. 25	5:54a	7:06a	8:33a	10:27a	12:49p	3:21p	5:51p	8:22p	10:53p	1:19a	3:14a	4:40a
Mar. 26	5:50a	7:02a	8:29a	10:23a	12:45p	3:17p	5:47p	8:18p	10:49p	1:15a	3:10a	4:36a
Mar. 27	5:47a	6:59a	8:26a	10:20a	12:42p	3:14p	5:44p	8:15p	10:46p	1:11a	3:07a	4:33a
Mar. 28	5:43a	6:55a	8:22a	10:16a	12:38p	3:10p	5:40p	8:11p	10:42p	1:08a	3:03a	4:29a
Mar. 29	5:39a	6:51a	8:18a	10:12a	12:34p	3:06p	5:36p	8:07p	10:38p	1:04a	2:59a	4:25a
Mar. 30	5:35a	6:47a	8:14a	10:08a	12:30p	3:02p	5:32p	8:03p	10:34p	1:00a	2:55a	4:21a
Mar. 31	5:31a	6:43a	8:10a	10:04a	12:26p	2:58p	5:28p	7:59p	10:30p	12:56a	2:51a	4:17a
Apr. 1	5:27a	6:39a	8:06a	10:00a	12:22p	2:54p	5:24p	7:55p	10:26p	12:52a	2:47a	4:13a
Apr. 2	5:23a	6:35a	8:02a	9:56a	12:18p	2:50p	5:20p	7:51p	10:22p	12:48a	2:43a	4:09a
Apr. 3	5:19a	6:31a	7:58a	9:52a	12:14p	2:46p	5:16p	7:47p	10:18p	12:44a	2:39a	4:05a
Apr. 4	5:15a	6:27a	7:54a	9:48a	12:10p	2:42p	5:12p	7:43p	10:14p	12:40a	2:35a	4:01a
Apr. 5	5:11a	6:23a	7:50a	9:44a	12:06p	2:38p	5:08p	7:39p	10:10p	12:36a	2:31a	3:57a
Apr. 6	5:07a	6:19a	7:46a	9:40a	12:02p	2:34p	5:04p	7:35p	10:06p	12:32a	2:27a	3:53a
Apr. 7	5:03a	6:15a	7:42a	9:36a	11:58a	2:30p	5:00p	7:31p	10:02p	12:28a	2:23a	3:49a
Apr. 8	4:59a	6:11a	7:38a	9:32a	11:54a	2:26p	4:56p	7:27p	9:58p	12:24a	2:19a	3:45a
Apr. 9	4:55a	6:07a	7:34a	9:28a	11:50a	2:22p	4:52p	7:23p	9:54p	12:20a	2:15a	3:41a
Apr. 10	4:51a	6:03a	7:30a	9:24a	11:46a	2:18p	4:48p	7:19p	9:50p	12:16a	2:11a	3:37a
Apr. 11	4:47a	5:59a	7:26a	9:20a	11:42a	2:14p	4:44p	7:15p	9:46p	12:12a	2:07a	3:33a
Apr. 12	4:43a	5:55a	7:22a	9:16a	11:38a	2:10p	4:40p	7:11p	9:42p	12:08a	2:03a	3:29a
Apr. 13	4:40a	5:52a	7:19a	9:13a	11:35a	2:07p	4:37p	7:08p	9:39p	12:04a	2:00a	3:26a

a = a.m.; p = p.m.; m = midnight; n = noon

(Continued)

Table B-3. *Continued*

Date	♈ ARI	♉ TAU	♊ GEM	♋ CAN	♌ LEO	♍ VIR	♎ LIB	♏ SCO	♐ SAG	♑ CAP	♒ AQU	♓ PIS
										12:01a		
Apr. 14	4:36a	5:48a	7:15a	9:09a	11:31a	2:03p	4:33p	7:04p	9:35p	11:57p	1:56a	3:22a
Apr. 15	4:32a	5:44a	7:11a	9:05a	11:27a	1:59p	4:29p	7:00p	9:31p	11:53p	1:52a	3:18a
Apr. 16	4:28a	5:40a	7:07a	9:01a	11:23a	1:55p	4:25p	6:56p	9:27p	11:49p	1:48a	3:14a
Apr. 17	4:24a	5:36a	7:03a	8:58a	11:19a	1:51p	4:21p	6:52p	9:23p	11:45p	1:44a	3:10a
Apr. 18	4:20a	5:32a	6:59a	8:54a	11:15a	1:47p	4:17p	6:48p	9:19p	11:41p	1:40a	3:06a
Apr. 19	4:16a	5:28a	6:55a	8:50a	11:11a	1:43p	4:13p	6:44p	9:15p	11:37p	1:36a	3:02a
Apr. 20	4:12a	5:24a	6:51a	8:46a	11:07a	1:39p	4:09p	6:40p	9:11p	11:33p	1:32a	2:59a
Apr. 21	4:08a	5:20a	6:47a	8:42a	11:03a	1:35p	4:05p	6:36p	9:07p	11:29p	1:28a	2:55a
Apr. 22	4:04a	5:16a	6:43a	8:38a	10:59a	1:31p	4:01p	6:32p	9:03p	11:25p	1:24a	2:51a
Apr. 23	4:00a	5:12a	6:39a	8:34a	10:55a	1:27p	3:57p	6:28p	9:00p	11:21p	1:20a	2:47a
Apr. 24	3:56a	5:08a	6:35a	8:30a	10:51a	1:23p	3:53p	6:24p	8:56p	11:17p	1:16a	2:43a
Apr. 25	3:52a	5:04a	6:31a	8:26a	10:47a	1:19p	3:49p	6:20p	8:52p	11:13p	1:12a	2:39a
Apr. 26	3:48a	5:00a	6:27a	8:22a	10:43a	1:15p	3:45p	6:16p	8:48p	11:09p	1:08a	2:35a
Apr. 27	3:44a	4:56a	6:23a	8:18a	10:39a	1:11p	3:41p	6:12p	8:44p	11:05p	1:04a	2:31a
Apr. 28	3:40a	4:52a	6:19a	8:14a	10:35a	1:07p	3:37p	6:08p	8:40p	11:01p	1:00a	2:27a
Apr. 29	3:36a	4:48a	6:15a	8:10a	10:31a	1:03p	3:33p	6:04p	8:36p	10:57p	12:56a	2:23a
Apr. 30	3:32a	4:44a	6:11a	8:06a	10:27a	12:59p	3:29p	6:00p	8:32p	10:53p	12:52a	2:19a
May 1	3:29a	4:41a	6:08a	8:03a	10:24a	12:56p	3:26p	5:57p	8:29p	10:50p	12:48a	2:15a
May 2	3:25a	4:37a	6:04a	7:59a	10:20a	12:52p	3:22p	5:53p	8:25p	10:46p	12:45a	2:12a
May 3	3:21a	4:33a	6:00a	7:55a	10:16a	12:48p	3:18p	5:49p	8:21p	10:42p	12:41a	2:08a
May 4	3:17a	4:29a	5:56a	7:51a	10:12a	12:44p	3:14p	5:45p	8:17p	10:38p	12:37a	2:04a
May 5	3:13a	4:25a	5:52a	7:47a	10:08a	12:40p	3:10p	5:41p	8:13p	10:34p	12:33a	2:00a
May 6	3:09a	4:21a	5:48a	7:43a	10:04a	12:36p	3:06p	5:37p	8:09p	10:30p	12:29a	1:56a
May 7	3:05a	4:17a	5:44a	7:39a	10:00a	12:32p	3:02p	5:33p	8:05p	10:26p	12:25a	1:52a
May 8	3:01a	4:13a	5:40a	7:35a	9:56a	12:28p	2:59p	5:29p	8:01p	10:22p	12:21a	1:48a
May 9	2:58a	4:09a	5:36a	7:31a	9:52a	12:24p	2:55p	5:25p	7:57p	10:18p	12:17a	1:44a
May 10	2:54a	4:05a	5:32a	7:27a	9:48a	12:20p	2:51p	5:21p	7:53p	10:14p	12:13a	1:40a
May 11	2:50a	4:01a	5:28a	7:23a	9:44a	12:16p	2:47p	5:17p	7:49p	10:10p	12:09a	1:36a
May 12	2:46a	3:57a	5:24a	7:19a	9:40a	12:12p	2:43p	5:13p	7:45p	10:06p	12:05a	1:32a
May 13	2:42a	3:53a	5:20a	7:15a	9:36a	12:08p	2:39p	5:09p	7:41p	10:02p	12:01a	1:28a
											11:57p	
May 14	2:38a	3:49a	5:16a	7:11a	9:32a	12:04p	2:35p	5:05p	7:37p	9:58p	11:53p	1:24a
May 15	2:34a	3:45a	5:12a	7:07a	9:28a	12:00n	2:31p	5:01p	7:33p	9:54p	11:49p	1:20a
May 16	2:30a	3:41a	5:08a	7:03a	9:24a	11:56a	2:27p	4:57p	7:29p	9:50p	11:45p	1:16a
May 17	2:26a	3:37a	5:04a	6:59a	9:20a	11:52a	2:23p	4:53p	7:25p	9:46p	11:41p	1:12a
May 18	2:23a	3:34a	5:01a	6:56a	9:17a	11:49a	2:20p	4:50p	7:22p	9:43p	11:38p	1:08a
May 19	2:19a	3:30a	4:57a	6:52a	9:13a	11:45a	2:16p	4:46p	7:18p	9:39p	11:34p	1:05a
May 20	2:15a	3:26a	4:53a	6:48a	9:09a	11:41a	2:12p	4:42p	7:14p	9:35p	11:30p	1:01a
May 21	2:11a	3:22a	4:49a	6:44a	9:05a	11:37a	2:08p	4:38p	7:10p	9:31p	11:26p	12:57a
May 22	2:07a	3:18a	4:45a	6:40a	9:01a	11:33a	2:04p	4:34p	7:06p	9:27p	11:22p	12:53a
May 23	2:03a	3:14a	4:41a	6:36a	8:58a	11:29a	2:00p	4:30p	7:02p	9:23p	11:18p	12:49a
May 24	1:59a	3:10a	4:37a	6:32a	8:54a	11:25a	1:56p	4:26p	6:58p	9:19p	11:14p	12:45a
May 25	1:55a	3:06a	4:33a	6:28a	8:50a	11:21a	1:52p	4:22p	6:54p	9:15p	11:10p	12:41a

a = a.m.; p = p.m.; m = midnight; n = noon

Date	♈ ARI	♉ TAU	♊ GEM	♋ CAN	♌ LEO	♍ VIR	♎ LIB	♏ SCO	♐ SAG	♑ CAP	♒ AQU	♓ PIS
May 26	1:51a	3:02a	4:29a	6:24a	8:46a	11:17a	1:48p	4:18p	6:50p	9:11p	11:06p	12:37a
May 27	1:47a	2:59a	4:25a	6:20a	8:42a	11:13a	1:44p	4:14p	6:46p	9:07p	11:02p	12:33a
May 28	1:43a	2:55a	4:21a	6:16a	8:38a	11:09a	1:40p	4:10p	6:42p	9:03p	10:58p	12:29a
May 29	1:39a	2:51a	4:17a	6:12a	8:34a	11:05a	1:36p	4:06p	6:38p	9:00p	10:54p	12:25a
May 30	1:35a	2:47a	4:13a	6:08a	8:30a	11:01a	1:32p	4:02p	6:34p	8:56p	10:50p	12:21a
May 31	1:31a	2:43a	4:09a	6:04a	8:26a	10:57a	1:28p	3:58p	6:30p	8:52p	10:46p	12:17a
Jun. 1	1:27a	2:39a	4:05a	6:00a	8:22a	10:53a	1:24p	3:54p	6:26p	8:48p	10:42p	12:13a
Jun. 2	1:23a	2:35a	4:01a	5:56a	8:18a	10:49a	1:20p	3:50p	6:22p	8:44p	10:38p	12:09a
Jun. 3	1:19a	2:31a	3:57a	5:52a	8:14a	10:45a	1:16p	3:46p	6:18p	8:40p	10:34p	12:05a
												12:01a
Jun. 4	1:15a	2:28a	3:54a	5:49a	8:11a	10:42a	1:13p	3:43p	6:15p	8:37p	10:31p	11:58p
Jun. 5	1:12a	2:24a	3:50a	5:45a	8:07a	10:38a	1:09p	3:39p	6:11p	8:33p	10:27p	11:54p
Jun. 6	1:08a	2:20a	3:46a	5:41a	8:03a	10:34a	1:05p	3:35p	6:07p	8:29p	10:23p	11:50p
Jun. 7	1:04a	2:16a	3:42a	5:37a	7:59a	10:30a	1:01p	3:31p	6:03p	8:25p	10:19p	11:46p
Jun. 8	1:00a	2:12a	3:38a	5:33a	7:55a	10:26a	12:57p	3:28p	5:59p	8:21p	10:15p	11:42p
Jun. 9	12:56a	2:08a	3:34a	5:29a	7:51a	10:22a	12:53p	3:24p	5:55p	8:17p	10:11p	11:38p
Jun. 10	12:52a	2:04a	3:30a	5:25a	7:47a	10:18a	12:49p	3:20p	5:51p	8:13p	10:07p	11:34p
Jun. 11	12:48a	2:00a	3:26a	5:21a	7:43a	10:14a	12:45p	3:16p	5:47p	8:09p	10:03p	11:30p
Jun. 12	12:44a	1:56a	3:22a	5:17a	7:39a	10:10a	12:41p	3:12p	5:43p	8:05p	9:59p	11:26p
Jun. 13	12:40a	1:52a	3:19a	5:13a	7:35a	10:06a	12:37p	3:08p	5:39p	8:01p	9:55p	11:22p
Jun. 14	12:36a	1:48a	3:15a	5:09a	7:31a	10:02a	12:33p	3:04p	5:35p	7:57p	9:51p	11:18p
Jun. 15	12:32a	1:44a	3:11a	5:05a	7:27a	9:58a	12:29p	3:00p	5:31p	7:53p	9:47p	11:14p
Jun. 16	12:28a	1:40a	3:07a	5:01a	7:23a	9:54a	12:25p	2:56p	5:27p	7:49p	9:43p	11:10p
Jun. 17	12:24a	1:36a	3:03a	4:57a	7:19a	9:50a	12:21p	2:52p	5:23p	7:45p	9:39p	11:06p
Jun. 18	12:20a	1:32a	2:59a	4:53a	7:15a	9:46a	12:17p	2:48p	5:19p	7:41p	9:35p	11:02p
Jun. 19	12:16a	1:28a	2:55a	4:49a	7:11a	9:42a	12:13p	2:44p	5:15p	7:37p	9:31p	10:58p
Jun. 20	12:12a	1:24a	2:51a	4:45a	7:07a	9:38a	12:09p	2:40p	5:11p	7:33p	9:27p	10:54p
Jun. 21	12:08a	1:21a	2:48a	4:42a	7:04a	9:35a	12:06p	2:37p	5:08p	7:30p	9:24p	10:51p
Jun. 22	12:05a	1:17a	2:44a	4:38a	7:00a	9:31a	12:02p	2:33p	5:04p	7:26p	9:20p	10:47p
Jun. 23	12:01a	1:13a	2:40a	4:34a	6:56a	9:27a	11:58a	2:29p	5:00p	7:22p	9:16p	10:43p
	11:57p											
Jun. 24	11:53p	1:09a	2:36a	4:30a	6:52a	9:23a	11:54a	2:25p	4:56p	7:18p	9:12p	10:39p
Jun. 25	11:49p	1:05a	2:32a	4:26a	6:48a	9:19a	11:50a	2:21p	4:52p	7:14p	9:08p	10:35p
Jun. 26	11:45p	1:01a	2:28a	4:22a	6:44a	9:15a	11:46a	2:17p	4:48p	7:10p	9:04p	10:31p
Jun. 27	11:41p	12:57a	2:24a	4:18a	6:40a	9:11a	11:42a	2:13p	4:44p	7:06p	9:00p	10:27p
Jun. 28	11:37p	12:53a	2:20a	4:14a	6:36a	9:07a	11:38a	2:09p	4:40p	7:02p	8:57p	10:23p
Jun. 29	11:33p	12:49a	2:16a	4:10a	6:32a	9:03a	11:34a	2:05p	4:36p	6:58p	8:53p	10:19p
Jun. 30	11:29p	12:45a	2:12a	4:06a	6:28a	9:00a	11:30a	2:01p	4:32p	6:54p	8:49p	10:15p
Jul. 1	11:25p	12:41a	2:08a	4:02a	6:24a	8:56a	11:26a	1:57p	4:28p	6:50p	8:45p	10:11p
Jul. 2	11:21p	12:37a	2:04a	3:58a	6:20a	8:52a	11:22a	1:53p	4:24p	6:46p	8:41p	10:07p
Jul. 3	11:17p	12:33a	2:00a	3:54a	6:16a	8:48a	11:18a	1:49p	4:20p	6:42p	8:37p	10:03p
Jul. 4	11:13p	12:29a	1:56a	3:50a	6:12a	8:44a	11:14a	1:45p	4:16p	6:38p	8:33p	9:59p
Jul. 5	11:09p	12:25a	1:52a	3:46a	6:08a	8:40a	11:10a	1:41p	4:12p	6:34p	8:29p	9:55p

a = a.m.; p = p.m.; m = midnight; n = noon

(Continued)

Table B–3. Continued

Date	♈ ARI	♉ TAU	♊ GEM	♋ CAN	♌ LEO	♍ VIR	♎ LIB	♏ SCO	♐ SAG	♑ CAP	♒ AQU	♓ PIS
Jul. 6	11:05p	12:21a	1:48a	3:42a	6:04a	8:36a	11:06a	1:37p	4:08p	6:30p	8:25p	9:51p
Jul. 7	11:01p	12:17a	1:44a	3:38a	6:00a	8:32a	11:02a	1:33p	4:04p	6:26p	8:21p	9:47p
Jul. 8	10:57p	12:13a	1:40a	3:34a	5:56a	8:28a	10:58a	1:29p	4:00p	6:22p	8:17p	9:43p
Jul. 9	10:54p	12:09a	1:37a	3:31a	5:53a	8:25a	10:55a	1:26p	3:57p	6:19p	8:14p	9:40p
Jul. 10	10:50p	12:06a	1:33a	3:27a	5:49a	8:21a	10:51a	1:22p	3:53p	6:15p	8:10p	9:36p
		12:02a										
Jul. 11	10:46p	11:58p	1:29a	3:23a	5:45a	8:17a	10:47a	1:18p	3:49p	6:11p	8:06p	9:32p
Jul. 12	10:42p	11:54p	1:25a	3:19a	5:41a	8:13a	10:43a	1:14p	3:45p	6:07p	8:02p	9:28p
Jul. 13	10:38p	11:50p	1:21a	3:15a	5:37a	8:09a	10:39a	1:10p	3:41p	6:03p	7:58p	9:24p
Jul. 14	10:34p	11:46p	1:17a	3:11a	5:33a	8:05a	10:35a	1:06p	3:37p	5:59p	7:54p	9:20p
Jul. 15	10:30p	11:42p	1:13a	3:07a	5:29a	8:01a	10:31a	1:02p	3:33p	5:55p	7:50p	9:16p
Jul. 16	10:26p	11:38p	1:09a	3:03a	5:25a	7:57a	10:27a	12:58p	3:29p	5:51p	7:46p	9:12p
Jul. 17	10:22p	11:34p	1:05a	3:00a	5:21a	7:53a	10:23a	12:54p	3:26p	5:47p	7:42p	9:08p
Jul. 18	10:18p	11:30p	1:01a	2:56a	5:17a	7:49a	10:19a	12:50p	3:22p	5:43p	7:38p	9:04p
Jul. 19	10:14p	11:26p	12:57a	2:52a	5:13a	7:45a	10:15a	12:46p	3:18p	5:39p	7:34p	9:00p
Jul. 20	10:10p	11:22p	12:53a	2:48a	5:09a	7:41a	10:11a	12:42p	3:14p	5:35p	7:30p	8:57p
Jul. 21	10:06p	11:18p	12:49a	2:44a	5:05a	7:37a	10:07a	12:38p	3:10p	5:31p	7:26p	8:53p
Jul. 22	10:02p	11:14p	12:45a	2:40a	5:01a	7:33a	10:03a	12:34p	3:06p	5:27p	7:22p	8:49p
Jul. 23	9:58p	11:10p	12:41a	2:36a	4:57a	7:29a	9:59a	12:30p	3:02p	5:23p	7:18p	8:45p
Jul. 24	9:54p	11:06p	12:37a	2:32a	4:53a	7:25a	9:55a	12:26p	2:58p	5:19p	7:14p	8:41p
Jul. 25	9:50p	11:02p	12:33a	2:28a	4:49a	7:21a	9:51a	12:22p	2:54p	5:15p	7:10p	8:37p
Jul. 26	9:46p	10:58p	12:29a	2:24a	4:45a	7:17a	9:47a	12:18p	2:50p	5:11p	7:06p	8:33p
Jul. 27	9:42p	10:54p	12:25a	2:20a	4:41a	7:13a	9:43a	12:14p	2:46p	5:07p	7:02p	8:29p
Jul. 28	9:39p	10:51p	12:21a	2:17a	4:38a	7:10a	9:40a	12:11p	2:43p	5:04p	6:59p	8:26p
Jul. 29	9:35p	10:47p	12:18a	2:13a	4:34a	7:06a	9:36a	12:07p	2:39p	5:00p	6:55p	8:22p
Jul. 30	9:31p	10:43p	12:14a	2:09a	4:30a	7:02a	9:32a	12:03p	2:35p	4:56p	6:51p	8:18p
Jul. 31	9:27p	10:39p	12:10a	2:05a	4:26a	6:58a	9:28a	11:59a	2:31p	4:52p	6:47p	8:14p
Aug. 1	9:23p	10:35p	12:06a	2:01a	4:22a	6:54a	9:25a	11:55a	2:27p	4:48p	6:43p	8:10p
			12:02a									
Aug. 2	9:19p	10:31p	11:58p	1:57a	4:18a	6:50a	9:21a	11:51a	2:23p	4:44p	6:39p	8:06p
Aug. 3	9:15p	10:27p	11:54p	1:53a	4:14a	6:46a	9:17a	11:47a	2:19p	4:40p	6:35p	8:02p
Aug. 4	9:12p	10:23p	11:50p	1:49a	4:10a	6:42a	9:13a	11:43a	2:15p	4:36p	6:31p	7:58p
Aug. 5	9:08p	10:19p	11:46p	1:45a	4:06a	6:38a	9:09a	11:39a	2:11p	4:32p	6:27p	7:54p
Aug. 6	9:04p	10:15p	11:42p	1:41a	4:02a	6:34a	9:05a	11:35a	2:07p	4:28p	6:23p	7:50p
Aug. 7	9:00p	10:11p	11:38p	1:37a	3:58a	6:30a	9:01a	11:31a	2:03p	4:24p	6:19p	7:46p
Aug. 8	8:56p	10:07p	11:34p	1:33a	3:54a	6:26a	8:57a	11:27a	1:59p	4:20p	6:15p	7:42p
Aug. 9	8:52p	10:03p	11:30p	1:29a	3:50a	6:22a	8:53a	11:23a	1:55p	4:16p	6:11p	7:38p
Aug. 10	8:48p	9:59p	11:26p	1:25a	3:46a	6:18a	8:49a	11:19a	1:51p	4:12p	6:07p	7:34p
Aug. 11	8:44p	9:55p	11:22p	1:21a	3:42a	6:14a	8:45a	11:15a	1:47p	4:08p	6:03p	7:30p
Aug. 12	8:41p	9:52p	11:19p	1:17a	3:39a	6:11a	8:42a	11:12a	1:44p	4:05p	6:00p	7:27p
Aug. 13	8:37p	9:48p	11:15p	1:14a	3:35a	6:07a	8:38a	11:08a	1:40p	4:01p	5:56p	7:23p
Aug. 14	8:33p	9:44p	11:11p	1:10a	3:31a	6:03a	8:34a	11:04a	1:36p	3:57p	5:52p	7:19p
Aug. 15	8:29p	9:40p	11:07p	1:06a	3:27a	5:59a	8:30a	11:00a	1:32p	3:53p	5:48p	7:15p

a = a.m.; p = p.m.; m = midnight; n = noon

120

Date	♈ ARI	♉ TAU	♊ GEM	♋ CAN	♌ LEO	♍ VIR	♎ LIB	♏ SCO	♐ SAG	♑ CAP	♒ AQU	♓ PIS
Aug. 16	8:25p	9:36p	11:03p	1:02a	3:23a	5:55a	8:26a	10:56a	1:28p	3:49p	5:44p	7:11p
Aug. 17	8:21p	9:32p	10:59p	12:58a	3:19a	5:51a	8:22a	10:52a	1:24p	3:45p	5:40p	7:07p
Aug. 18	8:17p	9:28p	10:55p	12:54a	3:15a	5:47a	8:18a	10:48a	1:20p	3:41p	5:36p	7:03p
Aug. 19	8:13p	9:24p	10:51p	12:50a	3:11a	5:43a	8:14a	10:44a	1:16p	3:37p	5:32p	6:59p
Aug. 20	8:09p	9:20p	10:47p	12:46a	3:07a	5:39a	8:10a	10:40a	1:12p	3:33p	5:28p	6:55p
Aug. 21	8:05p	9:16p	10:43p	12:42a	3:03a	5:35a	8:06a	10:36a	1:08p	3:30p	5:24p	6:51p
Aug. 22	8:01p	9:12p	10:39p	12:38a	3:00a	5:31a	8:02a	10:32a	1:04p	3:26p	5:20p	6:47p
Aug. 23	7:57p	9:08p	10:35p	12:34a	2:56a	5:27a	7:58a	10:28a	1:00p	3:22p	5:16p	6:43p
Aug. 24	7:53p	9:04p	10:31p	12:30a	2:52a	5:23a	7:54a	10:24a	12:56p	3:18p	5:12p	6:39p
Aug. 25	7:49p	9:01p	10:27p	12:26a	2:48a	5:19a	7:50a	10:20a	12:52p	3:14p	5:08p	6:35p
Aug. 26	7:45p	8:57p	10:23p	12:22a	2:44a	5:15a	7:46a	10:16a	12:48p	3:10p	5:04p	6:31p
Aug. 27	7:41p	8:53p	10:19p	12:18a	2:40a	5:11a	7:42a	10:12a	12:44p	3:06p	5:00p	6:27p
Aug. 28	7:37p	8:49p	10:15p	12:14a	2:36a	5:07a	7:38a	10:08a	12:40p	3:02p	4:56p	6:23p
Aug. 29	7:33p	8:45p	10:11p	12:10a	2:32a	5:03a	7:34a	10:04a	12:36p	2:58p	4:52p	6:19p
Aug. 30	7:30p	8:42p	10:08p	12:06a	2:29a	5:00a	7:31a	10:01a	12:33p	2:55p	4:49p	6:16p
				12:03a								
Aug. 31	7:26p	8:38p	10:04p	11:59p	2:25a	4:56a	7:27a	9:57a	12:29p	2:51p	4:45p	6:12p
Sep. 1	7:22p	8:34p	10:00p	11:55p	2:21a	4:52a	7:23a	9:53a	12:25p	2:47p	4:41p	6:08p
Sep. 2	7:18p	8:30p	9:56p	11:51p	2:17a	4:48a	7:19a	9:49a	12:21p	2:43p	4:37p	6:04p
Sep. 3	7:14p	8:26p	9:53p	11:47p	2:13a	4:44a	7:15a	9:45a	12:17p	2:39p	4:33p	6:00p
Sep. 4	7:10p	8:22p	9:49p	11:43p	2:09a	4:40a	7:11a	9:41a	12:13p	2:35p	4:29p	5:56p
Sep. 5	7:06p	8:18p	9:45p	11:39p	2:05a	4:36a	7:07a	9:37a	12:09p	2:31p	4:25p	5:52p
Sep. 6	7:02p	8:14p	9:41p	11:35p	2:01a	4:32a	7:03a	9:34a	12:05p	2:27p	4:21p	5:48p
Sep. 7	6:58p	8:10p	9:37p	11:31p	1:57a	4:28a	6:59a	9:30a	12:01p	2:23p	4:17p	5:44p
Sep. 8	6:54p	8:06p	9:33p	11:27p	1:53a	4:24a	6:55a	9:26a	11:57a	2:19p	4:13p	5:40p
Sep. 9	6:50p	8:02p	9:29p	11:23p	1:49a	4:20a	6:51a	9:22a	11:53a	2:15p	4:09p	5:36p
Sep. 10	6:46p	7:58p	9:25p	11:19p	1:45a	4:16a	6:47a	9:18a	11:49a	2:11p	4:05p	5:32p
Sep. 11	6:42p	7:54p	9:21p	11:15p	1:41a	4:12a	6:43a	9:14a	11:45a	2:07p	4:01p	5:28p
Sep. 12	6:38p	7:50p	9:17p	11:11p	1:37a	4:08a	6:39a	9:10a	11:41a	2:03p	3:57p	5:24p
Sep. 13	6:34p	7:46p	9:13p	11:07p	1:33a	4:04a	6:35a	9:06a	11:37a	1:59p	3:53p	5:20p
Sep. 14	6:30p	7:42p	9:09p	11:03p	1:29a	4:00a	6:31a	9:02a	11:33a	1:55p	3:49p	5:16p
Sep. 15	6:26p	7:38p	9:05p	10:59p	1:25a	3:56a	6:27a	8:58a	11:29a	1:51p	3:45p	5:12p
Sep. 16	6:23p	7:35p	9:02p	10:56p	1:21a	3:53a	6:24a	8:55a	11:26a	1:48p	3:42p	5:09p
Sep. 17	6:19p	7:31p	8:58p	10:52p	1:18a	3:49a	6:20a	8:51a	11:22a	1:44p	3:38p	5:05p
Sep. 18	6:15p	7:27p	8:54p	10:48p	1:14a	3:45a	6:16a	8:47a	11:18a	1:40p	3:34p	5:01p
Sep. 19	6:11p	7:23p	8:50p	10:44p	1:10a	3:41a	6:12a	8:43a	11:14a	1:36p	3:30p	4:57p
Sep. 20	6:07p	7:19p	8:46p	10:40p	1:06a	3:37a	6:08a	8:39a	11:10a	1:32p	3:26p	4:53p
Sep. 21	6:03p	7:15p	8:42p	10:36p	1:02a	3:33a	6:04a	8:35a	11:06a	1:28p	3:22p	4:49p
Sep. 22	5:59p	7:11p	8:38p	10:32p	12:58a	3:29a	6:00a	8:31a	11:02a	1:24p	3:18p	4:45p
Sep. 23	5:55p	7:07p	8:34p	10:28p	12:54a	3:25a	5:56a	8:27a	10:58a	1:20p	3:14p	4:41p
Sep. 24	5:51p	7:03p	8:30p	10:24p	12:50a	3:21a	5:52a	8:23a	10:54a	1:16p	3:10p	4:37p
Sep. 25	5:47p	6:59p	8:26p	10:20p	12:46a	3:17a	5:48a	8:19a	10:50a	1:12p	3:07p	4:33p
Sep. 26	5:43p	6:55p	8:22p	10:16p	12:42a	3:13a	5:44a	8:15a	10:46a	1:08p	3:03p	4:29p

a = a.m.; p = p.m.; m = midnight; n = noon

(Continued)

Table B–3. *Continued*

Date	♈ ARI	♉ TAU	♊ GEM	♋ CAN	♌ LEO	♍ VIR	♎ LIB	♏ SCO	♐ SAG	♑ CAP	♒ AQU	♓ PIS
Sep. 27	5:39p	6:51p	8:18p	10:12p	12:38a	3:10a	5:40a	8:11a	10:42a	1:04p	2:59p	4:25p
Sep. 28	5:35p	6:47p	8:14p	10:08p	12:34a	3:06a	5:36a	8:07a	10:38a	1:00p	2:55p	4:21p
Sep. 29	5:31p	6:43p	8:10p	10:04p	12:30a	3:02a	5:32a	8:03a	10:34a	12:56p	2:51p	4:17p
Sep. 30	5:27p	6:39p	8:06p	10:00p	12:26a	2:58a	5:28a	7:59a	10:30a	12:52p	2:47p	4:13p
Oct. 1	5:23p	6:35p	8:02p	9:56p	12:22a	2:54a	5:24a	7:55a	10:26a	12:48p	2:43p	4:09p
Oct. 2	5:19p	6:31p	7:58p	9:52p	12:18a	2:50a	5:20a	7:51a	10:22a	12:44p	2:39p	4:05p
Oct. 3	5:15p	6:27p	7:54p	9:48p	12:14a	2:46a	5:16a	7:47a	10:18a	12:40p	2:35p	4:01p
Oct. 4	5:12p	6:24p	7:51p	9:45p	12:10a	2:43a	5:13a	7:44a	10:15a	12:37p	2:32p	3:58p
Oct. 5	5:08p	6:20p	7:47p	9:41p	12:07a 12:03a	2:39a	5:09a	7:40a	10:11a	12:33p	2:28p	3:54p
Oct. 6	5:04p	6:16p	7:43p	9:37p	11:59p	2:35a	5:05a	7:36a	10:07a	12:29p	2:24p	3:50p
Oct. 7	5:00p	6:12p	7:39p	9:33p	11:55p	2:31a	5:01a	7:32a	10:03a	12:25p	2:20p	3:46p
Oct. 8	4:56p	6:08p	7:35p	9:29p	11:51p	2:27a	4:57a	7:28a	9:59a	12:21p	2:16p	3:42p
Oct. 9	4:52p	6:04p	7:31p	9:25p	11:47p	2:23a	4:53a	7:24a	9:55a	12:17p	2:12p	3:38p
Oct. 10	4:48p	6:00p	7:27p	9:21p	11:43p	2:19a	4:49a	7:20a	9:51a	12:13p	2:08p	3:34p
Oct. 11	4:44p	5:56p	7:23p	9:17p	11:39p	2:15a	4:45a	7:16a	9:47a	12:09p	2:04p	3:30p
Oct. 12	4:40p	5:52p	7:19p	9:13p	11:35p	2:11a	4:41a	7:12a	9:43a	12:05p	2:00p	3:27p
Oct. 13	4:36p	5:48p	7:15p	9:09p	11:31p	2:07a	4:37a	7:08a	9:40a	12:01p	1:56p	3:23p
Oct. 14	4:32p	5:44p	7:11p	9:05p	11:27p	2:03a	4:33a	7:04a	9:36a	11:57a	1:52p	3:19p
Oct. 15	4:28p	5:40p	7:07p	9:02p	11:23p	1:59a	4:29a	7:00a	9:32a	11:53a	1:48p	3:15p
Oct. 16	4:24p	5:36p	7:03p	8:58p	11:19p	1:55a	4:25a	6:56a	9:28a	11:49a	1:44p	3:11p
Oct. 17	4:20p	5:32p	6:59p	8:54p	11:15p	1:51a	4:21a	6:52a	9:24a	11:45a	1:40p	3:07p
Oct. 18	4:16p	5:28p	6:55p	8:50p	11:11p	1:47a	4:17a	6:48a	9:20a	11:41a	1:36p	3:03p
Oct. 19	4:12p	5:24p	6:51p	8:46p	11:07p	1:43a	4:13a	6:44a	9:16a	11:37a	1:32p	2:59p
Oct. 20	4:08p	5:20p	6:47p	8:42p	11:03p	1:39a	4:09a	6:40a	9:12a	11:33a	1:28p	2:55p
Oct. 21	4:05p	5:17p	6:44p	8:39p	11:00p	1:35a	4:06a	6:37a	9:09a	11:30a	1:25p	2:52p
Oct. 22	4:01p	5:13p	6:40p	8:35p	10:56p	1:32a	4:02a	6:33a	9:05a	11:26a	1:21p	2:48p
Oct. 23	3:57p	5:09p	6:36p	8:31p	10:52p	1:28a	3:58a	6:29a	9:01a	11:22a	1:17p	2:44p
Oct. 24	3:53p	5:05p	6:32p	8:27p	10:48p	1:24a	3:54a	6:25a	8:57a	11:18a	1:13p	2:40p
Oct. 25	3:49p	5:01p	6:28p	8:23p	10:44p	1:20a	3:50a	6:21a	8:53a	11:14a	1:09p	2:36p
Oct. 26	3:45p	4:57p	6:24p	8:19p	10:40p	1:16a	3:46a	6:17a	8:49a	11:10a	1:05p	2:32p
Oct. 27	3:41p	4:53p	6:20p	8:15p	10:36p	1:12a	3:42a	6:13a	8:45a	11:06a	1:01p	2:28p
Oct. 28	3:37p	4:49p	6:16p	8:11p	10:32p	1:08a	3:38a	6:09a	8:41a	11:02a	12:57p	2:24p
Oct. 29	3:33p	4:45p	6:12p	8:07p	10:28p	1:04a	3:34a	6:05a	8:37a	10:58a	12:53p	2:20p
Oct. 30	3:29p	4:41p	6:08p	8:03p	10:24p	1:00a	3:31a	6:01a	8:33a	10:54a	12:49p	2:16p
Oct. 31	3:25p	4:37p	6:04p	7:59p	10:20p	12:56a	3:27a	5:57a	8:29a	10:50a	12:45p	2:12p
Nov. 1	3:22p	4:33p	6:00p	7:55p	10:16p	12:52a	3:23a	5:53a	8:25a	10:46a	12:41p	2:08p
Nov. 2	3:18p	4:29p	5:56p	7:51p	10:12p	12:48a	3:19a	5:49a	8:21a	10:42a	12:37p	2:04p
Nov. 3	3:14p	4:25p	5:52p	7:47p	10:08p	12:44a	3:15a	5:45a	8:17a	10:38a	12:33p	2:00p
Nov. 4	3:10p	4:21p	5:48p	7:43p	10:04p	12:40a	3:11a	5:41a	8:13a	10:34a	12:29p	1:56p
Nov. 5	3:06p	4:17p	5:44p	7:39p	10:00p	12:36a	3:07a	5:37a	8:09a	10:30a	12:25p	1:52p
Nov. 6	3:02p	4:13p	5:40p	7:35p	9:56p	12:32a	3:03a	5:33a	8:05a	10:26a	12:21p	1:48p
Nov. 7	2:59p	4:10p	5:37p	7:32p	9:53p	12:28a	3:00a	5:30a	8:02a	10:23a	12:18p	1:45p
Nov. 8	2:55p	4:06p	5:33p	7:28p	9:49p	12:25a	2:56a	5:26a	7:58a	10:19a	12:14p	1:41p

a = a.m.; p = p.m.; m = midnight; n = noon

Date	♈ ARI	♉ TAU	♊ GEM	♋ CAN	♌ LEO	♍ VIR	♎ LIB	♏ SCO	♐ SAG	♑ CAP	♒ AQU	♓ PIS
Nov. 9	2:51p	4:02p	5:29p	7:24p	9:45p	12:21a	2:52a	5:22a	7:54a	10:15a	12:10p	1:37p
Nov. 10	2:47p	3:58p	5:25p	7:20p	9:41p	12:17a	2:48a	5:18a	7:50a	10:11a	12:06p	1:33p
Nov. 11	2:43p	3:54p	5:21p	7:16p	9:37p	12:13a	2:44a	5:14a	7:46a	10:07a	12:02p	1:29p
Nov. 12	2:39p	3:50p	5:17p	7:12p	9:33p	12:09a	2:40a	5:10a	7:42a	10:03a	11:58a	1:25p
Nov. 13	2:35p	3:46p	5:13p	7:08p	9:29p	12:05a	2:36a	5:06a	7:38a	9:59a	11:54a	1:21p
						12:01a						
Nov. 14	2:31p	3:42p	5:09p	7:04p	9:25p	11:57p	2:32a	5:02a	7:34a	9:55a	11:50a	1:17p
Nov. 15	2:27p	3:38p	5:05p	7:00p	9:21p	11:53p	2:28a	4:58a	7:30a	9:51a	11:46a	1:13p
Nov. 16	2:23p	3:34p	5:01p	6:56p	9:17p	11:49p	2:24a	4:54a	7:26a	9:47a	11:42a	1:09p
Nov. 17	2:19p	3:30p	4:57p	6:52p	9:14p	11:45p	2:20a	4:50a	7:22a	9:43a	11:38a	1:05p
Nov. 18	2:15p	3:27p	4:53p	6:48p	9:10p	11:41p	2:16a	4:46a	7:18a	9:39a	11:34a	1:01p
Nov. 19	2:11p	3:23p	4:49p	6:44p	9:06p	11:37p	2:12a	4:42a	7:14a	9:35a	11:30a	12:57p
Nov. 20	2:07p	3:19p	4:45p	6:40p	9:02p	11:33p	2:08a	4:38a	7:10a	9:31a	11:26a	12:53p
Nov. 21	2:03p	3:19p	4:41p	6:36p	8:58p	11:29p	2:04a	4:34a	7:06a	9:27a	11:22a	12:49p
Nov. 22	1:59p	3:11p	4:37p	6:32p	8:54p	11:25p	2:00a	4:30a	7:02a	9:23a	11:18a	12:45p
Nov. 23	1:55p	3:07p	4:33p	6:28p	8:50p	11:21p	1:56a	4:26a	6:58a	9:19a	11:14a	12:41p
Nov. 24	1:51p	3:03p	4:29p	6:24p	8:46p	11:17p	1:52a	4:19a	6:51a	9:12a	11:07a	12:34p
Nov. 25	1:48p	3:00p	4:26p	6:21p	8:43p	11:14p	1:48a	4:15a	6:47a	9:08a	11:03a	12:30p
Nov. 26	1:44p	2:56p	4:22p	6:17p	8:39p	11:10p	1:41a	4:11a	6:43a	9:04a	10:59a	12:26p
Nov. 27	1:40p	2:52p	4:18p	6:13p	8:35p	11:06p	1:37a	4:07a	6:39a	9:00a	10:55a	12:22p
Nov. 28	1:36p	2:48p	4:14p	6:09p	8:31p	11:02p	1:33a	4:03a	6:35a	8:56a	10:51a	12:18p
Nov. 29	1:32p	2:44p	4:10p	6:05p	8:27p	10:58p	1:33a	4:03a	6:35a	8:56a	10:51a	12:18p
Nov. 30	1:28p	2:40p	4:06p	6:01p	8:23p	10:54p	1:29a	3:59a	6:31a	8:52a	10:47a	12:14p
Dec. 1	1:24p	2:36p	4:02p	5:57p	8:19p	10:50p	1:25a	3:55a	6:27a	8:48a	10:43a	12:10p
Dec. 2	1:20p	2:32p	3:58p	5:53p	8:15p	10:46p	1:21a	3:51a	6:23a	8:45a	10:39a	12:06p
Dec. 3	1:16p	2:28p	3:54p	5:49p	8:11p	10:42p	1:17a	3:47a	6:19a	8:41a	10:35a	12:02p
Dec. 4	1:12p	2:24p	3:50p	5:45p	8:07p	10:38p	1:13a	3:44a	6:15a	8:37a	10:31a	11:58a
Dec. 5	1:08p	2:20p	3:46p	5:41p	8:03p	10:34p	1:09a	3:40a	6:11a	8:33a	10:27a	11:54a
Dec. 6	1:04p	2:16p	3:42p	5:37p	7:59p	10:30p	1:05a	3:36a	6:07a	8:29a	10:23a	11:50a
Dec. 7	1:00p	2:12p	3:38p	5:33p	7:55p	10:26p	1:01a	3:32a	6:03a	8:25a	10:19a	11:46a
Dec. 8	12:56p	2:08p	3:34p	5:29p	7:51p	10:22p	12:57a	3:28a	5:59a	8:21a	10:15a	11:42a
Dec. 9	12:52p	2:04p	3:30p	5:25p	7:47p	10:18p	12:53a	3:24a	5:55a	8:17a	10:11a	11:38a
Dec. 10	12:48p	2:00p	3:26p	5:21p	7:43p	10:14p	12:49a	3:20a	5:51a	8:13a	10:07a	11:34a
Dec. 11	12:44p	1:56p	3:22p	5:17p	7:39p	10:10p	12:45a	3:16a	5:47a	8:09a	10:03a	11:30a
Dec. 12	12:41p	1:53p	3:19p	5:14p	7:36p	10:07p	12:41a	3:13a	5:44a	8:06a	10:00a	11:27a
Dec. 13	12:37p	1:49p	3:15p	5:10p	7:32p	10:03p	12:38a	3:09a	5:40a	8:02a	9:56a	11:23a
Dec. 14	12:33p	1:45p	3:11p	5:06p	7:28p	9:59p	12:34a	3:05a	5:36a	7:58a	9:52a	11:19a
Dec. 15	12:29p	1:41p	3:07p	5:02p	7:24p	9:55p	12:30a	3:01a	5:32a	7:54a	9:48a	11:15a
Dec. 16	12:25p	1:37p	3:03p	4:58p	7:20p	9:51p	12:26a	2:53a	5:24a	7:46a	9:40a	11:07a
Dec. 17	12:21p	1:33p	3:00p	4:54p	7:16p	9:47p	12:22a	2:49a	5:20a	7:42a	9:36a	11:03a
Dec. 18	12:17p	1:29p	2:56p	4:50p	7:12p	9:43p	12:18a	2:45a	5:16a	7:38a	9:32a	10:59a
Dec. 19	12:13p	1:25p	2:52p	4:46p	7:08p	9:39p	12:14a	2:41a	5:12a	7:34a	9:28a	10:55a
Dec. 20	12:09p	1:21p	2:48p	4:42p	7:04p	9:35p	12:10a	2:41a	5:12a	7:34a	9:28a	10:55a

a = a.m.; p = p.m.; m = midnight; n = noon

(Continued)

Table B–3. Continued

Date	♈ ARI	♉ TAU	♊ GEM	♋ CAN	♌ LEO	♍ VIR	♎ LIB	♏ SCO	♐ SAG	♑ CAP	♒ AQU	♓ PIS
Dec. 21	12:05p	1:17p	2:44p	4:38p	7:00p	9:31p	12:06a / 12:02a	2:37a	5:08a	7:30a	9:24a	10:51a
Dec. 22	12:01p	1:13p	2:40p	4:34p	6:56p	9:27p	11:58p	2:33a	5:04a	7:26a	9:21a	10:47a
Dec. 23	11:57a	1:09p	2:36p	4:30p	6:52p	9:24p	11:54p	2:29a	5:00a	7:22a	9:17a	10:43a
Dec. 24	11:53a	1:05p	2:32p	4:26p	6:48p	9:20p	11:50p	2:25a	4:56a	7:18a	9:13a	10:39a
Dec. 25	11:49a	1:01p	2:28p	4:22p	6:44p	9:16p	11:46p	2:21a	4:52a	7:14a	9:09a	10:35a
Dec. 26	11:45a	12:57p	2:24p	4:18p	6:40p	9:12p	11:42p	2:17a	4:48a	7:10a	9:05a	10:31a
Dec. 27	11:41a	12:53p	2:20p	4:14p	6:36p	9:08p	11:38p	2:13a	4:44a	7:06a	9:01a	10:27a
Dec. 28	11:37a	12:49p	2:16p	4:10p	6:32p	9:04p	11:34p	2:09a	4:40a	7:02a	8:57a	10:23a
Dec. 29	11:33a	12:45p	2:12p	4:06p	6:28p	9:00p	11:30p	2:05a	4:36a	6:58a	8:53a	10:19a
Dec. 30	11:29a	12:41p	2:08p	4:02p	6:24p	8:56p	11:26p	2:01a	4:32a	6:54a	8:49a	10:15a
Dec. 31	11:26a	12:38p	2:05p	3:59p	6:21p	8:53p	11:23p	1:58a	4:29a	6:51a	8:46a	10:12a

a = a.m.; p = p.m.; m = midnight; n = noon

Table B–4. Adjustment of Rising Sign According to Place (in Minutes)

Place	♈ ARI	♉ TAU	♊ GEM	♋ CAN	♌ LEO	♍ VIR	♎ LIB	♏ SCO	♐ SAG	♑ CAP	♒ AQU	♓ PIS
Alabama												
Anniston	−17	−9	−2	+2	−2	−9	−17	−25	−32	−36	−32	−25
Birmingham	−13	−5	+2	+6	+2	−5	−13	−21	−28	−32	−28	−21
Dothan	−18	−7	+2	+7	+2	−7	−18	−29	−38	−43	−38	−29
Florence	−9	−2	+4	+6	+4	−2	−9	−16	−22	−24	−22	−16
Gadsden	−16	−8	−2	+2	−2	−8	−16	−24	−30	−33	−30	−24
Huntsville	−14	−7	−1	+1	−1	−7	−14	−21	−27	−29	−27	−21
Mobile	−8	+3	+13	+17	+13	+3	−8	−19	−29	−33	−29	−19
Montgomery	−15	−6	+3	+6	+3	−6	−15	−24	−33	−36	−33	−24
Selma	−12	−3	+6	+9	+6	−3	−12	−21	−30	−33	−30	−21
Tuscaloosa	−10	−1	+6	+10	+6	−1	−10	−19	−26	−30	−26	−19
Alaska												
Anchorage	−2	−49	−95	−123	−95	−49	−2	+45	+91	+119	+91	+45
Fairbanks	−10	−78	−144	−188	−144	−78	−10	+58	+124	+168	+124	+58
Juneau	+57	+20	−17	−36	−17	+20	+57	+94	+131	+150	+131	+94
Ketchikan	+45	+16	−9	−28	−9	+16	+45	+74	+99	+118	+99	+74
Nome	+1	−64	−129	−171	−129	−64	+1	+66	+131	+173	+131	+66
Yakutat	+18	−23	−64	−87	−64	−23	+18	+59	+100	+123	+100	+59

124

Place	♈ ARI	♉ TAU	♊ GEM	♋ CAN	♌ LEO	♍ VIR	♎ LIB	♏ SCO	♐ SAG	♑ CAP	♒ AQU	♓ PIS
Arizona												
Flagstaff	+26	+32	+38	+40	+38	+32	+26	+20	+14	+12	+14	+20
Phoenix	+27	+35	+43	+46	+43	+35	+27	+19	+11	+8	+11	+19
Prescott	+29	+36	+42	+45	+42	+36	+29	+22	+16	+13	+16	+22
Tucson	+23	+33	+42	+45	+42	+33	+23	+13	+4	+1	+4	+13
Yuma	+37	+46	+54	+57	+54	+46	+37	+28	+20	+17	+20	+28
Arkansas												
Blytheville	0	+5	+10	+12	+10	+5	0	−5	−10	−12	−10	−5
El Dorado	+11	+20	+27	+31	+27	+20	+11	+2	−5	−9	−5	+2
Fayetteville	+17	+22	+26	+29	+26	+22	+17	+12	+8	+5	+8	+12
Fort Smith	+18	+24	+29	+31	+29	+24	+18	+12	+7	+5	+7	+12
Little Rock	+9	+16	+22	+25	+22	+16	+9	+2	−4	−7	−4	+2
Pine Bluff	+8	+16	+22	+25	+22	+16	+8	0	−6	−9	−6	0
Texarkana	+16	+24	+32	+35	+32	+24	+16	+8	0	−3	0	+8
California												
Anaheim	−10	−2	+5	+8	+5	−2	−10	−18	−25	−28	−25	−18
Bakersfield	−5	+1	+6	+8	+6	+1	−5	−11	−16	−18	−16	−11
Barstow	−13	−6	−1	+2	−1	−6	−13	−20	−25	−28	−25	−20
Concord	+7	+10	+12	+13	+12	+10	+7	+4	+2	+1	+2	+4
El Centro	−19	−10	−2	+1	−2	−10	−19	−28	−36	−39	−36	−28
Eureka	+16	+15	+14	+13	+14	+15	+16	+17	+18	+19	+18	+17
Fremont	+7	+10	+13	+15	+13	+10	−2	−6	−10	−12	−10	−6
Fresno	−2	+2	+6	+8	+6	+2	−2	−6	−10	−12	−10	−6
Glendale	−8	−1	+6	+9	+6	−1	−8	−15	−22	−25	−22	−15
Long Beach	−8	0	+7	+10	+7	0	−8	−16	−23	−26	−23	−16
Los Angeles	−8	0	+6	+9	+6	0	−8	−16	−22	−25	−22	−16
Modesto	+3	+6	+9	+10	+9	+6	+3	0	−3	−4	−3	0
Oakland	+8	+11	+13	+14	+13	+11	+8	+5	+3	+2	+3	+5
Pasadena	−8	−1	+6	+9	+6	−1	−8	−15	−22	−25	−22	−15
Pomona	−10	−2	+4	+7	+4	−2	−10	−18	−24	−27	−24	−18
Redding	+9	+8	+7	+6	+7	+8	+9	+10	+11	+12	+11	+10
Redwood City	+8	+11	+14	+16	+14	+11	+8	+5	+2	0	+2	+5
Richmond	+8	+11	+13	+14	+13	+11	+8	+5	+3	+2	+3	+5
Riverside	−11	−3	+3	+6	+3	−3	−11	−19	−25	−28	−25	−19
Sacramento	+5	+7	+8	+9	+8	+7	+5	+3	+2	+1	+2	+3
Salinas	+6	+10	+14	+16	+14	+10	+6	+2	−2	−4	−2	+2
San Diego	−12	−3	+5	+9	+5	−3	−12	−21	−29	−33	−29	−21
San Francisco	+9	+12	+14	+15	+14	+12	+9	+6	+4	+3	+4	+6
San Jose	+7	+11	+14	+15	+14	+11	+7	+3	0	−1	0	+3
Santa Barbara	−2	+5	+11	+14	+11	+5	−2	−9	−15	−18	−15	−9
Santa Cruz	+7	+11	+15	+16	+15	+11	+7	+3	−1	−2	−1	+3

(Continued)

125

Table B–4. *Continued*

Place	♈ ARI	♉ TAU	♊ GEM	♋ CAN	♌ LEO	♍ VIR	♎ LIB	♏ SCO	♐ SAG	♑ CAP	♒ AQU	♓ PIS
Santa Monica	−7	+1	+7	+10	+7	+1	−7	−15	−21	−24	−21	−15
Santa Rosa	+10	+12	+14	+15	+14	+12	+10	+8	+6	+5	+6	+8
Stockton	+4	+7	+9	+10	+9	+7	+4	+1	−1	−2	−1	+1
Vallejo	+8	+11	+13	+14	+13	+11	+8	+5	+3	+2	+3	+8
Ventura	−4	+3	+10	+13	+10	+3	−4	−11	−18	−21	−18	−11
Colorado												
Boulder	+1	+1	+1	+1	+1	+1	+1	+1	+1	+1	+1	+1
Colorado Springs	−1	+1	+2	+3	+2	+1	−1	−3	−4	−5	−4	−3
Craig	+10	+9	+9	+8	+9	+9	+10	+11	+11	+12	+11	+11
Denver	0	0	0	+1	0	0	0	0	0	−1	0	0
Durango	+11	+14	+18	+19	+18	+14	+11	+8	+4	+3	+4	+8
Fort Collins	0	−1	−2	−3	−2	−1	0	+1	+2	+3	+2	+1
Grand Junction	+14	+15	+16	+17	+16	+15	+14	+13	+12	+11	+12	+13
Lamar	−10	−7	−5	−4	−5	−7	−10	−13	−15	−16	−15	−13
Pueblo	−2	0	+2	+3	+2	0	−2	−4	−6	−7	−6	−4
Sterling	−7	−8	−9	−10	−9	−8	−7	−6	−5	−4	−5	−6
Trinidad	−2	+2	+5	+7	+5	+2	−2	−6	−9	−11	−9	−6
Connecticut												
Bridgeport	−7	−8	−10	−11	−10	−8	−7	−6	−4	−3	−4	−6
Danbury	−6	−8	−10	−11	−10	−8	−6	−4	−2	−1	−2	−4
Hartford	−9	−12	−14	−15	−14	−12	−9	−6	−4	−3	−4	−6
New Haven	−8	−10	−11	−12	−11	−10	−8	−6	−5	−4	−5	−6
New London	−12	−14	−16	−17	−16	−14	−12	−10	−8	−7	−8	−10
Plainfield	−12	−14	−17	−18	−17	−14	−12	−10	−7	−6	−7	−10
Stamford	−6	−7	−9	−9	−9	−7	−6	−5	−3	−3	−3	−5
Waterbury	−8	−10	−13	−14	−13	−10	−8	−6	−3	−2	−3	−6
Delaware												
Dover	+2	+3	+4	+5	+4	+3	+2	+1	0	−1	0	+1
Georgetown	+2	+4	+5	+6	+5	+4	+2	0	−1	−2	−1	0
Wilmington	+2	+2	+2	+3	+2	+2	+2	+2	+2	+1	+2	+2
District of Columbia												
Washington	+8	+9	+10	+11	+10	+9	+8	+7	+6	+5	+6	+7
Florida												
Daytona Beach	+24	+37	+48	+53	+48	+37	+24	+11	0	−5	0	+11
Fort Lauderdale	+21	+37	+51	+57	+51	+37	+21	+15	−9	−15	−9	+15
Gainesville	+29	+42	+52	+57	+52	+42	+29	+17	+6	+1	+6	+17
Jacksonville	+27	+39	+49	+54	+49	+39	+27	+15	+5	0	+5	+15
Key West	+27	+45	+61	+67	+61	+45	+27	+9	−7	−13	−7	+9
Miami	+21	+39	+54	+60	+54	+39	+21	+3	−12	−18	−12	+3

Place	♈ ARI	♉ TAU	♊ GEM	♋ CAN	♌ LEO	♍ VIR	♎ LIB	♏ SCO	♐ SAG	♑ CAP	♒ AQU	♓ PIS
Orlando	+26	+40	+52	+57	+52	+40	+26	+12	0	−5	0	+12
Panama City	−17	−5	+5	+10	+5	−5	−17	−29	−39	−44	−39	−29
Pensacola	−11	+1	+11	+16	+11	+1	−11	−23	−33	−38	−33	−23
Saint Petersburg	+31	+46	+58	+64	+58	+46	+31	+16	+4	−2	+4	+16
Tallahassee	+37	+49	+59	+64	+59	+49	+37	+25	+15	+10	+15	+25
Tampa	+30	+45	+57	+62	+57	+45	+30	+15	+3	−2	+3	+15
West Palm Beach	+20	+36	+49	+55	+49	+36	+20	+4	−9	−15	−9	+4
Georgia												
Albany	+37	+47	+56	+60	+56	+47	+37	+27	+18	+14	+18	+27
Atlanta	+38	+46	+53	+56	+53	+46	+38	+30	+23	+20	+23	+30
Augusta	+28	+36	+43	+47	+43	+36	+28	+20	+13	+9	+13	+20
Columbus	+40	+49	+58	+61	+58	+49	+40	+31	+22	+19	+22	+31
Macon	+35	+44	+52	+55	+52	+44	+35	+26	+18	+15	+18	+26
Savannah	+24	+34	+42	+47	+42	+34	+24	+14	+6	+1	+6	+14
Valdosta	+33	+44	+54	+58	+54	+44	+33	+22	+12	+8	+12	+22
Hawaii												
Hilo	+20	+43	+61	+69	+61	+43	+20	−3	−21	−29	−21	−3
Honolulu	+31	+52	+70	+78	+70	+52	+31	+10	−8	−16	−8	+10
Lihue	+37	+57	+75	+82	+75	+57	+37	+17	−1	−8	−1	+17
Wailuku	+26	+47	+65	+74	+65	+47	+26	+5	−13	−22	−13	+5
Idaho												
Boise	+45	+39	+35	+33	+35	+39	+45	+51	+55	+57	+55	+51
Coeur d'Alene	−13	−25	−37	−42	−37	−25	−13	−1	+11	+16	+11	−1
Grangeville	−15	−24	−33	−36	−33	−24	−15	−6	+3	+6	+3	−6
Idaho Falls	+28	+23	+19	+16	+19	+23	+28	+33	+37	+40	+37	+33
Lewiston	−12	−22	−31	−35	−31	−22	−12	−2	+7	+11	+7	−2
Pocatello	+30	+26	+22	+20	+22	+26	+30	+34	+38	+40	+38	+34
Twin Falls	+38	+34	+31	+30	+31	+34	+38	+42	+45	+46	+45	+42
illinois												
Aurora	−7	−10	−12	−13	−12	−10	−7	−4	−2	−1	−2	−4
Champaign	−7	−7	−7	−7	−7	−7	−7	−7	−7	−7	−7	−7
Chicago	−9	−12	−14	−16	−14	−12	−9	−6	−4	−2	−4	−6
Decatur	−4	−4	−4	−4	−4	−4	−4	−4	−4	−4	−4	−4
East Saint Louis	+1	+3	+4	+5	+4	+3	+1	−1	−2	−3	−2	−1
Joliet	−8	−10	−13	−14	−13	−10	−8	−6	−3	−2	−3	−6
Mount Vernon	−4	−2	0	+1	0	−2	−4	−6	−8	−9	−8	−6
Peoria	−2	−3	−4	−5	−4	−3	−2	−1	0	+1	0	−1
Rockford	−4	−7	−10	−11	−10	−7	−4	−1	+2	+3	+2	−1
Springfield	−1	−1	−1	−1	−1	−1	−1	−1	−1	−1	−1	−1
Waukegan	−9	−12	−15	−16	−15	−12	−9	−6	−3	−2	−3	−6

(Continued)

Table B–4. Continued

Place	♈ ARI	♉ TAU	♊ GEM	♋ CAN	♌ LEO	♍ VIR	♎ LIB	♏ SCO	♐ SAG	♑ CAP	♒ AQU	♓ PIS
Indiana												
Anderson	+43	+43	+43	+43	+43	+43	+43	+43	+43	+43	+43	+43
Bloomington	+46	+47	+48	+49	+48	+47	+46	+45	+44	+43	+44	+45
Evansville	−10	−7	−5	−4	−5	−7	−10	−13	−15	−16	−15	−13
Fort Wayne	+41	+40	+38	+38	+38	+40	+41	+42	+44	+44	+44	+42
Gary	−14	−16	−19	−20	−19	−16	−14	−12	−9	−8	−9	−12
Indianapolis	+45	+45	+45	+46	+45	+45	+45	+45	+45	+44	+45	+45
Muncie	+42	+42	+42	+41	+42	+42	+42	+42	+42	+43	+42	+42
South Bend	+45	+43	+40	+39	+40	+43	+45	+47	+50	+51	+50	+47
Terre Haute	+50	+51	+51	+52	+51	+51	+50	+49	+49	+48	+49	+49
Iowa												
Cedar Rapids	+7	+4	+2	0	+2	+4	+7	+10	+12	+14	+12	+10
Council Bluffs	+23	+21	+20	+19	+20	+21	+23	+25	+26	+27	+26	+25
Davenport	+2	0	−2	−3	−2	0	+2	+4	+6	+7	+6	+4
Des Moines	+15	+13	+10	+9	+10	+13	+15	+17	+20	+21	+20	+17
Dubuque	+3	−1	−4	−5	−4	−1	+3	+7	+10	+11	+10	+7
Fort Dodge	+17	+13	+10	+9	+10	+13	+17	+21	+24	+25	+24	+21
Sioux City	+26	+22	+19	+18	+19	+22	+26	+30	+33	+34	+33	+30
Waterloo	+9	+5	+2	+1	+2	+5	+9	+13	+16	+17	+16	+13
Kansas												
Dodge City	+40	+43	+45	+46	+45	+43	+40	+37	+35	+34	+35	+37
Emporia	+25	+27	+29	+30	+29	+27	+25	+23	+21	+20	+21	+23
Garden City	+44	+47	+49	+50	+49	+47	+44	+41	+39	+38	+39	+41
Goodland	−13	−12	−11	−10	−11	−12	−13	−14	−15	−16	−15	−14
Great Bend	+35	+37	+39	+40	+39	+37	+35	+33	+31	+30	+31	+33
Kansas City	+19	+20	+21	+22	+21	+20	+19	+18	+17	+16	+17	+18
Manhattan	+26	+27	+28	+29	+28	+27	+26	+25	+24	+23	+24	+25
Mankato	+33	+33	+33	+34	+33	+33	+33	+33	+33	+32	+33	+33
Syracuse	−13	−10	−8	−7	−8	−10	−13	−16	−18	−19	−18	−16
Topeka	+23	+24	+25	+26	+25	+24	+23	+22	+21	+20	+21	+22
Wichita	+29	+32	+35	+36	+35	+32	+29	+26	+23	+22	+23	+26
Kentucky												
Covington	+38	+39	+40	+41	+40	+39	+38	+37	+36	+35	+36	+37
Hazard	+33	+37	+40	+42	+40	+37	+33	+29	+26	+24	+26	+29
Lexington	+38	+41	+43	+44	+43	+41	+38	+35	+33	+32	+33	+35
Louisville	+43	+45	+47	+48	+47	+45	+43	+41	+39	+38	+39	+41
Owensboro	−12	−9	−7	−6	−7	−9	−12	−15	−17	−18	−17	−15
Paducah	−6	−2	+1	+3	+1	−2	−6	−10	−13	−15	−13	−10
Somerset	+38	+42	+45	+47	+45	+42	+38	+34	+31	+29	+31	+34

Place	♈ ARI	♉ TAU	♊ GEM	♋ CAN	♌ LEO	♍ VIR	♎ LIB	♏ SCO	♐ SAG	♑ CAP	♒ AQU	♓ PIS
Louisiana												
Alexandria	+10	+21	+30	+34	+30	+21	+10	−1	−10	−14	−10	−1
Baton Rouge	+5	+17	+27	+31	+27	+17	+5	−7	−17	−21	−17	−7
Houma	+3	+15	+26	+31	+26	+15	+3	−9	−20	−25	−20	−9
Lafayette	+8	+20	+30	+35	+30	+20	+8	−4	−14	−19	−14	−4
Lake Charles	+13	+25	+35	+40	+35	+25	+13	+1	−9	−14	−9	+1
Monroe	+8	+20	+30	+34	+30	+20	+8	−4	−14	−18	−14	−4
New Orleans	0	+12	+23	+27	+23	+12	0	−12	−23	−27	−23	−12
Shreveport	+15	+24	+33	+36	+33	+24	+15	+6	−3	−6	−3	+6
Maine												
Augusta	−21	−27	−33	−35	−33	−27	−21	−15	−9	−7	−9	−15
Bangor	−25	−32	−39	−42	−39	−32	−25	−18	−11	−8	−11	−18
Eastport	−32	−40	−46	−50	−46	−40	−32	−24	−18	−14	−18	−24
Houlton	−29	−38	−47	−51	−47	−38	−29	−20	−11	−7	−11	−20
Millinocket	−25	−34	−42	−45	−42	−34	−25	−16	−8	−5	−8	−16
Portland	−19	−24	−29	−32	−29	−24	−19	−14	−9	−6	−9	−14
Presque Isle	−28	−38	−47	−52	−47	−39	−28	−18	−9	−4	−9	−18
Skowhegan	−21	−28	−35	−38	−35	−28	−21	−14	−7	−4	−7	−14
Maryland												
Annapolis	+6	+6	+6	+6	+6	+6	+6	+6	+6	+6	+6	+6
Baltimore	+7	+8	+9	+10	+9	+8	+7	+6	+5	+4	+5	+6
Bethesda	+9	+10	+11	+12	+11	+10	+9	+8	+7	+6	+7	+8
Cumberland	+15	+15	+16	+16	+16	+15	+15	+15	+14	+14	+14	+15
Frederick	+10	+11	+12	+12	+12	+11	+10	+9	+8	+8	+8	+9
Hagerstown	+11	+11	+12	+12	+12	+11	+11	+11	+10	+10	+10	+11
Salisbury	+2	+4	+6	+7	+6	+4	+2	0	−2	−3	−2	0
Massachusetts												
Boston	−16	−19	−22	−24	−22	−19	−16	−13	−10	−8	−10	−13
Brockton	−16	−19	−22	−23	−22	−19	−16	−13	−10	−9	−10	−13
Fall River	−15	−17	−20	−21	−20	−17	−15	−13	−10	−9	−10	−13
Hyannis	−19	−21	−24	−25	−24	−21	−19	−17	−14	−13	−14	−17
Lowell	−15	−19	−22	−24	−22	−19	−15	−11	−8	−6	−8	−11
New Bedford	−16	−18	−20	−21	−20	−18	−16	−14	−12	−11	−12	−14
Pittsfield	−7	−11	−14	−16	−14	−11	−7	−3	0	+2	0	−3
Springfield	−10	−13	−16	−17	−16	−13	−10	−7	−4	−3	−4	−7
Worcester	−13	−16	−19	−21	−19	−16	−13	−10	−7	−5	−7	−10
Michigan												
Ann Arbor	+35	+32	+29	+27	+29	+32	+35	+38	+41	+43	+41	+38

(Continued)

129

Table B–4. *Continued*

Place	♈ ARI	♉ TAU	♊ GEM	♋ CAN	♌ LEO	♍ VIR	♎ LIB	♏ SCO	♐ SAG	♑ CAP	♒ AQU	♓ PIS
Detroit	+32	+29	+26	+24	+26	+29	+32	+35	+38	+40	+38	+35
Flint	+35	+31	+27	+25	+27	+31	+35	+39	+43	+45	+43	+39
Grand Rapids	+43	+39	+35	+33	+35	+39	+43	+47	+51	+53	+51	+47
Kalamazoo	+42	+39	+36	+34	+36	+39	+42	+45	+48	+50	+48	+45
Lansing	+38	+34	+30	+29	+30	+34	+38	+42	+46	+47	+46	+42
Marquette	+50	+40	+30	+26	+30	+40	+50	+60	+70	+74	+70	+60
Pontiac	+33	+29	+26	+24	+26	+29	+33	+37	+40	+42	+40	+37
Saginaw	+36	+31	+27	+25	+27	+31	+36	+41	+45	+47	+45	+41
Sault Sainte Marie	+37	+27	+17	+13	+17	+27	+37	+47	+57	+61	+57	+47
Traverse City	+42	+35	+28	+25	+28	+35	+42	+49	+56	+59	+56	+49
Minnesota												
Albert Lea	+13	+8	+3	0	+3	+8	+13	+18	+23	+26	+23	+18
Bemidji	+20	+8	−3	−7	−3	+8	+20	+32	+43	+47	+43	+32
Duluth	+8	−3	−13	−17	−13	−3	+8	+19	+29	+33	+29	+19
Marshall	+23	+16	+10	+7	+10	+16	+23	+30	+36	+39	+36	+30
Minneapolis	+13	+5	−1	−5	−1	+5	+13	+21	+27	+31	+27	+21
Saint Cloud	+17	+8	+1	−3	+1	+8	+17	+26	+33	+37	+33	+26
Saint Paul	+12	+4	−2	−5	−2	+4	+12	+20	+26	+29	+26	+20
Mississippi												
Biloxi	−4	+8	+18	+23	+18	+8	−4	−16	−26	−31	−26	−16
Columbus	−6	+2	+9	+13	+9	+2	−6	−14	−21	−25	−21	−14
Greenville	+4	+12	+20	+23	+20	+12	+4	−4	−12	−15	−12	−4
Hattiesburg	−3	+8	+17	+21	+17	+8	−3	−14	−23	−27	−23	−14
Jackson	+1	+10	+19	+23	+19	+10	+1	−8	−17	−21	−17	−8
Meridian	−5	+5	+13	+17	+13	+5	−5	−15	−23	−27	−23	−15
Natchez	+6	+16	+25	+29	+25	+16	+6	−4	−13	−17	−13	−4
Oxford	−2	+5	+11	+14	+11	+5	−2	−9	−15	−18	−15	−9
Vicksburg	+4	+13	+22	+25	+22	+13	+4	−5	−14	−17	−14	−5
Missouri												
Cape Girardeau	−2	+2	+5	+6	+5	+2	−2	−6	−9	−10	−9	−6
Columbia	+9	+10	+11	+12	+11	+10	+9	+8	+7	+6	+7	+8
Jefferson City	+9	+11	+12	+13	+12	+11	+9	+7	+6	+5	+6	+7
Joplin	+18	+22	+25	+27	+25	+22	+18	+14	+11	+9	+11	+14
Kansas City	+19	+20	+21	+22	+21	+20	+19	+18	+17	+16	+17	+18
Kirksville	+10	+10	+9	+9	+9	+10	+10	+10	+11	+11	+11	+10
Saint Joseph	+19	+19	+19	+20	+19	+19	+19	+19	+19	+18	+19	+19
Saint Louis	+1	+3	+4	+5	+4	+3	+1	−1	−2	−3	−2	−1
Springfield	+13	+17	+20	+22	+20	+17	+13	+9	+6	+4	+6	+9
Montana												
Billings	+14	+5	−3	−7	−3	+5	+14	+23	+31	+35	+31	+23

Place	♈ ARI	♉ TAU	♊ GEM	♋ CAN	♌ LEO	♍ VIR	♎ LIB	♏ SCO	♐ SAG	♑ CAP	♒ AQU	♓ PIS
Bozeman	+24	+15	+8	+4	+8	+15	+24	+33	+40	+44	+40	+33
Butte	+30	+21	+12	+9	+12	+21	+30	+39	+48	+51	+48	+39
Glendive	−1	−12	−22	−27	−22	−12	−1	+10	+20	+25	+20	+10
Great Falls	+25	+13	+2	−3	+2	+13	+25	+37	+48	+53	+48	+37
Havre	+19	+5	−9	−14	−9	+5	+19	+33	+47	+52	+47	+33
Kalispell	+37	+24	+12	+6	+12	+24	+37	+50	+62	+68	+62	+50
Missoula	+36	+25	+15	+11	+15	+25	+36	+47	+57	+61	+57	+47
Nebraska												
Chadron	−8	−12	−16	−17	−16	−12	−8	−4	0	+1	0	−4
Columbus	+29	+27	+25	+24	+25	+27	+29	+31	+33	+34	+33	+31
Grand Island	+33	+32	+30	+30	+30	+32	+33	+34	+36	+36	+36	+34
Lincoln	+27	+26	+25	+24	+25	+26	+27	+28	+29	+30	+29	+28
McCook	+43	+43	+42	+41	+42	+43	+43	+43	+44	+45	+44	+43
North Platte	+43	+42	+41	+40	+41	+42	+43	+44	+45	+46	+45	+44
Omaha	+24	+22	+20	+19	+20	+22	+24	+26	+28	+29	+28	+26
Scottsbluff	−5	−8	−10	−11	−10	−8	−5	−2	0	+1	0	−2
Nevada												
Carson City	−2	−1	0	+1	0	−4	−2	−3	−4	−5	−4	−3
Elko	−18	−19	−20	−21	−20	−19	−18	−17	−16	−15	−16	−17
Ely	−21	−20	−19	−18	−19	−20	−21	−22	−23	−24	−23	−22
Las Vegas	−20	−15	−11	−8	−11	−15	−20	−25	−29	−32	−29	−25
Reno	−2	−1	−1	0	−1	−1	−2	−3	−3	−4	−3	−3
Tonopah	−12	−9	−7	−6	−7	−9	−12	−15	−17	−18	−17	−15
Winnemucca	−14	−15	−16	−17	−16	−15	−14	−13	−12	−11	−12	−13
New Hampshire												
Berlin	−15	−22	−28	−31	−28	−22	−15	−8	−2	+1	−2	−8
Concord	−14	−19	−22	−24	−22	−19	−14	−9	−6	−4	−6	−9
Keene	−11	−15	−19	−21	−19	−15	−11	−7	−3	−1	−3	−7
Manchester	−14	−18	−22	−24	−22	−18	−14	−10	−6	−4	−6	−10
Nashua	−14	−18	−22	−23	−22	−18	−14	−10	−6	−5	−6	−10
Portsmouth	−17	−21	−25	−27	−25	−21	−17	−13	−9	−7	−9	−13
New Jersey												
Atlantic City	−2	−1	0	+1	0	−1	−2	−3	−4	−5	−4	−3
Camden	0	0	0	0	0	0	0	0	0	0	0	0
Jersey City	−4	−5	−6	−7	−6	−5	−4	−3	−2	−1	−2	−3
Newark	−3	−4	−5	−6	−5	−4	−3	−2	−1	0	−1	−1
New Brunswick	−2	−3	−3	−4	−3	−3	−2	−1	−1	0	−1	−2
Paterson	−3	−4	−6	−6	−6	−4	−3	−2	0	0	0	−2
Phillipsburg	+1	0	−1	−2	−1	0	+1	+2	+3	+4	+3	+2
Trenton	−1	−1	−2	−3	−2	−1	−1	−1	0	+1	0	−1

(Continued)

Place	♈ ARI	♉ TAU	♊ GEM	♋ CAN	♌ LEO	♍ VIR	♎ LIB	♏ SCO	♐ SAG	♑ CAP	♒ AQU	♓ PIS
Vineland	0	+1	+1	+2	+1	+1	0	−1	−1	−2	−1	−1
New Mexico												
Alamogordo	+4	+13	+20	+24	+20	+13	+4	−5	−12	−16	−12	−5
Albuquerque	+7	+13	+19	+21	+19	+13	+7	+1	−5	−7	−5	+1
Clovis	−7	0	+7	+9	+7	0	−7	−14	−21	−23	−21	−14
Farmington	+12	+16	+20	+22	+20	+16	+12	+8	+4	+2	+4	+8
Gallup	+15	+21	+26	+28	+26	+21	+15	+9	+4	+2	+4	+9
Las Cruces	+7	+17	+25	+29	+25	+17	+7	−3	−11	−15	−11	−3
Roswell	−2	+6	+14	+17	+14	+6	−2	−10	−18	−21	−18	−10
Santa Fe	+4	+10	+15	+16	+15	+10	+4	−2	−7	−8	−7	−2
New York												
Albany	−5	−9	−12	−14	−12	−9	−5	−1	+2	+4	+2	−1
Binghamton	+4	+1	−2	−3	−2	+1	+4	+7	+10	+11	+10	+7
Buffalo	+16	+12	+8	+6	+8	+12	+16	+20	+24	+26	+24	+20
Elmira	+7	+4	+1	0	+1	+4	+7	+10	+13	+14	+13	+10
Hicksville	−6	−7	−8	−9	−8	−7	−6	−5	−4	−3	−4	−5
Jamestown	+17	+14	+11	+10	+11	+14	+17	+20	+23	+24	+23	+20
New York	−4	−5	−6	−7	−6	−5	−4	−3	−2	−1	−2	−3
Plattsburgh	−6	−13	−20	−23	−20	−13	−6	+1	+7	+11	+7	+1
Rochester	+10	+5	+1	−1	+1	+5	+10	+15	+19	+21	+19	+15
Rome	+2	−3	−7	−9	−7	−3	+2	+7	+11	+13	+11	+7
Southampton	−10	−11	−12	−13	−12	−11	−10	−9	−8	−7	−8	−9
Syracuse	+5	+1	−3	−5	−3	+1	+5	+9	+14	+15	+14	+9
Utica	+1	−3	−7	−9	−7	−3	+1	+5	+9	+11	+9	+5
Watertown	+4	−2	−7	−10	−7	−2	+4	+10	+15	+18	+15	+10
North Carolina												
Asheville	+30	+36	+40	+43	+40	+36	+30	+24	+20	+17	+20	+24
Charlotte	+23	+29	+35	+37	+35	+29	+23	+17	+11	+9	+11	+17
Fayetteville	+16	+23	+28	+31	+28	+23	+16	+9	+4	+1	+4	+9
Greensboro	+19	+24	+29	+31	+29	+24	+19	+14	+9	+7	+9	+14
Raleigh	+15	+20	+25	+27	+25	+20	+15	+10	+5	+3	+5	+10
Rocky Mount	+11	+16	+21	+23	+21	+16	+11	+6	+1	−1	+1	+6
Wilmington	+12	+20	+26	+29	+26	+20	+12	+4	−2	−5	−2	+4
Winston-Salem	+21	+26	+31	+33	+31	+26	+21	+16	+11	+9	+11	+16
North Dakota												
Bismarck	+43	+32	+23	+18	+23	+32	+43	+54	+63	+68	+63	+54
Bowman	−7	−16	−25	−29	−25	−16	−7	+2	+11	+15	+11	+2
Devil's Lake	+35	+22	+11	+5	+11	+22	+35	+48	+59	+65	+59	+48
Dickinson	−9	−20	−30	−34	−30	−20	−9	+2	+12	+16	+12	+2

Place	♈ ARI	♉ TAU	♊ GEM	♋ CAN	♌ LEO	♍ VIR	♎ LIB	♏ SCO	♐ SAG	♑ CAP	♒ AQU	♓ PIS
Fargo	+27	+16	+6	+2	+6	+16	+27	+38	+48	+52	+48	+38
Grand Forks	+28	+15	+4	−2	+4	+15	+28	+41	+52	+58	+52	+41
Jamestown	+35	+24	+14	+10	+14	+24	+35	+46	+56	+60	+56	+46
Minot	+45	+32	+20	+14	+20	+32	+45	+58	+70	+76	+70	+58
Williston	+54	+41	+29	+23	+29	+41	+54	+67	+79	+85	+79	+67
Ohio												
Akron	+26	+25	+23	+23	+23	+25	+26	+27	+29	+29	+29	+27
Athens	+28	+28	+29	+29	+29	+28	+28	+28	+27	+27	+27	+28
Canton	+25	+24	+23	+23	+23	+24	+25	+26	+28	+28	+28	+26
Cincinnati	+38	+39	+40	+41	+40	+39	+38	+37	+36	+35	+36	+37
Cleveland	+27	+25	+23	+22	+23	+25	+27	+29	+31	+32	+31	+29
Columbus	+32	+32	+32	+32	+32	+32	+32	+32	+32	+32	+32	+32
Dayton	+37	+37	+37	+38	+37	+37	+37	+37	+37	+36	+37	+37
Lima	+37	+36	+35	+34	+35	+36	+37	+38	+39	+40	+39	+38
Mansfield	+30	+29	+27	+27	+27	+29	+30	+31	+33	+33	+33	+31
Toledo	+34	+31	+30	+29	+30	+31	+34	+37	+38	+39	+38	+37
Youngstown	+23	+22	+20	+20	+20	+22	+23	+24	+26	+26	+26	+24
Zanesville	+28	+28	+28	+28	+28	+28	+28	+28	+28	+28	+28	+28
Oklahoma												
Altus	+37	+44	+50	+52	+50	+44	+37	+30	+24	+22	+24	+30
Enid	+32	+37	+41	+43	+41	+37	+32	+27	+23	+21	+23	+27
Guymon	+46	+50	+54	+56	+54	+50	+46	+42	+38	+36	+38	+42
Lawton	+34	+41	+47	+50	+47	+41	+34	+27	+21	+18	+21	+27
Muskogee	+21	+26	+31	+33	+31	+26	+21	+16	+11	+9	+11	+16
Oklahoma City	+30	+36	+41	+43	+41	+36	+30	+24	+19	+17	+19	+24
Ponca City	+28	+32	+36	+38	+36	+32	+28	+24	+20	+18	+20	+24
Stillwater	+28	+33	+38	+40	+38	+33	+28	+23	+18	+16	+18	+23
Tulsa	+24	+29	+34	+36	+34	+29	+24	+19	+14	+12	+14	+19
Oregon												
Baker	−8	−15	−22	−25	−22	−15	−8	−1	+6	+9	+6	−1
Bend	+4	−2	−7	−10	−7	−2	+4	+10	+15	+18	+15	+10
Corvallis	+12	+5	−1	−4	−1	+5	+12	+19	+25	+28	+25	+19
Eugene	+10	+4	−1	−4	−1	+4	+10	+16	+21	+24	+21	+16
Klamath Falls	+6	+3	0	−1	0	+3	+6	+9	+12	+13	+12	+9
Medford	+11	+8	+5	+4	+5	+8	+11	+14	+17	+18	+17	+14
Ontario	+47	+41	+36	+33	+36	+41	+47	+53	+58	+61	+58	+53
Pendleton	−6	−15	−23	−26	−23	−15	−6	+3	+11	+14	+11	+3
Portland	+10	+2	−6	−10	−6	+2	+10	+18	+26	+30	+26	+18
Roseburg	+12	+7	+4	+2	+4	+7	+12	+17	+20	+22	+20	+17
Salem	+11	+3	−3	−7	−3	+3	+11	+19	+25	+29	+25	+19

(Continued)

133

Table B–4. *Continued*

Place	♈ ARI	♉ TAU	♊ GEM	♋ CAN	♌ LEO	♍ VIR	♎ LIB	♏ SCO	♐ SAG	♑ CAP	♒ AQU	♓ PIS
Pennsylvania												
Allentown	+2	+1	0	0	0	+1	+2	+3	+4	+4	+4	+3
Altoona	+14	+13	+12	+12	+12	+13	+14	+15	+16	+16	+16	+15
Chambersburg	+11	+11	+11	+12	+11	+11	+11	+11	+11	+10	+11	+11
Erie	+20	+17	+15	+13	+15	+17	+20	+23	+25	+27	+25	+23
Harrisburg	+8	+8	+7	+7	+7	+8	+8	+8	+9	+9	+9	+8
Johnstown	+16	+16	+15	+15	+15	+16	+16	+16	+17	+17	+17	+16
Lancaster	+5	+5	+5	+4	+5	+5	+5	+5	+5	+6	+5	+5
New Castle	+21	+20	+18	+18	+18	+20	+21	+22	+24	+24	+24	+22
Philadelphia	+1	+1	+1	+2	+1	+1	+1	+1	+1	0	+1	+1
Pittsburgh	+20	+19	+18	+18	+18	+19	+20	+21	+22	+22	+22	+21
Reading	+4	+4	+3	+3	+3	+4	+4	+4	+5	+5	+5	+4
Scranton	+3	+1	−1	−2	−1	+1	+3	+5	+7	+8	+7	+5
Williamsport	+8	+6	+5	+4	+5	+6	+8	+10	+11	+12	+11	+10
York	+7	+7	+7	+8	+7	+7	+7	+7	+7	+6	+7	+7
Rhode Island												
Newport	−15	−17	−19	−20	−19	−17	−15	−13	−11	−10	−11	−13
Providence	−14	−17	−19	−20	−19	−17	−14	−11	−9	−8	−9	−11
Westerly	−13	−15	−17	−18	−17	−15	−13	−11	−9	−8	−9	−11
Woonsocket	−14	−17	−18	−21	−18	−17	−14	−11	−10	−7	−10	−11
South Carolina												
Bennettsville	+19	+26	+31	+34	+31	+26	+19	+12	+7	+4	+7	+12
Charleston	+20	+29	+37	+41	+37	+29	+20	+11	+3	−1	+3	+11
Columbia	+24	+32	+38	+42	+38	+32	+24	+16	+10	+6	+10	+16
Greenville	+30	+37	+42	+45	+42	+37	+30	+23	+18	+15	+18	+23
Greenwood	+29	+36	+43	+46	+43	+36	+29	+22	+15	+12	+15	+22
Myrtle Beach	+15	+23	+30	+33	+30	+23	+15	+7	0	−3	0	+7
South Dakota												
Aberdeen	+34	+26	+18	+15	+18	+26	+34	+42	+50	+53	+50	+42
Belle Fourche	−5	−12	−18	−21	−18	−12	−5	+2	+8	+11	+8	+2
Mitchell	+32	+26	+22	+20	+22	+26	+32	+38	+42	+44	+42	+38
Pierre	+41	+34	+29	+26	+29	+34	+41	+48	+53	+56	+53	+48
Rapid City	−7	−13	−18	−21	−18	−13	−7	−1	+4	+7	+4	−1
Sioux Falls	+27	+22	+17	+15	+17	+22	+27	+32	+37	+39	+37	+32
Watertown	+28	+20	+14	+11	+14	+20	+28	+36	+42	+45	+42	+36
Tennessee												
Chattanooga	+41	+48	+53	+56	+53	+48	+41	+34	+29	+26	+29	+34
Jackson	−5	+1	+5	+8	+5	+1	−5	−11	−15	−18	−15	−11
Johnson City	+29	+34	+39	+40	+39	+34	+29	+24	+19	+18	+19	+24
Knoxville	+36	+41	+46	+48	+46	+41	+36	+31	+26	+24	+26	+31

Place	♈ ARI	♉ TAU	♊ GEM	♋ CAN	♌ LEO	♍ VIR	♎ LIB	♏ SCO	♐ SAG	♑ CAP	♒ AQU	♓ PIS
Memphis	0	+6	+12	+14	+12	+6	0	−6	−12	−14	−12	−6
Nashville	−13	−8	−3	−2	−3	−8	−13	−18	−23	−24	−23	−18
Shelbyville	−14	−8	−3	−1	−3	−8	−14	−20	−25	−27	−25	−20
Union City	−4	+1	+5	+7	+5	+1	−4	−9	−13	−15	−13	−9
Texas												
Abilene	+39	+49	+57	+60	+57	+49	+39	+29	+21	+18	+21	+29
Amarillo	+47	+53	+59	+61	+59	+53	+47	+41	+35	+33	+35	+41
Austin	+31	+43	+53	+58	+53	+43	+31	+19	+9	+4	+9	+19
Beaumont	+16	+28	+39	+43	+39	+28	+16	+4	−7	−11	−7	+4
Brownsville	+30	+47	+61	+68	+61	+47	+30	+13	−1	−7	−1	+13
Corpus Christi	+30	+45	+57	+62	+57	+45	+30	+15	+3	−2	+3	+15
Dallas	+27	+36	+44	+47	+44	+36	+27	+18	+10	+7	+10	+18
El Paso	+6	+16	+25	+29	+25	+16	+6	−4	−13	−17	−13	−4
Fort Worth	+29	+38	+46	+49	+46	+38	+29	+20	+12	+9	+12	+20
Houston	+22	+35	+45	+50	+45	+35	+22	+9	−1	−6	−1	+9
Laredo	+38	+55	+69	+76	+69	+55	+38	+21	+7	0	+7	+21
Lubbock	+47	+55	+63	+66	+63	+55	+47	+39	+30	+26	+30	+39
Odessa	+49	+59	+68	+72	+68	+59	+42	+31	+22	+18	+22	+31
San Angelo	+42	+53	+62	+66	+62	+53	+34	+21	+10	+5	+10	+21
San Antonio	+34	+47	+58	+63	+58	+47	+34	+21	+11	+3	−1	+3	+11
Tyler	+21	+31	+39	+43	+39	+31	+21	+11	+3	−1	+3	+11
Waco	+29	+39	+48	+52	+48	+39	+29	+19	+10	+6	+10	+19
Wichita Falls	+34	+42	+48	+52	+48	+42	+34	+26	+20	+16	+20	+26
Utah												
Cedar City	+32	+35	+38	+39	+38	+35	+32	+29	+26	+25	+26	+29
Logan	+27	+25	+22	+21	+22	+25	+27	+29	+32	+33	+32	+29
Ogden	+28	+26	+25	+24	+25	+26	+28	+30	+31	+32	+31	+30
Provo	+27	+27	+26	+26	+26	+27	+27	+27	+28	+28	+28	+27
Salt Lake City	+28	+27	+26	+25	+26	+27	+28	+29	+30	+31	+30	+29
Vernal	+18	+17	+17	+16	+17	+17	+18	+19	+19	+20	+19	+19
Vermont												
Barre	−10	−16	−22	−24	−22	−16	−10	−4	+2	+4	+2	−4
Bennington	−7	−11	−15	−17	−15	−11	−7	−3	+1	+3	+1	−3
Brattleboro	−10	−14	−18	−20	−18	−14	−10	−6	−2	0	−2	−6
Burlington	−7	−14	−20	−23	−20	−14	−7	0	+6	+9	+6	0
Rutland	−8	−13	−18	−20	−18	−13	−8	−3	+2	+4	+2	−3
Virginia												
Arlington	+9	+11	+11	+12	+11	+11	+9	+7	+7	+6	+7	+7
Charlottesville	+14	+17	+19	+20	+19	+17	+14	+11	+9	+8	+9	+11
Danville	+18	+22	+26	+28	+26	+22	+18	+14	+10	+8	+10	+14

(Continued)

Table B–4. Continued

Place	♈ ARI	♉ TAU	♊ GEM	♋ CAN	♌ LEO	♍ VIR	♎ LIB	♏ SCO	♐ SAG	♑ CAP	♒ AQU	♓ PIS
Grundy	+29	+33	+36	+38	+36	+33	+29	+25	+22	+20	+22	+25
Lynchburg	+17	+21	+24	+25	+24	+21	+17	+13	+10	+9	+10	+13
Norfolk	+5	+9	+13	+14	+13	+9	+5	+1	−3	−4	−3	+1
Richmond	+5	+8	+11	+13	+11	+8	+5	+2	−1	−3	−1	+2
Roanoke	+20	+24	+27	+29	+27	+24	+20	+16	+13	+11	+13	+16
Winchester	+13	+14	+15	+16	+15	+14	+13	+12	+11	+10	+11	+12
Washington												
Bellingham	+9	−6	−19	−25	−19	−6	+9	+24	+37	+43	+37	+24
Everett	+8	−5	−16	−22	−16	−5	+8	+21	+32	+38	+32	+21
Longview	+11	+2	−7	−11	−7	+2	+11	+20	+29	+33	+29	+20
Olympia	+11	0	−10	−15	−10	0	+11	+22	+32	+37	+32	+22
Port Angeles	+13	0	−12	−17	−12	0	+13	+26	+38	+43	+38	+26
Seattle	+8	−4	−15	−20	−15	−4	+8	+20	+31	+36	+31	+20
Spokane	−11	−23	−35	−40	−35	−23	−11	+1	+13	+18	+13	+1
Tacoma	+9	−2	−13	−18	−13	−2	+9	+20	+31	+36	+31	+20
Vancouver	+10	+2	−6	−10	−6	+2	+10	+18	+26	+30	+26	+18
Walla Walla	−8	−17	−26	−30	−26	−17	−8	+1	+10	+14	+10	+1
Yakima	+1	−9	−19	−23	−19	−9	+1	+11	+21	+25	+21	+11
West Virginia												
Beckley	+25	+28	+30	+32	+30	+28	+25	+22	+20	+18	+20	+22
Charleston	+27	+29	+31	+32	+31	+29	+27	+25	+23	+22	+23	+25
Clarksburg	+21	+22	+23	+23	+23	+22	+21	+20	+19	+19	+19	+20
Huntington	+30	+32	+34	+35	+34	+32	+30	+28	+26	+25	+26	+28
Morgantown	+20	+20	+21	+22	+21	+20	+20	+20	+19	+18	+19	+20
Parkersburg	+26	+27	+28	+28	+28	+27	+26	+25	+24	+24	+24	+25
Wheeling	+23	+23	+23	+22	+23	+23	+23	+23	+23	+24	+23	+23
Wisconsin												
Appleton	−6	−12	−18	−21	−18	−12	−6	0	+6	+9	+6	0
Eau Claire	+6	−1	−8	−11	−8	−1	+6	+13	+20	+23	+20	+13
Green Bay	−8	−15	−21	−24	−21	−15	−8	−1	+5	+8	+5	−1
La Crosse	+5	−1	−6	−8	−6	−1	+5	+11	+16	+18	+16	+11
Madison	−2	−6	−10	−12	−10	−6	−2	+2	+6	+8	+6	+2
Milwaukee	−8	−12	−16	−18	−16	−12	−8	−4	0	+2	0	−4
Sheboygan	−9	−15	−20	−22	−20	−15	−9	−3	+2	+4	+2	−3
Superior	+8	−2	−12	−16	−12	−2	+8	+18	+28	+32	+28	+18
Wausau	−2	−10	−16	−20	−16	−10	−2	+6	+12	+16	+12	+6
Wyoming												
Casper	+5	+1	−3	−5	−3	+1	+5	+9	+13	+15	+13	+9
Cheyenne	−1	−3	−4	−5	−4	−3	−1	+1	+2	+3	+2	+1
Gillette	+2	−4	−10	−13	−10	−4	+2	+8	+14	+17	+14	+8

Place	♈ ARI	♉ TAU	♊ GEM	♋ CAN	♌ LEO	♍ VIR	♎ LIB	♏ SCO	♐ SAG	♑ CAP	♒ AQU	♓ PIS
Laramie	+2	0	−1	−2	−1	0	+2	+4	+5	+6	+5	+4
Rawlins	+9	+6	+4	+3	+4	+6	+9	+12	+14	+15	+14	+12
Rock Springs	+17	+15	+13	+12	+13	+15	+17	+19	+21	+22	+21	+19
Sheridan	+8	+1	−6	−9	−6	+1	+8	+15	+22	+25	+22	+15
Puerto Rico												
Mayagüez	+29	+49	+73	+81	+73	+49	+29	+9	−15	−23	−15	+9
San Juan	+24	+45	+67	+75	+67	+45	+24	+3	−19	−27	−19	+3
Virgin Islands												
Charlotte Amalie	+20	+41	+63	+71	+63	+41	+20	−1	−23	−31	−23	−1
Alberta												
Calgary	+36	+17	0	−8	0	+17	+36	+55	+72	+80	+72	+55
Edmonton	+34	+9	−14	−25	−14	+9	+34	+59	+82	+93	+82	+59
Grande Prairie	+54	+27	+2	−11	+2	+27	+54	+81	+106	+119	+106	+81
Medicine Hat	+23	+6	−9	−16	−9	+6	+23	+40	+55	+62	+55	+40
British Columbia												
Dawson Creek	0	−28	−55	−68	−55	−28	0	+28	+55	+68	+55	+28
Fernie	−20	−35	−49	−55	−49	−35	−20	−5	+9	+15	+9	−5
Kamloops	0	−19	−35	−43	−35	−19	0	+19	+35	+43	+35	+19
Prince George	+8	−18	−42	−53	−42	−18	+8	+34	+58	+69	+58	+34
Prince Rupert	+40	+13	−11	−23	−11	+13	+40	+67	+91	+103	+91	+67
Vancouver	+11	−4	−18	−24	−18	−4	+11	+26	+40	+46	+40	+26
Victoria	+12	−2	−14	−20	−14	−2	+12	+26	+38	+44	+38	+26
Manitoba												
Brandon	+40	+24	+8	+1	+8	+24	+40	+56	+72	+79	+72	+56
Dauphin	+40	+20	+2	−7	+2	+20	+40	+60	+78	+87	+78	+60
Flin Flon	+45	+19	−5	−18	−5	+19	+45	+71	+95	+108	+95	+71
Portage La Prairie	+33	+14	+1	−6	+1	+14	+33	+50	+65	+72	+65	+50
Winnipeg	+29	+13	−3	−10	−3	+13	+29	+45	+61	+68	+61	+45
New Brunswick												
Bathurst	+22	+9	−2	−7	−2	+9	+22	+35	+46	+51	+46	+35
Edmundston	+33	+21	+10	+5	+10	+21	+33	+45	+56	+61	+56	+45
Fredericton	+26	+17	+9	+6	+9	+17	+26	+35	+43	+46	+43	+35
Moncton	+19	+10	+1	−3	+1	+10	+19	+28	+37	+41	+37	+28
Saint John	+25	+17	+10	+7	+10	+17	+25	+33	+40	+43	+40	+33
Newfoundland												
Gander	+10	−4	−16	−22	−16	−4	+10	+24	+36	+42	+36	+24
Goose Bay	+30	+12	−2	−9	−2	+12	+30	+48	+62	+69	+62	+48

(Continued)

Table B–4. *Continued*

Place	♈ ARI	♉ TAU	♊ GEM	♋ CAN	♌ LEO	♍ VIR	♎ LIB	♏ SCO	♐ SAG	♑ CAP	♒ AQU	♓ PIS
Port aux Basques	+29	+17	+6	+1	+6	+17	+29	+41	+52	+57	+52	+41
Saint John's	+1	−11	−22	−27	−22	−11	+1	+13	+24	+29	+24	+13
Nova Scotia												
Amherst	+17	+8	0	−3	0	+8	+17	+26	+34	+37	+34	+26
Halifax	+15	+9	+4	+1	+4	+9	+15	+21	+26	+29	+26	+21
Sydney	+1	−9	−17	−21	−17	−9	+1	+11	+19	+23	+19	+11
Yarmouth	+25	+19	+14	+11	+14	+19	+25	+31	+36	+39	+36	+31
Ontario												
Hamilton	+19	+14	+11	+9	+11	+14	+19	+24	+27	+29	+27	+24
Kenora	+18	+1	−13	−20	−13	+1	+18	+35	+49	+56	+49	+35
Kitchener	+22	+17	+13	+11	+13	+17	+22	+27	+31	+33	+31	+27
London	+26	+22	+18	+16	+18	+22	+26	+30	+34	+36	+34	+30
Ottawa	+3	−5	−13	−16	−13	−5	+3	+11	+19	+22	+19	+11
Sudbury	+25	+15	+6	+2	+6	+15	+25	+35	+44	+48	+44	+35
Thunder Bay	+54	+39	+26	+20	+26	+39	+54	+69	+82	+88	+82	+69
Toronto	+18	+13	+8	+6	+8	+13	+18	+23	+28	+30	+28	+23
Prince Edward Island												
Charlottetown	+13	+3	−6	−10	−6	+3	+13	+23	+32	+36	+32	+23
Québec												
Chicoutimi	−16	−30	−43	−49	−43	−30	−16	−2	+11	+17	+11	−2
Gaspé	−40	−55	−68	−74	−68	−55	−40	−25	−12	−6	−12	−25
Montréal	−6	−15	−22	−26	−22	−15	−6	+3	+10	+14	+10	+3
Natashquan	+8	−10	−24	−31	−24	−10	+8	+26	+40	+47	+40	+26
Québec	−15	−26	−36	−40	−36	−26	−15	−4	+6	+10	+6	−4
Rivière-du-Loup	−22	−35	−46	−51	−46	−35	−22	−9	+2	+7	+2	−9
Sept-Îles	−32	−50	−64	−71	−64	−50	−32	−14	0	+7	0	−14
Saskatchewan												
Maple Creek	+18	+1	−14	−21	−14	+1	+18	+35	+50	+57	+50	+35
North Battleford	+12	−11	−31	−41	−31	−11	+12	+35	+55	+65	+55	+35
Prince Albert	+62	+38	+17	+5	+17	+38	+62	+86	+107	+119	+107	+86
Regina	+59	+41	+25	+17	+25	+41	+59	+77	+93	+101	+93	+77
Saskatoon	+63	+42	+23	+13	+23	+42	+63	+84	+103	+113	+103	+84
Swift Current	+71	+53	+37	+29	+37	+53	+71	+89	+105	+113	+105	+89
Northwest Territories												
Wrigley	+80	+24	−33	−68	−33	+24	+80	+136	+193	+228	+193	+136
Yellowknife	+40	−11	−63	−93	−63	−11	+40	+91	+143	+173	+143	+91
Yukon Territory												
Dawson	+77	+15	−48	−89	−48	+15	+77	+137	+202	+243	+202	+137
Whitehorse	+59	+13	−32	−58	−32	+13	+59	+105	+150	+176	+150	+105

Selected Bibliography

Ames, Louise Bates, and Ilg, Frances L. *Your Four-Year-Old: Wild and Wonderful.* New York: Delacorte Press, 1976.

———. *Your Three-Year-Old: Friend or Enemy.* New York: Delacorte Press, 1976.

———. *Your Two-Year-Old: Terrible or Tender.* New York: Delacorte Press, 1976.

Arroyo, Stephen, Ph.D. *Astrology, Psychology and the Four Elements: An Energy Approach to Astrology and Its Use in the Counseling Arts.* Davis, Calif.: CRCS Publications, 1975.

Caplan, Frank, general editor. *The First Twelve Months of Life: Your Baby's Growth Month by Month.* New York: Grosset and Dunlap, 1971.

Fraiberg, Selma H. *The Magic Years: Understanding and Handling the Problems of Early Childhood.* New York: Charles Scribner's Sons, 1959.

Gesell, Arnold, M.D.; Ilg, Frances L., M.D.; and Ames, Louise Bates, Ph.D. *Infant and Child in the Culture of Today: The Guidance of Development in Home and Nursery School.* Revised edition. New York: Harper and Row, 1974.

Hand, Robert. *Planets in Youth: Patterns of Early Development.* Rockport, Mass.: Para Research, 1977.

Liepmann, Lise. *Your Child's Sensory World.* Baltimore, Md.: Penguin Books, 1974.

Moore, Marcia, and Douglas, Mark. *Astrology, the Divine Science.* York Harbor, Me.: Arcane Publications, 1971.

Oken, Allan. *The Horoscope, the Road and Its Travelers.* New York: Bantam Books, 1974.

Orser, Mary, and Brightfield, Rick and Glory. *Instant Astrology.* Harper Colophon Books. New York: Harper and Row, 1976.

Parker, Derek and Julia. *The Compleat Astrologer.* New York: Bantam Books, 1975.

Spock, Benjamin, M.D. *Baby and Child Care.* Pocket Books. New York: Simon and Schuster, 1968.

Thomas, Alexander; Chess, Stella; and Birch, Herbert G. "The Origin of Personality." *Scientific American* 223 (1970): 102–109.

Index